Prai

The Church Planting Journey

"This book is set to reignite the church planting conversation! May Jesus Christ richly bless the reading of this book."

—Keith Shields - Executive Pastor Bow Valley Christian Church in Calgary, Alberta, Canada

"Knowledge is good. Insight about processes and structures are valuable. But it is rare indeed to find those things matched with real wisdom. Bob is not just "smart" about church planting. His expert guidance comes from an ideal mix of spiritual depth and experiential breadth. I hope every church planter, and church planting coach will make use of this book."

—Todd Hunter - Anglican Bishop, author of Christianity Beyond Belief

"Reading *The Church Planting Journey* I found myself saying, "YES! That's it!" again and again, even out loud, hoping the neighbors couldn't hear me. This book puts into practical steps and helpful diagrams the vision God is giving us into through his word."

—Tim Clark, Church Planter- Tokyo, Japan

"After interviewing hundreds of dynamic, forward thinking planters who've trained a new generation of planters, most of them had one thing in common; when asked who trained them, the name Bob Logan came up repeatedly. Read this book, and you'll find out why."

—Peyton Jones - Church Planting Trainer, Founder of Church Planter Magazine, Architect of Jump School Core Team Training, and author of Church Zero, and Reaching the Unreached

"We utilized Bob's work for many years to train church planters. This book is the best yet as he captures the essence of church planting as the overflow of disciplemaking, not the other way around. A must read!"

—Tammy Dunahoo - Vice President of U.S. Operations, The Foursquare Church

"Starting anything from scratch is an exhilarating, overwhelming, nerve-racking, humbling, intimidating, and yes, a marvelous life experience. Having a trail guide to help you navigate, prepare, respond, and progress is of utmost value. Bob Logan provides it. Not a cookbook, but an indispensable process tool for every person beginning the church planting journey."

> —John Wasem - Senior Director of Resource Development, Stadia Church Planting

"The right question asked to the right people at the right time can change history. Bob Logan is equipped to make sure you and your team asks the right questions and can help you get to your right answers for church planting. Bob Logan is a master teacher, practitioner, and coach. Reading this book will make your church planting journey more effective, efficient, and enjoyable"

> —Dr. John Jackson - President of William Jessup University (www.jessup.edu), speaker and author of books on leadership and transformation

"If you are or are planning to become a church planter or if you supervise church planters, it is imperative that you read Dr. Bob Logan's newest book, *The Church Planting Journey*. Buy it, read and study it, live it."

> —Robert Gill, global consultant and coach, Journey Deeper Ministries.

"One of the things I love the most about Bob's coaching and this book is the way he allows each planter to reflect deeply on the most important matters and pushes each to live into the calling God has given to them. If I were starting on the planting journey again, this is a volume that would sit on my desk, dog-eared from use and referred back to often."

> —Thomas M. Greener, DMin - Pastor, Camp Ground UMC, Fayetteville, NC

"For over four decades Bob Logan and Church Planting have been synonymous in the western world. A practitioner, author and international coach, Bob has spent the bulk of his ministry life on the cutting edge of all things Church Planting. His latest book *The Church Planting Journey* uses all of his years of experience as the foundation for looking at what is new in Church Planting in the 21st century. This book is not only relevant to anyone in ministry but also a must read for Church Planters, Denominational and Movement leaders!"

> —Colin Noyes - Director of ResourceZone International

Bob Logan is a wise and seasoned church planter and coach who shares foundational convictions and practical advice for those engaged in this challenging work. The church planting journey is often uncharted. This is an essential guide."

—Kurt N Fredrickson, DMin, PhD - Associate Dean for the Doctor of Ministry Program, Associate Professor of Pastoral Ministry, Fuller Seminary

"In this comprehensive work on church planting, Bob Logan, provides the planter with first-rate content and practical steps, checklists, and questions for the planter and launch team. This book is a must read for those embarking on the church planting journey."

—Billy Waters - Lead Pastor, Wellspring Church, Englewood, CO

"It's no surprise that once again the Lord is using Bob Logan to bring Spirit led inspiration and practical insight to church planters. *The Church Planting Journey* is a must read and helpful guide for everyone desiring to launch a new congregation."

—Dr. Stephen Fitch - President and Founder, The Eden Projects

"What I like about the *The Church Planting Journey* is the thoughtful integration of the practical principles and steps in planting churches with spiritual formation and discipleship. It is strategic, it is practical, and it is profoundly theological and spiritual. In my mind I don't need other books on church planting. This one has it all, and I will use it and implement its principles in my various spheres of influence."

—Per Christian Lunde - Lead Pastor Vintage Vineyard, Oslo, National Leader Vineyard Norway

"Bob is truly an expert in church planting. He not only knows how to speak about church planting, but he is a practitioner who does it with excellence and success. In *The Church Planting Journey*, Bob asks the right questions that need to be dealt with, and if the reader takes the time to answer the questions, our new church plants will benefit greatly."

—Jerry Conner - Pastor of Global Outreach and Church Planting, Pleasant Valley Baptist Church

"In *The Church Planting Journey*, Bob Logan has given ecclesial innovators a gift by combining his extensive practical experience with innumerable church starters and theological reflection that is currently unmatched within similar books. From the discerner, to the practitioner, to the national leader, this book has much to offer for all."

—Nick Warnes - Executive Director of Cyclical INC and Director of Cyclical LA

"*The Church Planting Journey* is greatly needed and right on time for the church today."

—Kendra Diehl - Vice President of Ministry Formation and Innovation, The Master's Institute, St. Paul MN

"Bob, as teacher and practitioner, pours his heart and soul into this book offering a wealth of help for planting healthy churches. A warning though, as you read this book, it will challenge you to return to the early church model of making disciples as the essential activity and focus of church planting."

—Nelson Roth, Discipleship Coach at Relevant Ministry and author of Relevant Discipleship Pathway

"Anyone seeking to grow a church that obeys the Great Commandment and lives into the Great Commission should keep the Bible on one corner of their desk and *The Church Planting Journey* on the other."

—The Rev. Dr. Adam T. Trambley, Rector, St. John's Episcopal Church, Sharon, PA

"In *The Church Planting Journey*, Bob does a masterful job distilling his expansive knowledge of initiating, developing, and establishing new churches. Writing for the current generation, I especially appreciate his continued emphasis on the core activity of discipling others in every aspect of the planting process. I highly recommend this book to church planters and their sending churches!"

—Mark Fields - Director of Global & Intercultural Ministry, Vineyard Missions

"In *The Church Planting Journey* there's no hype, fads, or trends. What you will get are timeless, field tested, fruitful principles. Put them into action and watch what God does!"

—Josh Miller - St. Thomas Church, Fort Collins, Colorado

Bob Logan brings decades of expertise, as he provides this needed update in transformational evangelism. In *The Church Planting Journey*, Bob apprises the reader of the importance of engaging an ever-changing culture, through intentional connection, relational sensitivity, and a passion towards understanding all of God's people. Unlike most other updates, one cannot afford to delay downloading the powerful insights presented through this book.

—Parnell M. Lovelace, Jr., MSW, D.Min. - Talbot School of Theology, Biola University and Lovelace Leadership Connection

"Church planting is a journey with steep hills, beautiful valleys, and sometimes distracting detours, but one we must pursue with all we are for the glory of God. Bob Logan has the wisdom and authority to guide us along that journey. The Church Planting Journey, is a comprehensive blueprint for disciplemaking and church multiplication. "

—Tom Camacho - Church planter, Intervarsity author, leadership trainer and coach

"In typical Bob Logan style, *The Church Planting Journey* provides more questions than answers. But don't let that fool you, Bob is an expert practitioner who embraces the value that every journey is unique. God will use this book to help you and your core group members discover what his mission will look like in your community."

—Dino Senesi - Denominational Church Planter Coaching Leader, Author of *Sending Well: A Field Guide to Great Church Planter Coaching*

"Bob Logan's magnum opus might be the single resource of its kind to engage the full range of questions and challenges faced by church planters. If you are eager to act upon the Great Commission, this is a must-have resource."

—Dennis Bachman - Executive Director / Lead Pastor at ViaCordis

"I was immediately engaged at the beginning of Chapter 1 with the emphasis on disciple-making from those formerly without Christ and the formation of churches from the communities of growing disciples."

—Joe Hernandez - Coach and Trainer, Global Gates Network

"Bob Logan has done it again. He's clarified the process, identified the principles and engaged leaders in church planting. Some things never change. Bob continues to capture the best thinking on church planting in *The Church Planting Journey*."

—Dr. Gary B. Reinecke - Executive Director, InFocus Ministries

"This isn't just another book to read on the subject of church planting. This is a most helpful resource to patiently work through on your journey to begin a healthy, local church-based, reproducing discipleship movement. This book is a gift to those of us pursuing biblical missional engagement in the world today!"

—Michael Gatlin - National Coordinator of Multiply Vineyard

ISBN —13 978-1-944955-54-0
ISBN —10 1-944955-54-2

Printed in the USA
2019—First Edition
28 27 26 25 24 23 22 21 20 19   10 9 8 7 6 5 4 3 2 1

The Church Planting Journey

By Robert E. Logan

Contents

Foreword

It's finally happened—I've found someone who validates what I think I've learned in 45 years of multiplying churches.

When Robert Logan intimates that formal training works best when administered at the point of need and that it is best done with brevity, he drills into the core of my experience. That the surrounding material provides an extremely practical framework for that training is pure genius. I love *The Church Planting Journey*.

I've discipled nearly 80 church planters who've discipled others, etc. We've tried to live Paul's admonition to pass what we learned to faithful people who can hand it off to others (2 Timothy 2:2). Beginning with a dozen people in a California beach town, our efforts spawned a movement that touches every continent and includes nearly a quarter of a million people. What we dug out in all those years fits neatly within the covers of this book.

There were no books on church planting when I began this journey. I managed to find one autobiography that covered the subject, but the author was a world away from a bunch of hippies who barely fit into their denomination. What we did unearth, we gleaned mostly from Acts and Ephesians. We learned the form of the early church from Acts 2 and its functions from Ephesians. We discovered that each Christ-follower is God's masterpiece created unto good works (Ephesians 2), but that those missional events won't occur without leaders living as equippers (Ephesians 4). This and a hungry love for scripture, in general, generated a value-based approach to church planting that served us well.

However, we are one group and we've evolved a singular approach to disciplemaking and church multiplication. We're good at what we do, but narrowly focused. This is where Bob comes in.

After struggling through a similar lack of tools in the beginning of his journey, God led him to coach church planters across a broad spectrum of communities and cultures. His wider vista is useful to me today—Bob's wisdom and tools help me coach others. I only wish I had enjoyed his wealth of insight back in 1971. Had it been available, more seed would have found its way to good soil.

The big takeaway for me is that Robert Logan esteems values above vision or deeds. He does this while mining *your own* thoughts and prayers for the vision and actions you'll need on your journey. A world awash in 'how-to' manuals often misses the former while superimposing the latter. To find both in such balance is a treasure.

It's a privilege to add these few words to the work of someone whom I so deeply admire.

Ralph Moore

Hope Chapel Founder

Introduction

As I sit down to write these words, I reflect that I now have more than forty years of experience in the field of church planting, and I am still actively involved. I love the hands-on work of church planting, the direct coaching of many planters, the involvement in developing church planting resources, and the work with denominational and network leaders to catalyze movements.

Not coincidentally, I've been thinking a lot about legacy lately. Although I don't yet have plans to retire, I do think this is a natural time to consider: What have I contributed? What do I still have to contribute? What is needed by the world today that I can help with?

One of the things I'm still most known for is *The Church Planter's Toolkit*, coauthored with Steve Ogne. Originally released in 1991, it was adopted and embraced by many, quickly becoming the go-to resource for church planters across denominations. Even today, it still forms the basis for most other church planting systems and approaches.

I'm especially grateful to have made this contribution, since I promised God many years ago—when I was a struggling church planter—that if I were ever in a position to help other church planters someday, I would. When I graduated from seminary in 1977, I quickly realized that no one was hiring inexperienced twenty-four-year-old pastors. So when the denominational leader of our regional association of churches approached me about starting a new church, I was open to it and accepted the invitation.

Janet and I moved to a newer, expanding community about forty miles east of Los Angeles. We felt a great deal of excitement as we anticipated the raising up of a new church and seeing people come to know Christ. I began knocking on doors and gathered a small group of unchurched people who had no connection with Jesus. It was wonderful to see their spiritual eyes opening as I gave them Bibles, and we started by looking at the table of contents.

A couple of months later, the euphoria wore off and I came to the startling realization: I didn't have the slightest idea what I was doing! And it would be only a matter of time (perhaps a year) before the people I was leading would come to the same conclusion.

My seminary education did not prepare me for at least 75 percent of what I was called to do, so I began to search for books and seminars that would help me learn how to plant a church. I only found two books—and neither was helpful. There were no church planting seminars. I had to figure it out on my own. I needed help. So I passionately cried out to God.

As I was praying and wrestling with the Lord, I got a vision in my mind of a seashore. All the church planters of the world were lined up on the California coast, and the voice of God came and gave them the assignment to swim to Catalina, an island some twenty-six miles off the California coast. The gun sounded and the planters waded into the water. Some sank, some swam, a few died of heart attacks on the shore just thinking about it. I noticed that those who made it to Catalina did not return to help those who were still in the water.

It was very upsetting to me that we were not learning from the failures, or successes, of others. Everyone was reinventing the wheel; planter after planter died repeating the same mistakes over and over. I cried out, "Why can't we learn from the mistakes of others?" I got even more angry over those who were swimming. I was not unhappy for their success; it was encouraging to see that it was possible. But none of them were coming back to the shore to help people like me, who were wading into the water. My frustration was intensifying.

It was at that moment that I cried out to God: "Lord, this is not right! We're not learning from the successes or failures of others. If you get me through this and ever allow me to get in a position to do something about this, that's what I want to change!"

Through a lot of wrong turns and mistakes, I eventually figured out how to plant churches. Community Baptist Church in Rancho Cucamonga, California grew (through the grace of God) to a worshiping attendance of 1,200 people (two-thirds previously unchurched). In my eleven years there, we also planted five or six new churches, and the church continued to plant more daughter churches after my departure. The original church recently celebrated its fortieth anniversary.

I had no idea that God would take seriously the prayer of a young, inexperienced church planter, and provide opportunities to live out the promise of that dream.

I've worn a lot of hats since then: pastor, coach, trainer, speaker, consultant, and author. I also have continued in my calling to church planting, having cofounded ViaCordis, a network of house churches, with Jon Van Bruggen. I'm not only grateful for my own experiences, but for the privilege of having coached hundreds of church planters over the last thirty-five-plus years. That vantage point has given me a wide window into how church planting has changed—and how it has remained the same—over the years.

What has changed and what has not

Planters still need to be hands-on and relational in their communities. More so than ever, our current approach needs to be intensely organic and personal. At the same time, planters need to be more intentional about setting up organizational dynamics so that they can reproduce. "Organic" and "organized" are not opposites; they're mutually necessary. For organic beings to reproduce, they must be inherently organized. What's missing from many current missional applications is the underlying structure needed to empower people to make it truly reproducible. We need to pay attention to those dynamics of an organism that allow it to grow and reproduce. Increased intentionality is needed in today's context.

> We are now planting churches in a world that isn't looking for churches.

Intentionality is a crucial point, especially for leaders who are naturally intuitive but aren't sure how to pass on ministry and leadership skills to others. By taking the time to identify the underlying principles that you're working from—and you *are* working from underlying principles—you can more easily translate those skills for those you're developing. In this way, we can aim for multiplication from the beginning.

As I look out at today's church planting landscape, I'm convinced that it's time to return to and take a fresh look at church planting tools and processes. However, I do want to be clear on one point: The principles of church planting haven't changed. You could still take the old toolkit and, with some cultural translation, figure out what to do.

But while the principles haven't changed, a lot of other things have. The world around us and the situations in which we are planting have changed. The possible ways the church can look have changed. The way the church is perceived from the outside has changed. We are now planting churches in a world that isn't looking for churches. It's not (usually) that people are hostile to churches; they just have no category for them.

This translation isn't just for the culture outside of the church, either. It's for current planters and pastors as well. The way we think of the church from the inside has changed, as has the vocabulary we use. The questions today's leaders are asking have changed. Here's just a sampling:

I hear questions wrestling with the proliferation of structures and models:
- What makes a church a church? Does ten people meeting in a living room count? Do people watching a screen at another location count?

I hear questions about the functions of the church:
- What is a church actually supposed to do? Deliver sermons? Serve the poor? Encourage Christians? Reach non-Christians? Develop leaders? Make disciples? Provide the sacraments? What is the nature of church?

I hear financial and leadership questions:
- Can a church planter really expect to make a living at this in today's world? To what degree does a "professional" leader differ from a lay leader? Who is "in charge"? Is *anyone* "in charge"?

And I hear questions about expectations:
- What expectations do Christians have of church? What expectations do non-Christians have of church? What expectations do pastors and planters have? And what do we do when those expectations inevitably come into conflict?

Why not make it easier on today's planter and do some of this cultural translation up front? Certainly we'll still need to figure out how to apply the basic principles to the specific situation; that will always be the case. But the less translation required for those principles to make sense in our current reality, the better.

In that sense, although the format is quite different, this book builds on my (and Steve's) original *Church Planter's Toolkit*. Yet I'm calling it *The Church Planting Journey*. I recognize the road is often winding, rocky, and uphill—and looks a little bit different for everybody. My prayer is that God will use the ideas and resources here to help and support the church planters venturing into today's world.

In some ways, this resource is the application of a lifetime of work, integrating the missional concept with discipleship and leadership. I've recently written three books on those topics: *The Missional Journey, The Discipleship Difference,* and

The Leadership Difference. This book brings those three concepts together as they apply to church planting. It's designed to answer questions like: How can planters create environments, relationships, and processes to work effectively with their people? And how can planters do that in such a way that it is not copying someone else's model, but rather is a truly customized principle-based approach that fits the uniqueness of what God wants to do in their context?

This resource is designed to help planters get their minds wrapped around not only what needs to be done, but how to work with others to make that happen, and how to do it in such a way that their work is reproducible—leading to a harvest thirty, sixty, one-hundredfold what was sown (Matthew 13:8).

Principle-based

I've worked with hundreds of church planters and dozens of denominations. The range includes a wide variety of communities, traditions, cultures, countries, ethnicities, histories, governing structures, and worship styles. These church plants and their leaders are all quite different. But what do they all need?

They all need principle-based tools that can be adapted to their context. Planters often know what they want to accomplish. What they need help with is the *how*. How do they get where they want to go? They need tools and they need a process to follow. That may look quite different with different churches, but there are still some underlying principles that apply.

This book introduces a variety of concepts and principles, then points you toward tools for each area that you can use or adapt. The end of each chapter also includes:

- Reflection questions you can use with your team, coach, or cohort
- A checklist of important action items for this area of the church plant
- A prayer guide you can use with your team, as well as one you can provide to outside intercessors

Many of these resources are readily adaptable. You can use them as-is, change the vocabulary or emphasis to fit your people or vision, or pare them down so you don't feel like David in Saul's armor. The point is to get right-sized, adaptable resources into the hands of planters that can be easily used alongside others on this journey of church planting.

There are other important recurring themes you'll notice throughout *The Church Planting Journey*. First, this book is not in linear order—because there is no linear order in church planting. A lot of tasks run concurrently, or in different order, so you'll need to jump back and forth between chapters. I've put them in rough order here, in four parts:

> Part 1: Get Ready: Personal Commitment and Readiness
> Part 2: Get Set: Preparation and Planning
> Part 3: Get Going: Living Out the Mission
> Part 4: Keep Growing: Ongoing Development and Multiplication

I recommend skimming through the entire resource once, then referencing back to the parts you need when you need them. Here are a handful more recurring themes you'll notice:

- Get a coach—and a cohort of peers. You should never do church planting alone, and you need people outside of your core team. Many of the resources referenced here are intended to be used with your coach or with a cohort of peers, as well as with your team. Getting a coach is the single most effective thing you can do as a church planter.

- Prayer matters. There are prayer guides at the end of every chapter for use with your team, with your intercessors, and personally. Listening to the direction of God and discerning his voice about your particular planting journey is crucial to the health and viability of your plant. I recommend assembling a team of at least three to five spiritually gifted and committed intercessors before you even get started with the planting process.

- This resource isn't just for you as an individual planter; it's for other new potential planters you'll go on to train, teach, and coach. We're not just training you to do it, but also equipping you to train others to do it. This is critically important. You can use this resource as a planter, and then turn around and use it to help develop new planters and guide them along the journey. You're not starting a service or a church—you're starting a movement.

- This isn't just about your church. As wonderful as your church may be, it takes all kinds in all places. The kingdom of God is much, much bigger than just one church. Live according to that truth, with open hands of generosity and with respect for churches different from your own.

My earlier work on *The Church Planter's Toolkit* was to help planters establish new churches. This resource goes beyond that. If you pay attention and apply the underlying principles, this book is designed to help you plant a church that goes on to plant churches—that goes on to launch a missional movement.

We plant now not just for ourselves or even just for our own generation, but for our children, their grandchildren, and their grandchildren . . . and all people who have yet to find Jesus through our existing churches. We want to plant churches that will last, and that will reach both people and churches. The church has changed form in many ways throughout history, but it never disappears; it abides, it lasts, it persists. It is a movement. It adapts and changes and—hopefully with our cooperation with the work of the Holy Spirit—will grow and flourish and multiply into the future until Jesus returns.

Get Ready:
Personal Commitment
and Readiness

Planting a church is not an endeavor to be entered into lightly. It requires a thorough assessment of yourself and the task ahead. Part 1 covers these chapter topics:

Chapter 1:
Developing Vision and Values

What is the point of church planting? After all, Jesus never commanded us to plant churches. What he did tell us to do is recorded in the Great Commission, the last instructions the resurrected Jesus gave to his disciples before his ascension:

> And Jesus came and said to them, "All authority in heaven and on earth has been given to me. [19] Go therefore and make disciples of all nations, baptizing them in the name of the Father and of the Son and of the Holy Spirit, [20] and teaching them to obey everything that I have commanded you. And remember, I am with you always, to the end of the age." (Matthew 28:18–20)

Jesus never commanded us to start churches: He commanded us to make disciples. After the disciples were empowered by the Holy Spirit, that's when churches happened. **Church planting is a byproduct of making disciples.** If you make disciples, they naturally form into groups and churches. Our mission—the one given us by Jesus—is to make disciples.

Disciples are those who love God with all their heart, mind, soul, and strength; those who love their neighbor as themselves; those who help others follow Jesus even as they themselves are following Jesus. Disciples are those who give themselves to God and allow him to transform their lives.

As a church, our core vision is to love God, love others, and make disciples. That's for everybody. If we keep our focus there, then churches will form, develop, and multiply. We don't want to just plant churches that draw people who are already Christians. We want to plant churches to make new believers. Disciplemaking is the reason for our existence.

The main point is making disciples who make disciples who make disciples— with all generations of disciples living out the Great Commission and the Great Commandment: Love God, love others, make disciples.

FOCUS YOUR VISION
- Free up time and energy
- Take a personal inventory
- Clarify what a disciple looks like
- Ensure a holistic reproducible process

START WHERE JESUS STARTED
- Look to the harvest
- Engage with unbelievers
- Serve and live alongside others
- Model kingdom values

DISCOVER RESPONSIVE PEOPLE
- Pray for discernment
- Dialogue to discover spiritual openness
- Select the few you're going to invest in
- Engage honestly and transparently

DEVELOP OTHERS HOLISTICALLY
- Invest consistently
- Listen and ask questions
- Assess people's starting points
- Engage in show-how training

STRETCH TOWARD WHAT'S NEXT
- Prayerfully determine what's next
- Focus the next challenge
- Strengthen an outward focus
- Follow through on what God is blessing

MOBILIZE OTHER DISCIPLERS
- Sharpen your skills
- Multiply disciples
- Develop skills in others
- Form new faith communities

This process outlines the basic progression of making disciples that Jesus has called us to. Churches are the byproduct of, and the vehicle for, that process. A church that isn't making disciples isn't a church. It may be a social club, social justice organization, or volunteer network, but it isn't a church.

The Holy Spirit was essential for the foundation of the church. Jesus said he would build his church. We are to make disciples. Jesus told the original twelve to wait until empowered by the promised Holy Spirit. Then they made disciples in response to the command of Jesus, and called the groups that were gathered as a result "church."

Acts 2:37–47, a familiar passage to church planters, gives us important insights into what the church is supposed to be and to do. A great exercise to walk through together with your core team is to read through the passage and make a list of all the actions of the early church. What did they do?

Above all—and in summary of the book of Acts—they made disciples. This is the primary work of the church. We take our cues from the Holy Spirit. It's not about God getting on board with our mission, but about us getting on board with his mission: the mission of making disciples.

One contemporary example of this disciplemaking movement in a western context is the ministry of Ralph Moore. He has focused his ministry on raising up new disciples who then go on to plant churches. Starting with just 12 people in Hermosa Beach, California in 1971, the Hope Chapel movement now has at least two thousand churches around the world. Some estimates are significantly higher. By staying focused on just one thing—making disciples who make more disciples—Ralph Moore launched a fruitful movement that has had international impact.

Your new church plant needs to be about making disciples. That said, each church goes about this mission in a slightly different way. You'll need to do some work—together with your coach and core team—to discern what that looks like in your case. So let's take a look at how Jesus' mission fits in with vision and values.

Putting a clear vision and values into words, and discussing them in your communities, is essential for getting on the same page. If you just say, "We want to be a good church," what does that mean? It could mean ten different things to ten different people.

Start with the roots

I've worked with enough planters to know that, by and large, most of them are "big-vision" people. I ask them about their vision and they begin describing it in great detail—which is wonderful. Yet I wonder if by starting with the vision, we might be missing something critical that needs to be addressed first: values.

The true, lived-out organizational values form the organizational culture. Culture, once established, is powerful and difficult to change, and often has the ability to overshadow and reshape the vision and mission. As Peter Drucker is credited with saying, "Culture eats strategy for breakfast." Therefore, we'll begin this chapter by looking more deeply at the sometimes unprocessed or unconscious values from which the church planting vision springs.

Here is an image that may be helpful, which I developed together with Steve Ogne: Picture the whole church as a tree. The values are the roots. You can't see them, but they are responsible for virtually everything that happens above the ground. The roots are ultimately what produces the fruit. They fuel the mission (the trunk), which results in the fruit. The vision, then, is of the whole tree in the preferred future—complete with fruit and surrounding orchard. It is a holistic perception of the role each of these things play in contribution to the overall vision.

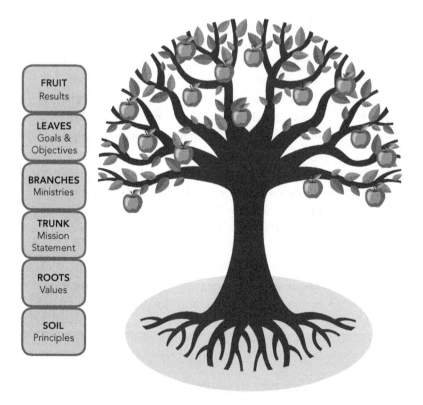

FRUIT
Results

LEAVES
Goals &
Objectives

BRANCHES
Ministries

TRUNK
Mission
Statement

ROOTS
Values

SOIL
Principles

What kind of roots do you need in place? How do your roots express the kingdom of God? What kind of church will reflect that DNA? How will your roots shape your thinking going forward?

Soil: principles

Principles, according to Stephen Covey, are "the guidelines for human conduct that are proven to have enduring, permanent value." They feel like self-evident natural laws: treat people fairly, do not steal, be honest. One church plant principle might be: "We listen to the Holy Spirit to direct our ministry."

Roots: values

Our values are the unwritten assumptions that guide our actions and determine our priorities. They are not statements of faith, doctrine, or theology, but they do stem from our beliefs about God. If we believe God is compassionate, kind, and loving, those beliefs become our values.

Trunk: mission statement

A mission statement expresses your objective and incorporates your values. Examples might include: "Practicing the way of Jesus together." "Living and loving like Jesus so that others become passionate, devoted followers of Christ who serve others." "Love God, love people, make disciples."

Branches: ministries

Each church likely has between three and five main "branches" through which its purpose will be accomplished. One church may have small groups, compassion ministry, worship celebration, and a discipleship path. Each branch must have a clearly stated purpose that it is seeking to accomplish.

Leaves: goals and objectives

Out of each main ministry area (branch) will flow specific goals and objectives. For example, compassion ministry might produce goals and objectives such as, "Host a weekly grief support group with people in the community," or "Partner with schools and other organizations to provide weekend backpacks filled with food for children in need."

Fruit: results

If the rest of the tree is healthy, you should see fruit: changed lives, community transformation, increased maturity, new disciples. If there is little to no fruit, check the rest of the tree. Is it planted in good soil? Are the roots healthy? Are the branches damaged? Ask yourselves, "Have we done everything we can to cooperate with what God is doing?"

Values

Consider which values you truly own. Which are currently lived out, rather than just stated? That's what will truly make the difference. Maybe you're thinking, "I haven't started the church yet. The values of the church will be different from the ones I'm currently living out." Don't be fooled—they won't. The values you currently live out will be the ones that grow in the church. If you don't reach out to people who don't know Jesus, your church won't

> The values you currently live out will be the ones that grow in the church.

either. If you don't live generously, your church won't either. Don't think values change when they move from the planter's personal life to the church—they simply deepen and expand.

The same is true of the values during the core-team stage. The long-term identity of your church depends on the lived-out values (the DNA) you start with. If you start with a tightly knit group of friends who share life deeply with each other but are not inclusive of others, you are unlikely to end up with an open, welcoming church that reaches out. If you start with a very loose relational style, you're unlikely to become a church with a clear, outcome-focused discipleship path that reproduces generations of disciples.

What *kind* of church do you want to start? What do you want it to look like in seven to ten years? It all depends on what you're going for—and whether you get there depends on what you're starting with. Values matter *now*. Although you'll periodically need to revisit to make sure you're still on track, do the hard work of establishing values now. It will make all the difference in the long run.

Values are:
- passionate, non-negotiable convictions that are expressed in consistent behavior. What we do demonstrates what we truly value.
- constant, motivational, and observable/discernible.
- core convictions that serve as the internal guidance system by which we make decisions, formulate plans, etc.
- evident in how a person or a group uses time and resources.
- the "why" behind the "what."

Values are not:
- statements of faith, belief, purpose, or theology. What is believed is not necessarily valued. For example, the demons believe in God (James 2:19), but they do not value him. You may believe in evangelism, but do you do it?
- methods or programs. These are the delivery systems for our values, not the values themselves. A *method* might be a weekly date night with your spouse, but the *value* is cultivating healthy family relationships.

Take an honest look in the mirror. What do you *really* value? What do you *really* believe? For each value, you should be able to point to specific behavioral examples in your life where that value has been demonstrated—both historically and recently. These beliefs-lived-out will create the basic DNA of your church. Just as the parent passes on DNA to the children, so your ministry as it grows and multiplies will pass on some essential DNA to whatever entities it creates: It's not you, but it's like you.

Now is the time to think through what kind of DNA you want to pass down, not when you're ready to start multiplying leaders or ministries or churches. It'll be too late then. Now is when you can make the decisions about what values to live out that will solidify your DNA as a church.

Every church is a little bit different, so let's delve into some options. Here's a stream-of-consciousness list of potential values. As you'll notice, they're in the form of questions. That's because different people often have vastly different definitions of what they mean by some of these values. You'll need to define your values clearly, and provide some behavioral descriptions of what they look like.

- What does **engagement with God** look like?
- What is **incarnational living**? What does it mean to live like Jesus lived?
- What does it mean to be **missional**?
- What is the **kingdom of God**?
- What is **discipleship**?
- What does **spiritual maturity** look like?
- What is **leadership**?
- What is **community**?
- What is the church supposed to **do**?
- How are we to **work together** with believers?

- How are we to **engage with those who don't yet know Jesus**?
- Who are we to **serve**? How are we to serve?
- What does it look like to follow the **leading of the Holy Spirit**?
- How does **God speak** today? To whom does he speak?

Based on your reflections, identify seven to twelve key values you want for your church—those you consider truly important. Brainstorm, get a lot of ideas, pray them through, then narrow your list down to four to six core values. Any more than that will be difficult to remember, and will have less impact in the years to come.

Next, consider what behaviors you (as an individual, team, and church plant) are engaging in that reflect those values. Are there some values not being reflected by behavior? What would look different if your behavior matched your stated value?

Here's an example from Vintage Vineyard Norway. From its inception, this church has articulated four values by which they navigate and calibrate everything they do:
- Generous lives
- Inclusive faith
- Authentic community
- Dynamic growth

You can see where these values would be central to those inside of a community, as well as appealing to those outside of it. A great deal of meaning and direction is packed into each of those values:

Generous lives—What does it mean to reflect the generosity of a God who has unconditionally given us everything? What does that look like in real life as we steward our time, energy, and money? Why does it matter?

Inclusive faith—What if there was a community with unrestricted access for everyone who wants to journey toward wholeness and a homecoming with their Designer? What if the place you were headed mattered more than where you were right now? How could we together create a culture where we always lead each other and new people to Jesus?

Authentic community—What could happen in a community where we are as real about our failures as we are about our successes? In what way could an authentic and transparent community speak to the culture of our day? If Jesus is the way, the truth, and the life, and the truth is what sets us all free —why would anyone *not* want to know him?

Dynamic growth—*Dunamis* is the Greek word for explosive power—the kind of power fueled by the Holy Spirit; the kind of power that turns death into life, that heals, and sets free. What if the only way to growth and maturity was to step out of our comfort zones, and embrace the adventure of trusting him, who loves us more than we could imagine?

Vision

Most of us, when we go on a trip, think about what it will be like when we get there. We don't just show up in Rome and then think, "Hmmm, what is there to do here?" Aside from the rare nomad who considers that kind of travel fun, most of us would, say, buy a guidebook beforehand, or at least look around online. There we could find a picture of the Coliseum. We'd look at it, imagining what it would be like to be there in person. We might visualize ourselves alongside a significant other, with the monument lit up at night; on a sunny day with our kids, getting an educational tour of the site; or backpacking and seeing the city on foot, and staying in hostels. Whatever it is we're visualizing, we'll call it our picture postcard—it's our ideal version of the future journey.

We can't know everything along the way—the delayed flight, the crowds of tourists, the rain on the one day we're there, the kind local person who helped us when we got lost. But the point is, we have expectations. They may be close to how the trip actually pans out, or they may be wildly off the mark. But how we envision our trip determines how we prepare for it. If we're thinking romantic getaway, we make different decisions about everything—from who we travel with, to what type of clothes we pack, to what kinds of restaurants we choose.

Church planting is similar. You, as the planter or planting team, need to imagine where you're going—what type of church you want to start. Even though you know you can't possibly get all of the details right in advance, you still need to imagine it, because the type of church you want to start determines the kind of choices you'll make to get there. If you want to start a house church, that requires different planning than a multisite church or a megachurch. Visualizing our picture postcard beforehand helps us decide on the best path to get there—even though no church ever ends up looking precisely like it did in our imagination.

Before planting a church, we need to spend some time clarifying our vision—praying over it, looking for it, imagining it, refining it, articulating it. Each church planter's vision will sound a little bit different. Listen to these three church planters and see how well you can imagine what they have in mind. Notice also how an articulation of the vision feels energizing. People are motivated by vision, not by need. Seeing only the needs can become overwhelming and paralyzing—unless there is a compelling vision that tells them they can make a difference.

Planter Hal: I want to start a church that doesn't look like a church. I'm thinking sofas instead of pews or auditorium seats—a place where people get to know each other, where they wear whatever they usually wear. College students in jean cutoffs and tattoos. I'm thinking stories and interactive dialogues instead of sermons. I don't mean a house church— I'm thinking maybe a gathering of fifty to one hundred. If it gets to be any more than one hundred, we'll have to branch off somehow, because the dynamic won't work anymore. I'm not sure where we'd meet, maybe a rental space in a strip mall . . . something like that. I envision peer discipleship relationships in groups of two to four people—somewhere people can get really honest with each other about what's going on in their lives. People learn best from peers. These smaller groups will create organic ways to reach out and serve the community around them, and out of those groups more leaders will emerge. I want younger people who aren't afraid to take a chance on a different kind of church.

Planter Richard: Too many churches are targeting the suburbs. What about those of us left in the decaying parts of the city? The parts that haven't been gentrified yet? The parts where the housekeepers and construction workers live? I want to create a church for people like me. We don't need to bring in a seminary-educated, white pastor—that would never work here. Almost no one in my neighborhood has been to college for more than a year or two. That doesn't mean we don't want what's best for our kids. A lot of us are new to this country, and we know that in one more generation our kids will have opportunities we've never had. It's for this reason that we work hard. But we want our kids to understand the core of the gospel message without any watering down, because they're going to need Jesus in the world out there. This church is going to be one that really "gets it" serving-wise. We understand the needs of our community and will serve with no shaming and no strings. We'll also elevate the elderly. Too many churches don't take advantage of their wisest people. I want them to be the mentors we so badly need. We will be a church that understands the value of the generations that came before us, using life-on-life mentoring to help everyone in our church continue to grow in their spiritual journey.

Planter Kristine: I'm tired of the whole big-church game. Usually there's just a lot of activity without much to show for it. More and more I think traditional church structures just burn out our volunteers. We spend so many volunteer hours on putting on worship services that we don't have the time to serve the community around us. We match our volunteers according to the needs of our machine rather than according to their gifts. We spend so much money on buildings and staffs that we don't give to the poor. I can't help thinking what Jesus would think if he walked into one of our nice, neat church services. I want to do something different: Lay-led house churches geared toward serving the city and giving to the urban poor—and we'll only gather everyone together monthly to conserve resources. I think something like this will really allow us to mobilize our leaders and challenge all of us toward a deeper kind of discipleship—a hands-on discipleship where every leader has a coach.

These three planters, if they accomplish their visions, will have created three very different churches—which is great. There's no one right paint-by-numbers approach. Consider how you can pray through your specific vision. When you make disciples, how are they living? How does the way they are living impact your church's vision and reputation? The kind of disciples you make matters. It informs how you do church together. This whole church thing is something we do in concert with others. Therefore, get a little more specific about what you're trying to produce—because it impacts the vision.

For example, if you want to plant a church that goes out of its way to demonstrate grace to those outside its walls, what will that look like on the individual-disciple level? What concrete actions will you take to model grace? What actions will the disciples you're making take that will indicate they're growing and living in grace? Some examples might include stopping on your run to help a neighbor who looks upset, inviting people from the community into your home, creating space for people to tell their stories and listening well in a way that honors them. How you are living will be observed—and imitated—by those in your church plant.

Consider carefully the values that undergird your actions. They will be demonstrated in how you live and work together, and in the kind of ministry you do together. Together, this makes up the broader vision and contribution God wants your church to make. It's not just a gathering of people in a room to sing songs or talk. What kind of disciples do you want to make? What are the actual outcomes? What's going to be different? What are you trying to produce in the people you're working with?

Spend some time visualizing all of this—and getting specific about it. Plenty of different models and structures can get us where we want, as long as we're walking in the footsteps of Jesus to plant a church that aligns with how we see him working in our communities. It takes all kinds of churches to build the kingdom.

Exercise: What's your vision?
Spend some time journaling about your ideal church. What do you
want it to look like? To feel like? To be about? Spend some time
dreaming.
- How can you love God with your whole life?
- How can you love others?
- How can you make disciples?
- How can you gather together?
- How can you develop leaders?

Five tests of a godly vision
A godly vision . . .
- is right for the times.
- promotes faith rather than fear.
- motivates people to action.
- requires some risk-taking.
- glorifies God, not people (or churches).

Reality check

By now you're probably really excited. Thinking about your vision and values is
energizing. You have a picture of a preferred future, an ideal church, the kind of
church you've always wanted to be a part of. But if you actually want to get there
someday, you need to stop right here and perform a reality check.

And the reality check is this: How is your current life reflecting these values? Or
is this just theory? Even though you're discerning God's call for planting this
church, if the intended values for the church aren't actually reflected in your life,
they aren't a reality to you personally—and you won't be able to plant a church
built on them.

A planter may say, "I want to plant a church that reaches the poor." But if she's
unwilling to get her hands dirty—actually getting to know the poor on their
own turf and understanding their world—she's not going to get far. Even if she's
successful in planting a church, it will likely be a very different kind of church.
It'll be one that reflects her values—the ones she actually lives out.

Exercise: Consider the values you've determined for your church. Audit each value by considering the strength and frequency of the behaviors you've listed, based on how you live them out. Think of multiple, concrete examples of times you've invested time, energy, or money into these values. Place a star next to those values for which you're able to think of multiple examples without difficulty. Consider how/whether you will be able to implement the values that don't have stars by them. Write your plan below.

_____

_____

_____

_____

_____

_____

Revisiting values again and again

Determining values is not a one-and-done exercise. You'll likely need to think through your values at the very beginning of your planting journey—which is why it's the topic of chapter 1—again with your core team when you have them recruited, and then again periodically along the way to assess whether your current path is staying in alignment with those values.

One of the reasons it's so important to identify and reconfirm values is that so often differing values—or differing expectations around values—are at the root of conflict. Over the years, churches attract all kinds of people with different values. If the ministry does not clearly and consistently articulate its values from the beginning, bringing a sense of unity, the church can be pulled apart by differing expectations.

Another reason why determining values is important in the long run is that much of strategic planning fails when values are not articulated early enough in the process, or are not revisited and reconfirmed. As the ministry grows and expands, the multiple paths of ministry options increase. If core values are *not* established, a clear direction is also difficult to establish. To grow well, you need to know what you want to become.

A vision of the kingdom

The vision we have of the kingdom shapes what we do as we move toward accomplishing our vision. What would the kingdom look like in your particular context, with your particular people? What would it look like lived out and multiplied across the surrounding community? What would it look like to those who don't yet know Jesus?

Before you start building and multiplying something, make sure it's something truly worth building and multiplying. Make sure your vision is consistent with what God has called you to do, and that it reflects the kingdom of God: "*Your kingdom come, Your will be done, on earth as it is in heaven*" *(Matthew 6:10).*

Journey Guide for Chapter 1
Developing Vision and Values

As a church plant, we need to develop vision and values in ways that align with our view of discipleship. Disciplemaking is the reason for our existence. After all, we don't want to just plant churches that draw people who are already Christians. We want to plant churches to make and multiply disciples. This chapter considers the connection between our vision and values and our core purpose of disciplemaking. You can use the questions and other resources in this journey guide to help you explore that connection more fully in your own context.

Checklist: for the road ahead

- ☐ Time has been regularly set aside for prayer and reflection.
- ☐ Values have been clarified and distilled into four to six primary values.
- ☐ Behavioral examples have been provided for each value.
- ☐ Church values have been rooted in personal values.
- ☐ Values have been processed with the core team.
- ☐ Values have been lived out and practiced regularly.
- ☐ The vision has been birthed out of prayer.
- ☐ The vision has been rooted in Scripture.
- ☐ The vision has been clarified and confirmed.
- ☐ The vision statement has been written out.

Discipleship focus: Disciplemaking
As you are beginning the process of planting a church based on discipleship, be sure not to neglect your own discipleship. For this reason we've included personal discipleship questions in the journey guides at the end of each chapter.

Inward focus:

- • Pray, study, and write out your definition of a disciple.
- • Describe the last time you asked questions about someone's spiritual journey and listened without injecting your own opinion.
- • In what ways do you think active listening could grow you as a disciple?

Outward focus:

- • What are you personally doing to foster relationships with unbelievers at this time?
- • How might active listening impact your outreach (disciplemaking) efforts?

Strategic questions: for you and your coach

- How are you connecting with what God is doing? What's your part?
- What does your vision of the kingdom of God look like? What would it look like in your particular context?
- How can you clarify the vision? Reality-check the vision? Confirm the vision?
- What values are embedded in your vision? How are they currently lived out?
- How do you want to see your values lived out in the future?
- In what ways are you listening and discerning God's voice?
- What do you sense God is saying to you? How will you respond?

Discussion questions: for you and your team

- What do you see as the most central values of our church plant?
- How are we currently living those values out?
- What could we do to live those values out more fully?
- What do you imagine God wants to accomplish in and through our church?
- Let's each take a turn going around and having each of us describe the vision in our own words.

Guided prayer: for you personally

"Where there is no vision, the people perish" (Proverbs 29:18a, KJV).

- God, what are you saying to me?
- How can I listen for your voice?
- What do you need to change in me to create the kind of church you desire?

Guided prayer: for use with your team

Pray together with your team through each of these themes:

- God, show us the vision you want for us.
- Help us to align our lives with the values we want to see in this new church.
- Please allow this church and our team to reflect you as accurately as possible to the community around us.

Guided prayer: for your intercessors

As you're in the exploration stage of church planting, it's important to have others praying for you. Ask friends and family members to begin praying with you for discernment about whether you should plant a church, and about what that process might look like for you. You can easily email the selection below to those who are praying for you—it will be themed differently in each chapter.

Please pray that we would:
- hear God's voice regarding what this new church should look like.
- discern God's leading as to how to shape the vision and values it will be built upon.
- be wise, as we build a solid foundation for the church.
- live in such a way that we reflect God to one another and to the surrounding community.

Action guide: a place for planning your next steps

1.

2.

3.

Chapter 2:
Confirming Your Calling

There was a prospective church planter who had been very successful in numerous ministries. Every ministry he was a part of flourished, grew, and was excellent. He was successful in many different contexts, and had a kind of star quality within his denomination. Then he embarked on his first church plant—and it failed miserably.

Everyone was stunned. After all, if anyone could be predicted to have ministry success, it was this guy. They thought, "We need to figure out what went wrong." When they connected with me to help them answer that question, I realized I was doing my first autopsy.

Because this man's resume and ministry experience was so impressive, the sponsoring group did not do a church planter assessment. So I decided I needed to do a behavioral interview with this man, to measure his competencies as a church planter.

I discovered that in every situation where he was successful, it was within a preexisting structure with resources and people at his disposal. In that context he could connect the pieces, lead, and have things flourish. What he did not have was a single example of him starting anything from scratch.

Had the group done its homework beforehand, they likely would have realized that they needed to do a significant hive-off—starting with one hundred people or so—in order for this plant to work. This ministry leader had many strengths, but starting from scratch was not one of them. He had no experience with it. (This leader went on to have a very successful ministry in other ways. He was great with teams and pastored growing churches.)

This chapter is designed to help you sift out your personal connection to church planting and the part God wants you to play. With a calling as big as church planting, there are many different roles. Sometimes people come in thinking they want to be church planters, but determine that God could better use their gifts in a partnership, staff, or support role. There are many, many different ways to be involved in church planting, and discerning yours is key to overall effectiveness.

Start with this important question: Why do you want to plant a church? Motivations matter, and there are plenty of poor reasons to do good things: power, lack of oversight, desire to be in the spotlight. Take some time for reflection and be honest with yourself.

Remember also that not all the most important roles are the most visible roles. Consider the character in C. S. Lewis' *The Great Divorce* who appeared glorious and greatly honored in the afterlife.

> "Is it? . . . is it?" I whispered to my guide.
> "Not at all," said he. "It's someone ye'll never have heard of. Her name on earth was Sarah Smith and she lived at Golders Green."
> "She seems to be . . . well, a person of particular importance?"
> "Aye. She is one of the great ones. Ye have heard that fame in this country and fame on Earth are two quite different things."[1]

The rest of this chapter is designed to help you determine your calling as a church planter—and to seek confirmation in that calling from the body of Christ.

Begin, continue, and end with spiritual formation
All leaders, no matter how gifted or how naturally talented, must continue to walk in and rely upon the Holy Spirit, and to continue in their personal spiritual formation. Discipleship is the foundation of all leadership—and that's certainly true of planters. If we are not first and foremost disciples of Jesus, we have no business leading. That's true at any level of leadership, and in any role.

Discipleship is ongoing, no matter how long we have been followers of Jesus. Although we may have a strong foundation, we'll need to continue to abide in Jesus if we want to be able to serve effectively as a church planter. For that is ultimately where our strength and vision come from.

There are many ways to continue in your spiritual formation: prayer, meditating on God's Word, meeting with a spiritual director, listening to the Holy Spirit alongside a coach, gathering together with other planters and potential planters for fellowship and accountability, continuing to serve with humility in ways that are not always considered "leadership." We never stop learning, no matter our age, experience, or position within the church.

[1]C. S. Lewis, The Great Divorce (New York: HarperCollins, 2001), 118.

Reflect and meditate on these passages:
• John 15:1–17: The vine and the branches
• John 13:1–17: Jesus washes the disciples' feet
What can you glean about continuing in discipleship and spiritual formation from each of these passages?

The job description of a church planter

A young child, when asked what she wanted to be when she grew up, said she was going to be a pastor. The adult was surprised and asked what made her want to choose that profession. The girl responded without hesitation, "Because you only have to work one morning a week."

A surprising number of people—even adults—may think that pastors (and by extension, church planters) have a light work schedule. That assumption leads to an important question: What do church planters actually do?

If you read chapter 1, it will not come as a surprise that the main job of a church planter is to make disciples who make disciples. Without that, other activities are rather pointless. So what does it mean to make disciples?

There is a certain school of thought, common among planters who describe themselves as missional and incarnational, that the job of a church planter is really just hanging out; go to where the people are, and have a beer with them. Although that may be one activity a planter engages in, let me just tip my hand right now and say that being an effective church planter is about much more than just hanging out and having a beer with the unchurched. It involves actually making disciples, intentionally bridging into discipleship. Being both relational and intentional are required as we bridge into discipleship.

> The planter functions as the lead disciplemaker; that's the core essence of your job description.

Relational + intentional = purposefully making disciples

Consider what you're doing now to make disciples. If you're not currently making disciples, it's unlikely that you'll suddenly begin once you have the title "church planter." And if you're not making disciples, don't expect those who are part of your core team or church plant to be making disciples either. The planter functions as the lead disciplemaker; that's the core essence of your job description.

How you go about making disciples may look quite different in different church planting settings, but consider these questions, to think through how it could look in your setting and to form a coherent job description:

- What do you see as the purpose of the planter position?
- What gifts and passions are needed?
- Who will you work with most directly?
- Who will you be accountable to?
- Who or what will you be responsible for?
- What specific goals will you have?
- How many hours per week will you need, to attain those goals?

What does it look like to live as a church planter?
Just as a person in ministry needs to already be living as a disciple (chapter 1), the same is true of a church planter. How you are living personally matters.

Consider John. He started a painting business. He has people who work for him that he has invested in, and they feel like they are part of the business. Some have been trained in specialty areas, and one has left to begin a business of her own. John provides excellent customer service for his clients, reaching out to them personally to discover their needs and determine whether those needs are being met. John is gregarious and builds relationships quickly. He is approachable and listens well, staying involved in the neighborhood community he works and lives in. He is able to flex with the changing demands and scheduling inherent to the business, but still forecasts project completion dates for individual projects.

In short, John is already engaging in the kinds of skills, activities, and behaviors that church planters need to have.

Many years ago I took part in a qualitative research study led by psychologist Dr. Charles Ridley, to answer the question, "What competencies are needed to be an effective church planter?" Through his very in-depth research and interview process, he identified thirteen essential competencies that make for an effective church planter. See if some of these look familiar, as you consider what you know about John the painter.

1. **Personal motivation**—demonstrates the ability to be a self-starter who works with diligence and excellence
2. **Visionizing capacity**—pictures a preferred future, initiates plans, and builds significant projects from the ground up to realize that preferred future
3. **Creating ownership of ministry**—passes on the baton of ministry by making disciples who make disciples and reproducing leaders who raise up other leaders
4. **Spousal cooperation**—works together effectively in both marriage and in ministry, maintaining individual and family health
5. **Reaching the unchurched**—connects with and influences people toward a closer relationship with Christ and the church
6. **Relationship-building**—initiates connections with new people and authentically engages them in deepening relationships
7. **Commitment to church growth**—understands, embraces, and effectively implements principles of church planting and growth
8. **Responsiveness to community**—discerns the culture of the local context and implements redemptive ministries that meet the needs of people
9. **Gift utilization**—discerns, develops, and deploys others to serve in their area of giftedness
10. **Flexibility and adaptability**—negotiates change and manages multiple tasks while staying centered on the overall vision
11. **Building body cohesiveness**—orchestrates widely differing people to function as a unified group
12. **Resilience**—stays the course in the face of major setbacks, disappointments, and opposition
13. **Exercises faith**—evidences a strong, vital relationship with God and willingly takes significant risks to pursue God's calling

Think about it: John took the risk to start his own business. He works well with people both inside and outside his organization. He adapts to change and sudden shifts in timing. He invests in his employees. He knows the people he works for and listens to them.

The essential qualities of a church planter haven't changed. You still need to reach people and engage with them. You still need to get them to buy into the vision, and keep going when it gets tough. You still need your spouse (if married) to be fully on the same page with you. Although not all church planters fully possess all of these qualities—and your team members can certainly help supplement some of them—all these qualities should be present to some degree. The more qualities you possess, and the more fully they are expressed, the higher the likelihood of your success as a church planter.

I should add that the first six of these competencies are considered what Ridley calls "knockout factors." This means that if a planter is rated low in any one of these, his or her effectiveness as a planter is limited (a yellow light). Low ratings on two or more would raise serious concerns (a red light).

Yet all thirteen of these competencies should be in place to some degree before you begin planting. For instance, if you have not exercised faith in ways that require risk in the past, there is no reason to believe that you will suddenly become willing to do so just because you have been approved as a church planter. That holds true even if you really want this particular role. Likewise, if you have not demonstrated generally good relationship-building skills in the past, it's unlikely you'll begin displaying them in the future just because you understand they're important. Past behavior is the best predictor of future behavior. You need to be already living into your calling. It's a matter of provenness. That doesn't mean that only people who have planted churches in the past can do so in the future—it means that people who have already exhibited these qualities in arenas other than church planting are likely to exhibit them again as planters.

How then do we assess our past track record of qualities? Through a formal church planter assessment.

Getting an assessment

Almost all church groups and denominations do some sort of assessment on prospective planters, at least in an informal sense. As a planter, you'd be foolish not to take advantage of as full an assessment as is available. Most groups evaluate the character and doctrine of those they deploy. Yet a more formal—and beneficial— assessment process examines the level of provenness demonstrated by your past behavior. A more formal assessment broadens the scope of evaluation by addressing additional areas of consideration:

- Strengths
- Necessary skills, competencies, and giftedness
- Character qualities
- Emotional and marital stability
- Theological understanding
- Philosophy of ministry

If you are a prospective planter, insist on a thorough assessment process. Rather than seeing it as a threat to your plans, look at it as confirmation from the community that you are truly being called and that you are well-suited for this particular role. A good assessment also provides clarity on growth areas for you, and often results in resources and referrals that can help you in those areas.

Behavioral interviewing

One of the most effective assessment methods is behavioral interviewing. Again, past behavior is the best indicator of future success. Experience and vision are important, but are not accurate predictors of future success. A behavioral interview acts as the foundation of any strong assessment process.

Here are a few examples of how behavioral interviewing differs from standard interviewing:

- Standard: What are your thoughts on serving the community in the planting area?
- Behavioral: How have you ministered in ways that improve the quality of life in your community?

- Standard: How do you see discipling fitting into your church plant?
- Behavioral: Tell me about some of your current discipling relationships. What have you done to make disciples who make disciples?

- Standard: How do you plan to face the inevitable challenges of church planting?
- Behavioral: How do you see that your work gets completed when it is disrupted by emergencies or other unforeseen circumstances?

You'll know if you're receiving a good behavioral interview if the interviewer is asking behavioral questions, such as those above. If the interviewer is satisfied with generalizations and not asking follow-up questions to get at specific behaviors, they're clearly not skilled in behavioral interviewing.

Follow-up questions should stem from each inquiry as the interviewer digs deeper into specific examples. You'll notice in the examples above that the focus remains on the past and present, rather than the future. Most church planters are quite comfortable talking about an ideal future and their vision for it, but what actually needs to be assessed here is how your real-life past behaviors could contribute to such a preferred future.

You may be used to responding to questions with theory, ideas, and abstractions if people have not pressed you for more than that. In the case of a planter assessment, bring some actual behavioral examples to the table. You can do some pre-work by reflecting on stories and specific examples that shed light on how you've demonstrated key behaviors in the past. The more concrete examples of past behavior you can provide, the more helpful it will be to an assessor—and ultimately, to you.

One area where you will need to deal with the more abstract sense of your calling—but then will also need to delve into more practical how-to considerations—is in the area of making a living financially while planting a church.

Bivocational options

Tentmaking isn't just a metaphor. The apostle Paul literally worked as a tentmaker to earn money while he lived and ministered in Corinth:

> *After this Paul left Athens and went to Corinth. ² There he found a Jew named Aquila, a native of Pontus, who had recently come from Italy with his wife Priscilla, because Claudius had ordered all Jews to leave Rome. Paul went to see them, ³ and, because he was of the same trade, he stayed with them, and they worked together—by trade they were tentmakers. ⁴ Every sabbath he would argue in the synagogue and would try to convince Jews and Greeks. (Acts 18:1–4)*

Many church planters start out bivocational—serving both as pastor and in the marketplace—and some remain so throughout their ministry. Sometimes it's an economic necessity, but choosing this route brings additional advantages, including economic independence from the church and more relationship-building opportunities with people who don't know Jesus.

I met Gerardo, a bivocational church planter, on a trip to Honduras. He has started six churches in eleven years, and—like virtually all Honduran church planters—also has a day job. Gerardo works as a mechanic; he owns his own auto shop, which is attached to his home. Mechanics in Honduras are basically on-call, like doctors, so he doesn't have garage hours and works a flexible schedule. Sometimes he needs to travel to where the car has broken down. Gerardo's wife is home taking care of their children, ages four to nineteen, so she can receive visitors whenever people come in with their cars. It's a very fluid lifestyle.

Gerardo considers his ministry to be his primary calling, and fixing cars what he does to support his family. Sometimes he has to go out and fix cars at night, and other times he cannot because he has a prior ministry commitment.

What I really liked about Gerardo are his hands. When we had lunch together, his hands were dirty from working on cars. That night at church, he was wearing nicer clothes, but his hands were still dirty, even though he had washed them. They are the permanently dirty hands of an auto mechanic.

This is the way of the vast majority of church planters in Honduras, where— according to local ministry leaders—more than 235 churches have been planted and are led by bivocational people. Through Gerardo and his wife, I clearly saw the joy of serving the Lord and seeing fruitfulness emerge. His sacrifice didn't even feel like a sacrifice to him, such was his genuine joy.

Another bivocational church planter, this one American, comments on the importance of choosing the right job:

> If you're planning to be a bivocational planter, it's important that you have a job that gives you as much freedom as possible. I originally had a job in sales, but high pressure and the church don't mix well. I also had a job for a while in inventory planning and control, which is my area of expertise. It was a rather demanding job, though. Everywhere I went I had my laptop going. I just couldn't do that and be effective in church planting at the same time, so I left that job too. I'm currently working for a temporary agency doing administrative jobs. It's not taxing or stressful. When I leave at 5:00 p.m., I can leave it all at work so I'm able to concentrate on the ministry. My hours are flexible; I tell them when I want to work and when I'm not available.

Church leadership must be understood as a calling rather than a career. While one might be able to make a living leading in God's kingdom, he or she must be willing to lead whether there is a paycheck or not. Jesus made a sharp distinction between a true shepherd who would give his life for the sheep and a hired laborer who would not.

Denomination or network?

You may have known from the very beginning what denomination you're planting with, but that's not the case for all planters. What denomination you're a part of—or if you're a part of one at all—has significant bearing on your church structure. Some groups will require a certain type of board or oversight; some will work within districts. With any given group, you'll need to figure out what the requirements are and what elements are up to you to decide.

I strongly counseled one church planter early on to find a denomination or network of some kind. He chose not to. Three or four years after I had finished my coaching relationship with him, he had a crisis and called me. I said, "Well, this is a place where I would tell you to connect with your network." He was asking me to become his network leader, but as a coach that's not my function.

I believe that it's dangerous for a church planter to have too much of a spirit of independence. You can't read Scripture and not believe in some form of connectedness. What that looks like can certainly be debated, but our local congregations are not intended to be isolated. Help will be needed at some point.

I'd suggest that every planter connect with a denomination or network of some kind. Each group is different and works differently with the churches it is planting. Even if you're leaning toward nondenominational church planting, at some point your church will need the help of some type of outside network. It's a given. Connections and support will be especially crucial for those inevitable times when you're in trouble.

Below are some questions to ask yourself, to discern whether a particular denomination/network is a good fit for you. How you answer these questions is largely a matter of personal preference:

- How well do your church values fit with the values of the denomination/network?
- How excited do you sense the denomination/network is about the type of ministry you'd be doing?
- What tensions, either theologically or in practice, are you aware of?
- Do your measurements of success align with how the denomination/network measures success?
- What vision does the denomination/network have for church multiplication?
- What training and coaching is provided? What ongoing resourcing?
- What expectations does the denomination/network have for church planters and pastors? How willing are to you make these commitments?
- What type of financial support would you or your church receive, and what would be required in exchange for that support?

Every denomination works differently, but here are some possible advantages:

- Connectedness and support
- Coaching and training
- Cohort groups

- Accountability
- Financial funding
- Name recognition for the church

If a denomination isn't right for you, look into other options beyond your own congregation. Increasingly, looser networks of churches band together for support, accountability, and the sharing of resources. Each network is different in what it provides—and what it expects from its churches. Some networks have no financial ties but share a common statement of faith. Others share certain resources and have standards that they expect all of their member churches to meet. Local church autonomy varies greatly from network to network, and from denomination to denomination. When conversing with groups you're considering, make sure they're very clear about what they provide, what they expect, and what level of commitment is needed.

Every planter needs some type of confirmation from, and connection to, the larger body of Christ. It shouldn't just be you who thinks you should be planting but some sort of sending body—whether that's a denomination, a parent church, or a network of churches. Some type of covering needs to come from others, not just you and God. In this way, local churches can support each other when needed, and correct each other when *that's* needed.

If you find yourself unwilling to accept any type of oversight or accountability, set aside some time to reflect on that and consider what might be going on under the surface. Talk with a coach or trusted friend.

Networks and denominations provide the very important role of confirming a planter's calling. While anyone's gifts and abilities can be used in a church planting setting, the call of the lead church planter should be heard and confirmed in various ways. Many leaders have attempted to plant a church because of the desire to "see it done right," to "do my own thing," to "prove it can be done," or out of frustration with the established church. These desires do not constitute a call to lead a church planting effort.

One of the reasons to be certain of your call is because church planting *will* be disappointing and frustrating at times. Again, denominations and networks can help in this regard. You can look to others for prayer and support during challenging times, as well as have others who can validate your sense of calling when you doubt yourself.

Taking ministry context into account

Even if you have the right competencies to be a planter, you still need to be in the right situation. Unless you have a missionary or cross-cultural gift, you'll tend to reach people who are like you, and are your age and younger. I met a planter at a seminar in Boston who was starting a church there. He told me he'd been there well over a year and wondered why he had only reached a handful of people. I asked him, "How much time are you spending in reaching new people?" He was spending about twenty-five hours a week in direct outreach. I asked, "So what kinds of things are you doing?" He described all the right kinds of activities. I told him I couldn't give him a quick answer, but I could take him out to lunch.

At lunch, I asked him to tell me his story. He was from New Mexico; he went to an ordinary college without much name recognition, his parents had ordinary jobs —a teacher and a plumber, I think. I asked about his wife. She came from a similar educational background in North Carolina. They had preschool-aged children.

Then I asked, "Who are you trying to reach with your church plant?" He replied: the Harvard community, students, and others connected with the university. I asked about the number of people in the community who had preschool-aged children; there were very few in that demographic. I asked him how he had come to choose this particular community to reach, and he responded that God had told him to in prayer.

"Can I make a comment?" I asked. "Either you heard God wrong or—if you heard correctly—God is calling you to be a Jeremiah. You will work your heart out and labor with little to no response and suffer an awful lot." He was simply not a cultural fit with the people he was trying to reach.

Following the seminar, my wife and I took a few days to enjoy Boston. As we were driving around, we got lost. We found ourselves in a neighborhood ten miles from where this man was trying to plant a church. There were tons of young children and families and people with middle-class jobs. If he'd planted there, he would have flourished. Coming all the way from New Mexico, he only missed the will of God by ten miles.

The application is this: Understand who you are, where you're from, your educational background, your parents and grandparents—because you'll be best at reaching people who are like you. I grew up in the outskirts of Los Angeles, at the very edge of development at that time. There were orange groves past our house, dirt streets, and a newly built high school. My father was an engineer, and there are teachers and mechanics in my family tree. Both of my parents came to California early in life from the Midwest.

When I got the call to plant in Rancho Cucamonga, I hadn't picked it. My denomination had chosen three planting sites, I had third choice, and this was the one left over. That's how God called me. I didn't come to the realization of divine placement until years later. Looking back now, I have no doubt that it was God's sovereign leading. Rancho Cucamonga was exactly where I had grown up, culturally speaking. It was on the current edge of Los Angeles development. There were no traffic lights. Housing was affordable, attracting teachers, engineers, and high-level blue-collar construction jobs . . . mainly moving in from the Midwest.

Think of where you grew up. Where are there places like that today? People everywhere need to be reached. Unless you have a track record of being able to do cross-cultural ministry effectively, why not plant near those you're most likely to reach? Demographic research to understand those you're serving is a must. In some ways, the question of *who* God is calling you to serve might be more important than the *where*.

Modeling kingdom values and kingdom cooperation

Before you get too far down the path of becoming a church planter, reflect again on how you're living as a disciple. How is your life, currently lived, reflecting Jesus to those around you?

As you consider your calling, one of the most important and foundational questions to come back to is how you are personally living out kingdom values. How are you living incarnationally? How are you growing as a disciple and discipling others? How are you caring for the least and the lost? How are you modeling generosity and humility as you lead? Unless you build on this foundation, nothing else will hold. All the skills and giftedness in the world won't be able to shore up the structure.

For that reason, be sure to live into the values of your calling in the present moment. Commit to generosity from the beginning. Commit to serving the least of these and remembering the poor from the beginning. Commit to a posture of humility from the beginning. These are the foundations of the kingdom of God.

Make it a practice to cooperate with other local churches and ministries. You're not setting out to build a ministry business that competes with other ministry businesses for market share. At least that's not how God intended it. There are more than enough people who need God to go around. Different churches, far from competing with one another, have a vested interest in helping and strengthening one another. That's true even when they are geographically close. The stronger each local church becomes, the stronger the church universal becomes. That's the spirit of kingdom cooperation. Pray diligently for churches nearby, possibly even with them. We are all on the same team.

We see this approach modeled by the apostle Paul:

> At present, however, I am going to Jerusalem in a ministry to the saints; [26] for Macedonia and Achaia have been pleased to share their resources with the poor among the saints at Jerusalem. [27] They were pleased to do this, and indeed they owe it to them; for if the Gentiles have come to share in their spiritual blessings, they ought also to be of service to them in material things. [28] So, when I have completed this, and have delivered to them what has been collected, I will set out by way of you to Spain. (Romans 15:25–28)

It's important to note that this sharing of resources cut across the important racial, ethnic, and economic lines of the day.

Ultimately, the church is not many—it's one. We aren't to compete against other churches and ministries for people or resources. Your personal call is just one small part of the church universal. We can help and support one another—all of us becoming stronger in the process.

Questions to consider as you practice kingdom cooperation:
- **How can you take a posture of humility?** Just as you personally don't have it all together, neither does your church or ministry. It's easy to point fingers at other groups and say, "We're better than them." Don't fall into that trap. You may have different issues, but you can learn from one another. Don't consider yourselves better than others, and reflect on times you have been prideful and why.
- **Who is already there?** Consider the community around you. Who is already at work there? Are there churches already present? What other ministries, small groups, or leaders are there? You're probably not the first on the scene. Even if they are from different backgrounds, you can cooperate with one another.

- **How can you help?** Given who is already there and the work they've been doing, how can you come alongside? Maybe they've been praying for a certain resource or gift—and you are God's answer. How can you bless what they are doing, even if it's not of direct benefit to your organization?
- **Where can you partner?** As you cooperate with other ministries in the area, there may be some you have a natural affinity with. What type of ongoing partnerships might be mutually beneficial for both the ministries and the community? Be willing to be a part of what God might have for you, even if it wasn't part of your own plan.

Journey Guide for Chapter 2
Confirming Your Calling

JOURNEY GUIDE

Jesus told us to count the cost before beginning
to build something. Before planting a church, we
need to carefully consider our personal calling.
Doing this well often includes prayer and discernment, assessment, confirmation by
our community, and a consideration of how we will address the many practicalities
of planting a church. Walk through the checklist and questions below to help you
consider your own calling and what God may have for you.

Checklist: for the road ahead

- ☐ Spiritual growth has been evaluated.
- ☐ Motivations for planting have been evaluated.
- ☐ The planter has been assessed and confirmed.
- ☐ Planter strengths have been affirmed, and growth areas pinpointed.
- ☐ Essential ministry functions have been identified.
- ☐ The giftedness/role of planter's spouse (if married) has been clarified.
- ☐ Bivocational options have been assessed.
- ☐ Network and denominational connections have been explored.
- ☐ Kingdom values have been confirmed.

Discipleship focus: Spiritual Responsiveness

Considering your own calling is an essential component of personal discipleship.
Take time to reflect on the questions below.

Inward focus:
1. How do you understand God's call for your life?
2. What kind of "checks" do you perform to make sure you are
   hearing correctly?
3. How do God's calling and your desires fit together?

Outward focus:
1. What are some ways you can use your gifts for the benefit of
   others?
2. How would the church be different if you lived out your calling
   as fully as possible?

Strategic questions: for you and your coach

- What did the results of your planter assessment indicate? What are your takeaways from those results? What recommendations were made?
- What confirmations and cautions have you received from others as you look toward planting?
- How have you cultivated your capacity to listen to God about your church plant?
- In what ways are you personally engaged with people who don't yet know Jesus?
- What are your thoughts on bivocational church planting?
- What networks or denominational groups are you considering connecting with? What are the benefits and drawbacks of each?
- How have you dealt with your motivations for church planting? In what ways has God changed your attitudes?

Discussion questions: For you and your team

- In what ways are you currently continuing in your growth in each of the qualities needed to be an effective church planter?
- What does reliance on God look like for you in this season of your life? What action steps are you sensing God would have you take?
- What gifts and skills do you bring to the table? How might they be used in church planting?
- How can you support and encourage others in the use of their gifts?

Guided prayer: for you personally

Then I heard the voice of the Lord saying, "Whom shall I send, and who will go for us?" And I said, "Here am I; send me!" (Isaiah 6:8)

- God, what am I willing to give up to follow your calling?
- How open am I to other roles you may be calling me to?
- What are the potential "dark sides" to my desire to plant a church (e.g., power, lack of oversight, desire to be in the spotlight)?
- To whom will I turn for help and support when the road is difficult?

Guided prayer: for use with your team

Pray together with your team through each of these themes:

- God, please give each of us a clear vision of the role you have for us on this team.
- Please show each of us how you want us to grow.
- Help us look for ways we can encourage, support, and pray for one another—especially those of us with different giftings.

• Please allow this church and our team to reflect kingdom values to the world around us, and to cooperate with other churches and ministries in humility and generosity.

Guided prayer: for your intercessors

Please pray that we would:

- discern God's leading regarding each team member's contribution to the church plant.
- understand the ways each of us needs to grow and develop.
- work together well even in the midst of our differences.
- move toward our surrounding community with a heart of love and generosity.

Action guide: a place for planning your next steps

1.

2.

3.

Chapter 3:
Maximizing Your Learning

You may have noticed, when perusing the table of contents, that there was no chapter on "church planter training." This is that chapter. This chapter is about how people *really* learn, and the best contexts for you to learn, grow, and develop in your church planting skills.

Most people think of training academically, with a beginning and an end. Due in part to our culture and modernist influence, our default means of equipping planters is cognitive rather than relational. We focus on information, and then try to download it using a classroom-based approach.

Now, I am not against church planting training; after all, Steve Ogne and I developed the original curriculum for the "church planter's bootcamp," which many groups have adapted. You do need an overview of the process, and you do need a strategic plan before you get started. But what I recommend, rather than a lengthy training curriculum, is an orientation covering the basics—followed by engaging in relational environments where you can learn on the job. The best trainings are principle-based and result in an actual plan, then are followed up with coaching and peer networks for implementation and support.

Learning on the job means making mistakes—it's an essential part of learning. That's why you need a coach, and peers to learn from. That's the ideal context for holistic development and learning: basic orientation, opportunity for hands-on ministry, a coach to help guide you along the way, and peers to provide support and encouragement.

In some denominations and networks, an internship or residency of some kind is required. Often this practicum is done in an existing church by serving as an assistant pastor of some kind. While pastoring and planting are two different things, there are certainly skills that cross over. Internships have the added benefit of learning what you're moving toward in a planting situation: a fully functioning church. But the primary benefit of an internship is that it's an experience-based, hands-on learning environment with some built-in support. Look particularly for residencies that are focused on preparing the planter to launch a new church, rather than those that simply use the would-be planter as a ministry assistant for whatever the pastor needs done.

As planters, we need to move toward a character and competency-based training process, not just an academic one. This chapter lays out the fundamental pieces that you should seek out in a holistic, effective planter-training process.

Orientation

Orientation—what most people call training—should be brief. The temptation is to sign up for something lengthy that includes all of the information you may ever need. Don't succumb to that temptation. Most of what is taught will be forgotten—especially if you are trying to absorb too much that you aren't yet ready to use.

A good orientation should be the rough equivalent of reading this book: Just hit the highlights, and then work with your coach to explore what that looks like in your context with your people. Orientation should cover only enough information to get you started; the details fall into place as you go.

I've found that people learn best when they have an immediate need for the information being taught. For example, take conflict management. I have a teaching process, slides, relevant Scripture passages, and some stories to illustrate the important principles. It's good material and many people have sat through it and taken copious notes. But what happens when people run into real-life, messy human conflicts as they're trying to lead? Do they immediately recall the principles? No. They usually go into crisis mode and want to talk with someone about how to handle this particular situation. It's at *that* critical point that we can be pointed back to the general principles, given additional resources as needed, and discern how best to approach a given conflict.

At the beginning, you only need the basics to get started. Much of the rest will come on an as-needed basis, assuming you have a coach and support network. Coming face to face with real-life ministry situations has a way of making lessons stick. Orientation is only one part of a much larger process.

Opportunities for experience and room for failure

As author George Whitman wrote, "All the world is my school and all humanity is my teacher." We learn best through experience. When you're just starting out, you need a place where you can have the freedom to try things—and sometimes to fail.

When you have difficulty leading a core team gathering one night, your coach can say, "*This* is what we were talking about when we touched on group facilitation and developing leaders. Let's look back at some of that material and see how it applies here." Then you can go back to the next gathering prepared with a better understanding of how to lead in the midst of group dynamics.

Ideally, a good learning environment for planters just starting out should:
- provide access to multiple opportunities for leadership development (small groups, teaching, discipleship, one-on-one leadership development, outreach, etc.).
- evidence a healthy leadership development attitude: "We're here to develop you to do what God has called you to do" vs. "You're here to help me out and do whatever I would like to have off my plate."
- be highly relational, team-oriented, and involve a coaching component that provides a feedback loop.
- place significant emphasis on excellence, yet give permission to fail.
- be a place where significant ministry is happening and leadership is being modeled well.
- be home to supportive relationships and grace.

This is the messy part, where most of the mistakes happen. This is also the exciting part where you are really learning. It takes time to get started well; you will not learn everything all at once. No initial orientation, however well done, can personalize training to this degree or cover everything that needs to be covered. Real skills are learned on an as-needed basis. You're in the figuring-it-out-stage—and at that stage, you absolutely need a good coach to help you reflect, learn, and cement those learnings.

You need a coach
I firmly believe that everyone needs a coach. I've been in ministry for many decades now, and *I* still need a coach. Yet coaching is even more essential during the early stages of a church plant. I wish I'd had one when I was at the beginning of my planting journey. New planters need a guide—someone who will listen and provide focused attention; someone who will help discern ways to move forward in your particular context; someone to come alongside you as you learn, providing direction, encouragement, and feedback; someone to act as a sounding board for your questions and help you process your options.

A coach is someone who comes alongside a planter to help you find out what God wants you to do, and then help you do it. By encouraging and challenging others in the early church, Barnabas empowered people for ministry. Without him, many others would not have been able to accomplish great things for God.

The overall goal of coaching is to help the planter succeed. Planters need to discover for themselves what God wants them to do. Coaches will aid this process, but they do not direct it. Coaching is not about telling others what to do. Instead, it's about helping others to discover it for themselves. In this way, coaching can be both nondirective and results-oriented. Good coaches:
- ask powerful questions.
- practice active listening.
- raise awareness and increase principle-based thinking.
- provide outside perspective.
- facilitate development of multiple options.
- enable planters to prioritize and focus action plans.
- provide encouragement and support to stay on track.

In addition to a great deal of anecdotal evidence, a denominational research study by Ed Stetzer demonstrated that planter coaching resulted in a broader ministry impact in terms of church growth (measured by attendance)[2]. New church developers who met weekly with a mentor or coach started churches that were almost twice the size of those who did not meet with a mentor. Obviously, size is not the only indicator of health and success, but it does correlate with growth.

Getting a good coach is the single most important recommendation I have for any church planter—and the lacking ingredient in most attempts at church planting. Real planter development—the kind fostered through coaching—is not just about accomplishing the task but also about developing the whole person.

You need a supportive community of peers
In addition to a coach, you need a community of like-minded peers. These are other planters and ministry leaders—people who get it, people who can validate you by saying, "Yes, this is hard," and "Yes, this is worth it." It may be called a network, planter community, cohort, collective, or incubator—but in any case, it is a group of peers.

The type of support provided by this group is different than that provided by family, friends, or a church community. It's like a doctor talking with other doctors, or a

[2]Ed Stetzer, Planting Missional Churches (Nashville: Broadman & Holman, 2006), 102–103.

teacher talking with other teachers. These are people who understand experientially what you are facing because they're right there too, facing similar issues. They get it.

The apostle Paul provides a picture of how this type of mutual support takes place:

> For you know that we dealt with each of you as a father deals with his own children, [12]encouraging, comforting and urging you to live lives worthy of God, who calls you into his kingdom and glory. (1 Thessalonians 2:11–12, NIV)

Note that the support is multifaceted: encouraging, comforting, and urging. It's not just providing encouragement, but challenge as well. The dynamic is similar to what makes Alcoholics Anonymous so powerful to so many. These are peers—people who get it because they too share your struggles. They can provide encouragement because they understand. Yet, a challenge from them—"You can do this"—also carries much more weight, precisely because they understand.

Support from other church planters can be particularly powerful, in a way that is different from the support that others provide. Back in 1990 Steve Ogne and I put together something called the New Church Incubator (NCI). Planting teams from across an area would gather monthly with their coaches in the NCI for support, ongoing skill training, and implementation planning. Within this environment, coaches could work with planters, and planters could provide feedback and ideas to each other. Between each monthly gathering, each planter would meet individually with their coach to process and focus their efforts to move forward.

Ask your coach or your denomination or network about getting connected with other planters in a supportive network. Even if you want to put together an ad hoc gathering of church planters yourself, you'll be amazed at how little you need to give them to make that kind of gathering incredibly helpful. Just ask them to start sharing what is working well for them and what is not working well . . . then sit back and watch the ideas flow.

Gathering monthly for prayer, encouragement, sharing, and trouble-shooting has many benefits:
- Recognizing that you are not alone
- Normalizing your experiences
- Getting insights from others on how to move forward
- Learning from the mistakes of others
- Sharing from your own pain, and beginning to experience greater healing
- Being challenged to align your life and ministry with God's mission

One word of caution on peer learning communities: Do not turn them into mini-training sessions. These are not times to bring in new content or additional teaching. Set these times aside for the purposes of encouragement, relationship-building, and idea-sharing.

> *Let the word of Christ dwell in you richly; teach and admonish one another in all wisdom; and with gratitude in your hearts sing psalms, hymns, and spiritual songs to God. [17]And whatever you do, in word or deed, do everything in the name of the Lord Jesus, giving thanks to God the Father through him. (Colossians 3:16–17)*

The key message is this: Don't go it alone. Partner with others, learn from others, get equipped, have a coach, share with peers. Be in an ongoing developmental mode. Connect your key leaders with other key leaders. If you're married, connect your spouse with other planter spouses. Don't fall into the trap of thinking you know everything, or that you can figure it all out yourself.

There was a time when there were no planting resources and very little coaching. Fortunately, that is not the situation now. Things have changed, so explore your options. Consider who you need to connect with, even for personal support and accountability. You need to have people who will ask you the hard questions in a safe environment. Often the most helpful people are peer church planters who are in similar situations and facing similar struggles.

Living with purpose
Creating a holistic context for learning includes not only having a coach and a peer network, but also living intentionally with a sense of purpose. Your sense of purpose as a church planter impacts everything else in your life: how you choose to spend your time, how you prioritize your responsibilities, the daily decisions you make. Life is your training ground. What will you do with it?

It's surprising how much of good leadership relies on good time management. There are always many, many possible things to do, and many demands on your time. Yet we must all make decisions about how to best use our time during particular seasons of ministry. There are certainly times for putting out fires, dealing with crises, or taking on difficult challenges, but if we're spending most of our time that way, we don't have the availability for long-range planning for the development of the new church and its health.

Consequently, we need to be intentional about how we choose to spend our time. What will make the most difference? What can *only* we do? What will further the overall mission most effectively? It's a matter of choices and priorities. Each planter might make somewhat different choices, depending on his or her gifts, best contributions, and season of life and ministry. There's no one right answer all the time.

To manage our time well, we must:

- Discern what's important: Before we can manage time well, we need to take some time to discern what's truly the best use of our time. Jesus regularly took time away to pray (Mark 1:35). We need to do the same, listening to the Spirit to hear from him about how to invest our time.
- Recognize what's necessary: It may sound good to say we want to spend all of our time doing ministry, but we need to take a hard look at our real-life situation. What relationships do we need to maintain? What are our current responsibilities? In different seasons of life, we may have aging parents, young children, or spouses with medical challenges.
- Focus our kingdom investment: After considering what's required, we can then consider what ministry should look like in this season of life. What should our contribution be? We can't do everything, but we should do something. What will that something be? Focus on it.
- Use our time intentionally: Once we know what we're supposed to focus on, we need to be intentional about our time. "Seeing how things go" is a recipe for wasted opportunities. At the same time, that doesn't mean we never relax. On the contrary, using our time intentionally means proactively building in the rest we need—and protecting it from interruption. In this way, we can schedule our time to align with our priorities.
- Evaluate and adjust as we go: The life of a church planter seldom goes according to plan. There will be interruptions, and things we need to attend to. We can regularly reflect on how we are managing our time. What's working? What's not working? How can we build in the amount of flexibility we need while still remaining focused on what's truly important? These are key questions for ongoing effective time management.

As church planters, you need to keep your family relationships, health, and spiritual lives on track so that you and your ministry are sustainable over the long haul. As Bobby Clinton often said, "Ministry flows out of being, not doing." Church planting is a marathon, not a sprint.

The best leaders take long-term care of themselves. That includes not only having a coach and supportive peer community, and setting clear priorities and using time well, but also engaging in a pattern of lifelong learning. Only an insecure leader pretends to know it all. The most effective leaders are those who never stop learning and move forward in humility.

Training, learning, and developing don't stop once you've successfully planted a church. Keep learning, keep discerning, and see what God has for you next. In the classroom of life, you are never finished learning, even as you are teaching others.

Pass it on

Teaching others is an essential part of continuing learning. Just as you need to be making disciples while growing as a disciple, the same is true of leadership. You will continue developing as a leader much more effectively as you help develop others. The two things fuel each other. So what does that mean, in practical terms?

Start passing on the coaching you're receiving to the key leaders you're developing. They warrant the same kind of investment, and you will grow from the experience as well. Share the things you're learning in your ministry with other planters in your peer networks. As you reach out, you will benefit your own ongoing learning and development as well.

> The most effective leaders are those who never stop learning and move forward in humility.

Ultimately, everything living is meant to multiply itself. As a leader, you develop more leaders who go on to develop more leaders who go on to develop more leaders. Coach those you raise up; some of them may be the next generation of church planters. The end goal is never your own church plant, but the ongoing growth and movement toward the kingdom of God.

Coaching, leadership development, and learning environments aren't for you alone. They are to be expanded as part of the DNA throughout the whole church and beyond. Effective church planters invest at least 20 percent of their time in developing others. If that's not the case, it likely means we're either spending too much time pushing papers or too much time doing all the work of the ministry ourselves. So the question becomes, "Who am I intentionally developing?" In many cases, we're not getting the leadership results we want because we're not putting in the necessary investment ourselves.

That investment doesn't always remain within our own ministry or congregation though. Sometimes people's development means they need to move on and multiply more leaders elsewhere. That means we can't hang onto people—they need to be free to leave and go somewhere else that God maybe be calling them. Ultimately, leadership development is not done for the sake of our own organization, but for the sake of the kingdom. Jesus said, *"For whoever wants to save their life will lose it, but whoever loses their life for me and for the gospel will save it" (Mark 8:35).* If we truly want to develop leaders, we must be willing to lose them, we must be willing to give them away. We may lose them, but what a contribution for the kingdom.

Journey Guide for Chapter 3
Maximizing Your Learning

Planters and their teams need to be fully
equipped to start a healthy new church. Although
traditional training is often beneficial, the most
crucial pieces of preparedness include getting a coach and becoming part of a peer
network. This type of relational yet strategic support is essential and reinforces
ongoing learning and reflection throughout the process. What will training,
preparation, and support look like in your case? Work through this journey guide to
think through your options and determine the best path forward.

Checklist: for the road ahead

☐ Initial connections have been made into environments where ministry is
happening.
☐ The planter has been connected to a coach.
☐ A brief orientation of the planting process has been covered.
☐ Connection to a peer network has taken place.
☐ Permission has been given for both experimentation and failure.
☐ A feedback loop has been established for follow-up, reflection, and
learning.
☐ Priorities have been assessed, and time is being managed accordingly.
☐ An attitude of ongoing learning has been embraced.
☐ Investment in the development of others has been affirmed.

Discipleship focus: Personal Transformation
A significant part of preparedness for planting is being in an ongoing process of
personal transformation. To what degree are you willing to have God continue to
sharpen, shape, and change you? A good coach will help you maintain a posture of
learning and openness.

Inward focus:
1. What character qualities do you consider your strengths?
2. What character qualities do you consider your weaknesses?
3. How have you approached improving your weaknesses?
4. What practices might help you increasingly bear the fruit of the
Spirit?

Outward focus:
1. In what ways are you intentionally representing Jesus in your
community?
2. How are you called to join in with what you see God already
doing?

Strategic questions: for you and your coach

- Who are the people that make up your support network? What roles do each play? With which peers can you share freely?
- How could you connect to a peer network that gathers regularly? What would you want from that gathering? What could you contribute to that gathering?
- In what ministry environments do you have the freedom to experiment and fail?
- Where do you currently spend most of your time? How does this investment compare to your priorities, and/or where God has called you to invest your time?
- What time do you have set aside for reflection and prayer?
- How can you be intentional about furthering your learning? What ministry skills do you sense you need to develop further?
- How can you best replicate learning environments for those you lead? What will have to change in you so that you can facilitate learning more effectively?

Discussion questions: For you and your team

- What are some ways we can create a supportive environment for learning?
- How can we support one another when we fail? When we succeed?
- What time have we set aside for sharing of experiences and reflection on them?
- How could we become more intentional about aligning our time with our priorities?
- What skills would each of you like to develop? How could we support you in doing that?
- How could we open up or multiply our learning environments for the development of others?

Guided prayer: for you personally

So deeply do we care for you that we are determined to share with you not only the gospel of God but also our own selves, because you have become very dear to us. (1 Thessalonians 2:8)

- God, how can I open myself up to the support of others?
- Who are you bringing into my life that I can learn from?
- Where do I need to step out and try something new in ministry?
- How willing am I to risk failure?
- How can I be a part of supporting others as they learn?

Guided prayer: for use with your team

Pray together with your team through each of these themes:

- God, as you lay a foundation of mutual support, learning, and grace among us, please help us to express those qualities to one another.
- Please show each of us new ministry skills you want us to grow in.
- Please give us the humility to try, even when we are uncertain of success.
- Please bring the people into our lives that you want us to learn from, especially those who do not yet know you.
- Help us to be a support to those around us through listening, encouragement, challenge, and prayer.

Team assignment between now and next time we meet: Find a way to pray creatively:

- Meet with a prayer partner.
- Take prayer walks in the neighborhood.
- Organize or participate in concerts of prayer.
- Other ideas?

Guided prayer: for your intercessors

Please pray:

- for me personally: that I would hear God's voice and respond in a spirit of loving obedience.
- for the community we are serving: that God would be at work there, and that we would see what he is already doing in the hearts of the people.
- for strategic direction for the ministry of the church.
- that we would bring in more intercessors to pray on behalf of this new church plant as it grows.

Action guide: a place for planning your next steps

1.

2.

3.

Chapter 4: Understanding the Planting Process

This chapter is basically a bird's eye view of church planting from 35,000 feet. You can give this chapter to your team to help them understand what the overall planting process looks like. Big-picture people will like it; for those of you looking for more detail, know that all the other chapters in the book will flesh out these concepts in much more concrete ways.

Let's first begin with some foundational assumptions of church planting: what it is for, why we do it, and what we are hoping to accomplish. The main point of church planting is not actually planting a church—the main point is making disciples. Planting churches is a byproduct of disciplemaking. Look at it this way: If we plant churches without making disciples, we are actually just rearranging people who already know Jesus. So throughout the whole church planting process, we need to keep our eyes on the main point of what Jesus asked us to do: Make disciples.

And what is a disciple? Jesus said, *"A disciple is not above the teacher, but everyone who is fully qualified will be like the teacher" (Luke 6:40)*. As disciples, we are to become Christlike. We are to live and love like Jesus and to help others follow him. We are to live by the Great Commandment—love God and love others—and the Great Commission—make disciples. There is both an inward character development and an outward lifestyle development. Taken together, this is what spiritual transformation looks like for a disciple of Jesus.

The church planting life cycle

Many years ago, Dr. Don Stewart introduced me to the concept of church planting as a life cycle. It's been an incredibly helpful paradigm. I've used it for years, and it still works wonderfully.

Think of the process of how a baby is born. It begins with preparation: A couple discerns the calling to have a child, assesses their own readiness to become parents, and decides when the time is right. There is also a lot of dreaming and imagining during this stage, as well as getting various support systems and community in place to help, because they know help will be needed.

Next is conception: the very beginning when the seed is planted and the new life is just beginning to take shape. It may not look like much from the outside, but this is where the idea becomes the reality. All that will be there is already there in DNA form, just not fully developed.

Then comes the prenatal development stage. This phase is vital and cannot be rushed. It's now that every system the body will need develops and becomes functional: circulation, breathing, the nervous system, vision, hearing, etc. All of this must be done before birth. If a child is born before all of the essential systems are in place and working, that is known as a premature birth and can result in serious health problems or even death.

Finally, when everything is ready, the baby is born. This event is cause for great community-wide celebration.

Life continues with ongoing growth and development. Muscles that were already in place are strengthened and the baby can hold her own head up now. Vision, already functional, becomes sharper. The brain grows at an amazingly rapid pace. New skills such as grasping and crawling are developed as the baby moves toward independence.

Eventually that baby, when fully grown into a woman, can engage in the reproductive process herself, this time from the vantage point of a mother. The DNA that is in her can be passed on to her children. If she lives a long and healthy life, she can go on to see children, grandchildren, and great-grandchildren.

This analogy can be readily applied to church planting.

For now, let's look at each stage of the life cycle—and what needs to be accomplished during each stage before successfully moving on to the next. This point is key: You must fulfill the agenda and requirements of each stage before moving on to the next—or there will be problems.

Preparation

The preparation stage is often a highly personal one for the planter. It's a season of deciding whether or not to go forward. It's a time of learning about what planting will involve and require. It's a time of discerning whether God is really calling you (and your spouse, if you have one) to this type of ministry. Preparation is the "counting the cost" stage. Prayer and discernment are essential, as is getting the perspectives, confirmation, and support of other people who know you well.

Key tasks of the preparation stage are listed here. These tasks must be engaged fully and accomplished before moving forward to the next phase.

- Spend time in prayer, self-reflection, and discernment.
- Affirm your commitment to make and multiply disciples.
- Mobilize intercessors to pray for wisdom and direction.
- Deepen your understanding of the church planting process.
- Count the cost before you start.
- Confirm God's calling to plant a church.
- Seek out and establish healthy accountability.

Conception

Conception is bringing the idea of a church plant into reality—taking those first concrete steps. Essentially, it's similar to a planning and design stage. What should be included and what should be left out? Conception is when the structure of a new church is created and flesh is put onto it. A great deal of thought must go into this stage, to ensure that all the basic essentials are present.

Here are the key tasks of the conception phase that will need to happen before the church can really begin to take root and begin growing. Unless every item is in place, complications may develop during future stages.

- Get to know your ministry focus group.
- Gather and develop a core team.
- Discern an appropriate ministry model.
- Create a financial plan and raise any needed funds.
- Develop a proposal that outlines your strategic plan.
- Engage a coach.

Prenatal

The prenatal stage of a church plant consists of getting all of the essential systems ready before the church looks like a church to outsiders. There's a ton happening at a rapid pace, but it's all behind the scenes. Whatever the church needs to do after it officially launches absolutely needs to be happening now, even if it may be in a smaller or different capacity.

For example, during the prenatal stage the baby "breathes" amniotic fluid. If it does not practice breathing before birth, its lungs will not be strong enough after birth. In the same way, if a church plant is not making disciples before it launches, it will not suddenly make disciples when it launches and/or goes public.

Every woman who has given birth remembers the late prenatal stage; you just want that baby out *right now*. But all of the essential systems must be functioning first if you want a healthy baby. If they are not, do not induce labor—the baby isn't ready.

Stop and check beforehand: Are you currently engaging culture? Are you currently making disciples? Are you currently multiplying disciplemaking communities? If the answer to any of these is no, focus on these areas before any kind of public launch.

Here are the key tasks that need to be addressed before the birth of your church:
- Cast vision widely.
- Engage culture relationally and serve sacrificially.
- Share the gospel in word and deed.
- Make disciples who make disciples.
- Develop leaders through show-how training and coaching.
- Gather and multiply disciplemaking communities.

Birth

Birth is not so much a phase as an event. For many churches, the first public worship service represents birth. However, not all churches hold public worship services—including house churches, cell churches, or churches in countries where Christianity is illegal. Even if you don't have a worship gathering, you can still be a church and fulfill all the functions of being a church. After all, you're not starting a service, you're starting a church. Worship happens as soon as people start coming to Christ; it's just done in a different venue.

For these churches without public worship gatherings, birth occurs when all essential processes are fully functional. It's more of a seamless transition as the new church continues engaging culture, making disciples, and forming disciplemaking communities. The distinguishing feature is not so much the presence or absence of public worship services as it is the full functionality of the church. As an event marker rather than a true phase, birth is a continuation of a life already begun.

Here are the key tasks that need to have been addressed by birth (again, some will not apply to churches without corporate worship gatherings):

- Clarify your worship philosophy.
- Put functioning systems and ministry teams in place.
- Design connection spaces for children and newcomers.
- Expand worship gatherings appropriate to the culture.
- Provide strategic leadership for ministry teams.

Ongoing growth

Just because a church has launched publicly does not mean it's all finished and the job is done. There is still a lot of growing up to do. Although human development from infancy to adulthood can take between fifteen to twenty-five years, church development is closer to three to four years. During this season, a church must continue all the basic functions of being a church while also becoming increasingly independent.

It's perfectly healthy and normal for a newborn infant to be fed by its mother. But if a ten-year-old cannot feed herself, something is seriously wrong. Skills need to be added as a church grows. Here are the key things that should be accomplished during this stage of ongoing growth before moving on to reproduction:

- Model and communicate the vision continually.
- Create paths for assimilation of newcomers.
- Mobilize and equip people according to their spiritual gifts.
- Strengthen the coaching culture to empower people.
- Develop a leadership multiplication pathway.
- Discern and focus where God is working.
- Evaluate and change for continual improvement.
- Gather regularly to celebrate what God is doing.

Reproduction

The rule of the created order is that when an organism reaches maturity, it will reproduce. The same holds true for the local church: If it is healthy, it will reproduce as soon as it reaches a certain degree of maturity.

However, consider carefully how you are defining maturity. Just as no woman of childbearing age knows everything she's ever going to need to know to raise a baby, no church that has reached adulthood ever feels quite ready to plant another church. There are always things that still need to be put into place for one's own congregation. No one is ever really "ready" for children—you become ready as you have them and grow into this new role.

But don't let that stop you from engaging in church planting. Just as it is biologically, the longer you wait, the more difficult it is to conceive and give birth. It's largely a matter of stepping out in faith once basic readiness has been reached. God will meet your own needs, even as you give away time, energy, and resources to church planting.

Remember, without reproduction, the church is extinguished in one generation. We were created to reproduce: humans, churches, all living organisms. Reproduction is part of our natural job description. In most cases, churches should reproduce by their third year after birth so that multiplication is woven into the DNA. In most contexts, churches that do not reproduce within three years rarely become church-planting churches.

Often the reason reproduction doesn't happen is because churches don't plan for it. One of the best ways to foster church planting is to have planting apprentices starting along with you. In a couple of years, you can hive off some groups to go with them. It's not as hard as it seems, especially if you have multiplying disciplemaking communities at your core.

Here are some of the key tasks of reproduction:

- Cultivate deeper compassion and vision for the harvest.
- Focus action plans for starting and multiplying churches.
- Pray that God raises up workers to send out.
- Invest time, energy and resources to raise up disciplemaking leaders.
- Multiply to the fourth, fifth and sixth generations.
- Monitor reproduction rates.
- Give glory to God as you continue to make disciples of all nations.

The church lifecycle and the structure of this book

The chapters in *The Church Planting Journey* book expands the concept of the lifecycle. You can see the general alignment between the chapter structure I have chosen and the church planting lifecycle. Therefore, if you'd like more detailed information, checklists or coaching questions that focus on a particular stage of the lifecycle, you can see where to look.

Preparation (Part 1: Get Ready)
- Chapter 1: Developing Vision and Values
- Chapter 2: Confirming Your Calling
- Chapter 3: Maximizing Your Learning
- Chapter 4: Understanding the Planting Process
- Chapter 5: Preparing for Challenges and Discouragement

Conception (Part 2: Get Set)
- Chapter 6: Building Your Core Team
- Chapter 7: Knowing Who You're Reaching
- Chapter 8: Designing Effective Ministry
- Chapter 9: Establishing Financial Support
- Chapter 10: Developing Your Proposal

Prenatal (Part 3: Get Going)
- Chapter 11: Casting Vision
- Chapter 12: Engaging Culture
- Chapter 13: Making Disciples
- Chapter 14: Multiplying Disciplemaking Communities

Birth
- Chapter 15: Launching Public Worship

Ongoing growth (Part 4: Keep Growing)
- Chapter 16: Developing Leaders
- Chapter 17: Organizational Evaluation and Development
- Chapter 18: Planning Strategically
- Chapter 19: Navigating Growth and Change

Reproduction
- Chapter 20: Multiplying Movements

Growing pains

As churches go through different phases of their lifecycle, different types of leadership may be required. A catalytic planter may be exceptionally suited for the conception phase and prenatal stage, conceiving a ministry, and maybe even birthing it. However, the ongoing growth stage will require more organization, overseeing, and maintenance. Some planters are suited for making this transition, while others are better off moving on to other startup ventures.

Part of understanding the life cycle of a church is recognizing that these phase changes are coming and preparing accordingly. You'll need to figure out how to shift gears periodically, in order to smooth the transition into long-term growth. Pay attention to the sound and feel that indicate a need to shift gears. What worked well at one stage may not work well at the next stage.

Five key ingredients of multiplying movements

1. Multiplication movements are empowered by God: Supernatural involvement is necessary.
2. Multiplication movements are culturally relevant: They must connect to the hearts of people.
3. Multiplication movements focus outward: The core of our testimony to others is serving them without an agenda.
4. Multiplication movements identify spiritually responsive people and encourage them to follow Jesus in community with disciples.
5. Multiplication movements use reproducible methods: Whether it's disciples, leaders, groups, ministries, or churches, all must be set up to multiply, so that as the harvest comes in, capacity increases.

Seeing beyond the horizon

A church that is actively involved in making disciples in its own community will also look out on the fields of humanity far and near and see them as ripe for the harvest. It will reach across multiple cultures, generations, and languages. It will multiply both locally and globally. You and I are Christians today because the church has faithfully multiplied itself across every generation. Let us continue that tradition.

As a church plant, you are moving toward something much greater than just your own congregation; you are contributing toward the coming of the kingdom of God. Someday, all the harvest fields will be reached, and the word of the Lord will go out across every nation.

> *After this I looked, and there was a great multitude that no one could count, from every nation, from all tribes and peoples and languages, standing before the throne and before the Lamb, robed in white, with palm branches in their hands.* [10]*They cried out in a loud voice, saying,*
> *"Salvation belongs to our God who is seated on the throne, and to the Lamb!"*
> *(Revelation 7:9–10)*

That's why we are making disciples. That's why we are planting churches.

Journey Guide for Chapter 4
Understanding the Planting Process

JOURNEY GUIDE

This chapter outlines the basic lifecycle of the
church planting process, using the analogy
of childbirth. It begins with preparation and
reflection on the desire to have a child, then moves to the conception phase and
shaping of the very earliest DNA. From there, all the systems grow and strengthen
in the prenatal stage. When systems are fully functional, the baby is born and
continues with growth and development, finally moving toward reproduction in the
next generation. The journey guide below is designed to help you process questions
of the church planting lifecycle on your own, with your coach, and with your team.

Checklist: for the road ahead
- ☐ An orientation to the planting process has been provided.
- ☐ The plant's current place in that planting process has been identified.
- ☐ Plans have been made for how and when to move into the next stage of
  the process.
- ☐ The ways multiple phases of the planting process can be addressed
  simultaneously have been clarified.
- ☐ Ways to live out sacrificial service have been planned at every stage of
  the church plant.
- ☐ Ways to live out authentic relationships have been planned at every stage
  of the church plant.
- ☐ Prayer support has increased.

Discipleship focus: Experiencing God
Planting a new church gives you a front row seat to the miracle of seeing a new faith
community born. Stop to experience God in the midst of that.
Inward focused:
  1. When are you most aware of God's presence and love?
  2. When are you most able to live out that presence and love?
  3. When are you most in a state of awe? To what frame of mind
     does that bring you?
Outward focused:
  1. How could you share your experience of God with others in
     ways that might communicate well to them?
  2. Brainstorm creative ways to help others connect to God and to
     scripture.

Strategic questions: for you and your coach

- As you look at the overall planting process, where do you see yourself?
- What stages have you handled well? What future stages look like they may be challenging?
- What key tasks still need to be addressed before moving on to the next stage? How will you address them?
- How is your church plant practicing sacrificial service right now?
- How is your church plant practicing authentic relationships right now?
- How would you describe your personal prayer for the church plant?
- How do you encourage prayer among your team and other intercessors? What action steps are you sensing God would have you take to grow prayer support for the church plant?

Discussion questions: for you and your team

- Looking at the planting process, where do you see us now? Where do you sense God wanting to us to grow?
- How are we currently practicing sacrificial service? What are some additional ways we could do so?
- How are we currently practicing authentic relationships? What are some additional ways we could do so?
- How are we currently practicing discipleship? What are some additional ways we could do so?
- How can we better support our new church in prayer?

Guided prayer: for you personally

You must understand this, my beloved: let everyone be quick to listen, slow to speak, slow to anger. (James 1:19)

- God, where are you leading this new church next?
- How can we grow toward where you want us to be?
- How can we best honor you and live out the kingdom of God in our current stage of church planting?
- How can I best position myself to listen to you? To others?

Guided prayer: for use with your team

Pray together with your team through each of these themes:

- God, show us how you want us to live out the kingdom of God at this stage of our church plant.
- Help us live out sacrificial service.
- Help us invest in authentic relationships.
- Help us cooperate with the discipleship process.

Guided prayer: for your intercessors

Please pray that we would:

- continue listening to the voice of God, as we seek to move forward in accordance with his leading.
- steward well the resources God has given us in alignment with his kingdom purposes.
- live lives of sacrificial service toward others.
- invest in authentic relationships with each other and with those outside the church.
- open ourselves to what God wants to do in our discipleship.

Action guide: a place for planning your next steps

1.

2.

3.

Chapter 5:
Preparing for Challenges and Discouragement

Part of the purpose of going over the church planting life cycle in the previous chapter was to prepare you for what church planting can look like. Yet, you can never really know beforehand. Inevitably, things will not go according to plan, and the story of your church plant will not unfold neatly along those life-cycle stages. There will always be something unexpected. I want you to go in prepared for that reality, with eyes wide open. Church planting is one of the most exciting and most challenging things you will ever do. It's not always smooth sailing. In fact, it's a spiritual battle.

I remember leading a time of prayer about church planting with some denominational leaders. I was having each of them spend some time praying aloud about what they were sensing from God. One pastor said, "We'll be engaged in spiritual battle." This guy was from a conservative denomination that did not at all lean charismatic, so I was surprised.

I took him out to lunch, and asked him about his background. I said, "It's interesting what you shared about church planting being a spiritual battle. Why is that?" His response was immediate: "Well, it's biblical, of course." "I agree," I responded. "But spiritual warfare? How do you justify that to your tribe?"

He went on to quote Matthew 16:18: "*And I tell you, you are Peter, and on this rock I will build my church, and the gates of Hades will not prevail against it.*" Then he explained, "'Build my church'—that's church planting. And the 'gates of hell'— that's spiritual warfare. I spend two days training new church planters in my denomination on this. We also talked about Ephesians 6:12–13. In church planting, we're helping people transfer kingdoms, and there's an opposition to that in the heavenly realms. Planters need to be prepared for that."

Indeed. More than ever in a western context, we are becoming cognizant of the reality of the spiritual battle. Don't go into church planting lightly. It's scary. The unexpected will happen. Sometimes it will be your fault and sometimes not, but it's a guarantee that things will go wrong at some point. This happens to every planter, without exception.

You'll face opposition, challenges, obstacles, spiritual warfare, and discouragement. You'll want to quit. Yet it's also truly exciting and thrilling to be gathering and reaching people who previously had no relationship with Jesus. That's the tension inherent in church planting.

This chapter is designed to give some air time to the mistakes, the problems, the unexpected, the times things go wrong. Even when you're doing really good work—and you're doing it right—there will be times when you get tired, discouraged, or the unexpected happens. And I want you to be prepared for that eventuality.

The leadership challenge

Without exception, every church planter I know of has gone through a leadership challenge at some point. This can be a test of the values, a test of the vision, an attempted shift in focus, a challenge of the worship style, or a takeover of the board. The surface issue can be almost anything, but a leadership challenge arises when a group of people within the church plant want to take it in a different direction than the planter.

This challenge sometimes comes earlier if you are getting off to a rocky start. If you had a great start it can be delayed, but I have yet to meet an exception, so be prepared. Most planters are blindsided by it. Trust God and your call and you can navigate through it. Don't assume it means you did something wrong. A leadership challenge at some point is normal. If you think that you are the exception, know that it's coming.

Navigating leadership challenges

Because leadership challenges look different, it can sometimes be difficult both to identify them and to handle them. Sometimes the issue is a spiritual one; other times it's a management one. Those two different problems would necessarily have different solutions.

The first step is discerning what you're dealing with. Then, depending on the particular challenge you're facing, here are some potential strategies:

Rehearse the goodness of God. At many difficult times in my planting experience, it has helped me to take a look at the good things God was doing. Going over a mental list of blessings—progress that was being made, lives that were being changed—can go a long way in lifting a planter's perspective.

Take a break. Many times, as I've been coaching planters facing discouragement, I ask, "When is the last time you took a full day off?" When they can't remember, I suggest taking a sabbath. We were not meant to work nonstop. Work is difficult, and we need life rhythms with built-in rest and enjoyment.

Review your calling. How did God lead you to this place? Revisit the time of your calling and recommit to it. If God has called you to play a part in building his church, he will pave a way to make it possible. Remember your vision and your values. Remember what God has called you to and be faithful.

Avoid isolation. Maintain connections with family and friends. Have people you can talk honestly with. Keep a strong connection with your coach, and really confide in him or her, reflecting on your learnings. Don't get isolated or consumed by the work; you need outside perspectives.

Pray in the opposite spirit. Particularly when the issue is a spiritual one, you can pray against it. Discern what type of spirit you are facing, and then determine its biblical opposite. If you find yourself planting in an area where greed is predominant, pray against greed and practice generosity. When you face a spirit of fear, pray for hope. The best way to get rid of the darkness is to turn on the lights. Ask God to fill the space with his light.

Delegate. Sometimes when you are growing, you find yourself with too many things to oversee. You become overextended and stretched too thin. In these cases, you are facing a management issue. Prioritize and reprioritize what's most important for you to do. This will often mean increasing delegation and the development of other leaders.

Focus on your next faithful step. Take time to reflect and seek God's perspective. Prioritize and reprioritize. Ask God to help you determine the most important issue to address now. Then seek the guidance of the Holy Spirit to identify what needs to be done next—and with whom.

Jesus' job is to build the church. Your job is to follow the Spirit. I have always found that reality comforting as a church planter. I can pray to God, "Jesus, you said you'd build the church. Please do that—and show me what you want me to do. What do you want me to do now? Who do I need to connect with?"

My leadership challenge

Although your own leadership challenge may look quite different, I'll tell you about the biggest one I faced when planting Community Baptist Church (CBC). Things were going well, and we were about three years into the plant. Every year before New Year's I would pray for a theme for the year, and that theme would give me some direction for the next year. As I was seeking God this particular year, I had a clear sense of the Lord saying, "This will be the year that determines whether CBC will continue as an innovative, outward-focused church, or become a more traditional inward-focused church." I remember thinking how odd that was, as that issue wasn't really a struggle for us at the time. Two-thirds of the people we were reaching were unchurched, and the culture of the church reflected that reality.

> Jesus' job is to build the church. Your job is to follow the Spirit.

Then three weeks into the new year, a group of about twenty-five people came to our church from a very traditional, inward-focused church that was in decline, about thirty minutes away. Our location was much more convenient for these people, and they all went through the newcomers' classes and became members. Within a few months, they were having secret prayer meetings to try to change the direction and vision of the church. They wanted adult Sunday school instead of small groups. They wanted more hymns and less music that appealed to the unchurched. They wanted an altar call at the end of the service instead of the effective ways we were bringing people into a personal relationship with Christ. They wanted more congregational involvement in decision-making, so that members could vote on almost everything.

Now none of these things are wrong in and of themselves, but they were not a good fit with the people we had been reaching. This group was trying to make the church into the kind of church they wanted without regard for outreach effectiveness. And the scary thing was, they were beginning to convince some of my most key leaders. I practiced good leadership, casting vision, listening, processing people, taking dozens and dozens of meetings on the subject, but it was clear that the tide was turning.

Finally I came to the conclusion that there was nothing more I could do. I prayed, "This is not good. Lord, if you don't do something, they are going to win. They will undo all the work we have done in planting this church. I've done everything

I know to do to try to counteract it. There is nothing more I can do. Either change their hearts or get them out of here." I realized that was a serious prayer. It was the first time I had ever prayed such a thing. Yet I felt that this group was doing lasting damage to the church. I did nothing more; I just prayed.

A few weeks later, in July, that whole group of twenty-five people chose to leave. That next Sunday they were all gone. Yet, although it was the middle of summer, our overall attendance went up that Sunday. I felt God was validating that shift. We had faced the leadership challenge and had made it through. We began to grow more, and better. Although I believe I had practiced good leadership, it wasn't down to that. Good leadership wasn't enough. God had to show up. It was up to his moving ahead.

Outcomes

When a leadership challenge goes well, it often leads to increased faith and confidence that God is at work. Ministries often flourish after testing. When a leadership challenge does not go well, planters can feel hurt and doubt their calling. In either case, much growth can happen by reflecting on the situation and learning from it. Sometimes there's nothing to be done differently—it's more of a matter of understanding and acceptance. God can use these challenges to develop your leadership in ways it needs to grow.

When I gave an early draft of this book to some church planters for their feedback, one of them validated the breadth of topics covered. He said, "A lot of what is in here is advice I had ignored early on and now wish I had listened to. To those just starting out I would say this: Don't cut corners. It will come back to bite you. Just because you've had some ministry success in the past doesn't mean you can skip over the topics covered in this book. It's all necessary. These are vital practices that you ignore or shortcut at your peril."

So I say to you: Be prepared. You *will* face a leadership challenge. There has been no exception with any planter I've ever met. It can be a test of values or direction, it can be a direct challenge to your personal leadership, but every planter will face something. Generally speaking, the better your plant is doing at the beginning, the longer it will be before the challenge arrives. If you're off to a rockier start, it may come sooner. But it will come. It always comes. You can get through it and be stronger for it, and it will pave the way for kingdom growth.

Now let's get on with the specifics of what God is calling you to do.

Journey Guide for Chapter 5
Preparing for Challenges and Discouragement

JOURNEY GUIDE

Leadership challenges are an inevitable part of
any church plant. Planters and their teams need
to be prepared to face discouragement with
flexibility and faith, with reliance on systems of support that they have put into
place beforehand. The journey guide below is designed to help you count the cost
beforehand and consider the challenges and difficulties that may come your way so
you can most effectively prepare to face them.

Checklist: for the road ahead

☐ The reality of the challenges ahead has been accepted.
☐ A posture of faith, flexibility, and humility has been adopted, and
   regularly exercised.
☐ A coaching relationship has been established.
☐ A network of peer support has been established.
☐ A clear sense of calling to church planting has been embraced.
☐ A clear dedication to prayer and discipleship has been demonstrated.
☐ An expectation of, and preparation for, spiritual warfare has been
   established.

Discipleship focus: Personal Transformation

One of the most difficult aspects of church planting is that—at some point—things
will not go well and you will need to get constructive feedback from others. Keep an
attitude of humility and listening to God in your own journey discipleship as you
seek out helpful feedback from others, even when it's difficult.

Inward focused:

1. Who has given you unsolicited feedback that was constructive
   and helpful? What did you do with that feedback?
2. Who have you asked for feedback lately? Who else might be in a
   good position to give it?
3. What makes it difficult for you to ask for and receive feedback?
   What steps might you take to address those roadblocks?

Outward focused:

1. What relationships in your life and in your community need
   restorative work?
2. List steps you can take to work toward that restoration.

Strategic questions: for you and your coach

- What is your understanding of the relationship between church planting and spiritual warfare? What does it look like?
- What is your default way of responding to challenges? What additional responses would you like to practice?
- What can you do now to prepare for the inevitable challenges coming your way?
- What will you need to figure out in the moment?
- What reality do you want me (your coach) to remind you of when you face a leadership challenge?

Discussion questions: for you and your team

- In what ways are you expecting challenges? In what ways, if any, are you expecting things to go smoothly?
- If we're successful in accomplishing our vision, what pushback and resistance might we get from the world and/or from dark spiritual forces?
- What does God promise us in our challenges and spiritual battles? What does he not promise us?
- What should our posture to meet those challenges look like?
- How can we spiritually prepare ourselves beforehand?

Guided prayer: for you personally

Reflect on Numbers 11:10–15, a time when Moses faced a leadership challenge.

- Lord, when have I felt how Moses felt? How have I responded in the past?
- Please help me consider how to respond to future leadership challenges.
- Remind me that it's okay to feel emotions, just as Moses felt his, but give me the grace to ask for help, look for solutions, and rely on you in the midst of challenges.

Guided prayer: for use with your team

Pray aloud Ephesians 6:10–18 three times; then, open the floor for spontaneous prayer from team members.

> *Finally, be strong in the Lord and in the strength of his power.* [11] *Put on the whole armor of God, so that you may be able to stand against the wiles of the devil.* [12] *For our struggle is not against enemies of blood and flesh, but against the rulers, against the authorities, against the cosmic powers of this present darkness, against the spiritual forces of evil in the heavenly places.* [13] *Therefore take up the whole armor of God, so that you may be able to withstand on that evil day, and having done everything, to stand*

firm. [14] Stand therefore, and fasten the belt of truth around your waist, and put on the breastplate of righteousness. [15] As shoes for your feet put on whatever will make you ready to proclaim the gospel of peace. [16] With all of these, take the shield of faith, with which you will be able to quench all the flaming arrows of the evil one. [17] Take the helmet of salvation, and the sword of the Spirit, which is the word of God.

[18] Pray in the Spirit at all times in every prayer and supplication. To that end keep alert and always persevere in supplication for all the saints.

Guided prayer: for your intercessors

Please pray that we would:

- meet the inevitable challenges to church planting in a way that glorifies God.
- engage in ministry in a manner of humility and reliance on the Holy Spirit.
- remember our calling when we face difficult times.
- rely on our community for support and encouragement.
- be faithful with what God is calling us to do, leaving the results in his hands.

Action guide: a place for planning your next steps

1.

2.

3.

Get Set: Preparation and Planning

After doing a thorough assessment of yourself and the planting process, we now turn to the initial planning and preparation stage. Part 2 covers these topics:

Chapter 6:
Building Your Core Team

A number of years ago, *Forbes* magazine published an article called "Two for the Money," which shared the results of a research project studying startup businesses. Those businesses that began as partnerships were four times more likely to succeed than those launched by solo entrepreneurs.

At first those conducting the study thought that might be due to division of labor according to strengths, e.g., one person on the outside doing sales, the other on the inside doing development.

But they discovered that the core factor was actually time management. In businesses that started as partnerships, there was a subconscious accountability to make sure each person was spending time on what was truly essential. By contrast, solo entrepreneurs often spent monumental amounts of time on minutiae—areas of low priority. As a result, they became scattered in their focus.

There are many reasons to work together with a team in church planting:
- Support and encouragement
- Complementary gifts and skills
- Gaining wisdom through different perspectives
- Sharing the burden of ministry
- Maintaining focus on the truly important

Having the right core team in place is essential for a successful church plant. Who will you be walking through this journey alongside? Who will you be working with on a daily basis? When some leave, you want there to be enough others to carry on the work. Your core team are your essential coworkers in this church planting endeavor. You want to make sure you're walking through it with the right people. This is not an area to rush through, but one to take time over and invest in.

Jesus as a model of team building

Look at this brief passage from the book of Matthew:

> *From that time Jesus began to proclaim, "Repent, for the kingdom of heaven has come near."*
> *[18] As he walked by the Sea of Galilee, he saw two brothers, Simon, who is called Peter, and Andrew his brother, casting a net into the sea—for they were fishermen. [19] And he said to them, "Follow me, and I will make you fish for people." [20] Immediately they left their nets and followed him. (Matthew 4:17–20)*

As you think of starting a team, look at Jesus and how he formed his leadership community—the twelve disciples:

- He first began to preach the vision (Matthew 4:17).
- He looked for disciples in nontraditional places rather than from among existing religious leaders (Matthew 4:18).
- He gave a clear call, with a step to action (Matthew 4:19).
- He waited to see if they would follow through on that commitment (Matthew 4:20).

Don't be discouraged if you have difficulty recruiting a core team at the beginning. This stage is often a challenging one for planters. Not even everyone Jesus called decided to follow him:

> *Jesus answered, "If you want to be perfect, go, sell your possessions and give to the poor, and you will have treasure in heaven. Then come, follow me." [22] When the young man heard this, he went away sad, because he had great wealth. (Matthew 19:21–22)*

Do not start by trying to get anyone and everyone you can on board; be selective. The people on your core team will have a sizeable impact on the future DNA of the church, so they need to be the right people. This point is key, more so than most planters realize.

Ask God for discernment

Pray. And then pray again. The Holy Spirit needs to be involved in your decision-making process. Ask for discernment about who should be a part of your team. Ask those who have shown interest to pray also; they too will need discernment about their decision. There really is no substitute for this step—and it's probably the most important one if you want the right people on your team. Before Jesus chose the Twelve, he spent the whole night in prayer:

> *Now during those days he went out to the mountain to pray; and he spent*

the night in prayer to God. [13] And when day came, he called his disciples and chose twelve of them, whom he also named apostles. (Luke 6:12–13)

Casting vision to potential team members

As you recruit team members, you'll need to make sure they embrace your vision and share your values. This will require many conversations. Ask questions to find out what they're looking for in a church plant. Any values they express need to be demonstrated behaviorally—see how their values are currently playing out in their lives. Sometimes you may be using the same words as someone else, but not defining them the same way, so ask for examples. Take the time to dialogue, listen, ask questions, and get to know people.

Are these people who are already engaging in their own discipleship and disciplemaking? If they're not willing to build redemptive relationships and serve people who are not yet followers of Jesus before your church begins, they are unlikely to do it afterward. People certainly don't have to be perfect, but they do need to be willing to try and to be faithful. Personal engagement in making disciples must be the core DNA of the church.

> Don't recruit only people who are just like you.

Trust your intuition: Often it is the Holy Spirit giving you guidance. If something doesn't feel right, it's okay to point people in a different direction for their ministry outlet. Not everyone will be a good fit for your team and that's okay.

Remember to cast vision regularly; it's not a one-and-done kind of thing to check off your list. Put prompts on your calendar or phone if you need to, so that you return to the vision regularly and remind your team of the purpose you're trying to accomplish together.

Consider who you need

As part of the discernment process, consider who you may need. Don't recruit only people who are just like you. Respect people who are different in skill and passion. As you consider what kinds of people you need on your team, brainstorm a list of categories to look for.

- What roles, gifts or skills might be necessary (administrator, organizer, evangelist, visionary)?
- Consider the demographics of your team in light of who you want to reach. We'll address this issue more in a future chapter, but if your team is a gathering of white males in their 50s, how well will that fit with who you

will be serving? You'll need at least some people from the group you're reaching.

- Consider also who may already share your passion for those you're serving. People on your team must share a sense of calling.
- And of course, consider character qualities such as faithfulness, teachability, commitment to the vision, courage, and humility.
- Think broadly and break out of the "us vs. them" mentality. If you want to reach lower-income broken families, what about inviting a lower-income single mom to be a part of your team? If you want to reach addicts, who are some addicts in recovery who may be willing to team with you? As you start engaging more actively in ministry, more and more of the leaders you'll be developing will be those from the groups you're reaching.
- Don't fall into the trap of looking only for obvious ministry leaders. Jesus primarily chose fishermen and tax collectors. How different would his ministry have looked had he chosen mainly well-to-do religious leaders?

If you are stumped for names on this step, you need to spend more time living among the people you'll be reaching before you assemble a formal team. Only by getting to know people on a personal level will you understand them enough to put together a meaningful team that will actually reach them.

Different gift sets for different ministry leaders: APEST
One way that competencies of church leaders has been recently popularized is the APEST model. Knowing who you are and how you fit into APEST can help determine both how you plant and who you need around you. Behavioral interviewing and assessment help with this process as well.

The basic idea is that there are five different types of leaders, who work together in complementary ways. This concept, sometimes called a "4/11" team, is based on Ephesians 4:11: *"The gifts he gave were that some would be apostles, some prophets, some evangelists, some pastors and teachers."* These five roles are vital to the body of the church, provide specific strengths, and must be filled to create a movement.

- Apostle: one sent to lay a foundation for the expansion of the church with a specific, God-given assignment
- Prophet: one who hears and speaks a specific word from God to a distinct person or persons
- Evangelist: one who is called to passionately seek out opportunities to share the gospel with others, and lead them toward acceptance of Christ
- Shepherd: one who has an overwhelming concern for the continuing care of a specific community

- Teacher: one responsible for progressive growth in understanding and application of the truth

Each leader has one or more of these gifts. For example, today's senior pastor role in a large seeker-sensitive congregation likely leans heavily on being a teacher and evangelist, while enlisting others in the community to provide shepherding and assuming the foundation for the church has already been laid by the work of an apostle.

Who you are and which of these roles you more naturally lean toward affects how you plant, as well as who else you will need. Any of these roles can be used by God to plant a church, but each will need different forms of support.

For instance, the "start and go" team best functions as a team of two: an apostle and a prophet. This team, from the outset, does not plan to stay or pastor the churches. It plans to leave when the movement has been started, and must raise up a "stay and grow" team for that transition. The "stay and grow" team, usually comprised of an evangelist/shepherd/teacher combination, does its best planting along with a team or core group, and plans to remain with the church after it is established.

It is important to note that these five roles are often fluid rather than static. One may begin in one role and transition to another. Twice, Paul refers to himself as a teacher, herald (evangelist), and apostle (1 Timothy 2:7; 2 Timothy 1:11).

Your particular role mix can also give you direction regarding the type of ministry model that will likely work best for you. A leader who is strong in shepherding may excel using a house-church model, while an apostle does best in an unpredictable environment that is regularly moving toward new frontiers.

Who you will need on your team
Who you are in your giftedness and leadership style is also an important indicator of who else you will need on your church plant team. Whether partners, core team members, or spouses (depending on their role), you will need people different from yourself but complementary—as well as people who share your basic vision and values.

You won't really know who you need on your team until you know what roles God is calling you to play, based on your giftedness and calling. Once you know that, consider the gaps. What other critical roles will need filling for a healthy church start?

Some roles may be needed immediately; others may be needed in the future as the church grows. Here is a list of common church planting functions. Consider each aspect of APEST as well, and continue filling in missing pieces you will need:

- Visionary
- Outreach
- Serving
- Hospitality
- Bridge-builder
- Organizer
- Teacher
- Intercessor
- Helps/support
- Giving
- Administration
- Evangelist
- Mobilizer

However you want to label them, these functions are critical. Know who you are and how you lead. What roles have you identified that will be needed to complement your own skills and gifting? Keep a list, and begin praying over it and asking God for guidance.

Clarifying expectations and commitments

When inviting others to be a part of the core team, you'll need to be clear about expectations. What exactly are you asking them to do? Live missionally? Build a community of disciples? Offer hospitality? Be part of a launch team? What commitments are necessary? What will it cost them? How much time will be involved? People need these questions answered, so they know what they are committing to.

You'll also want to let them know what they can expect from you. Will you disciple them? Invest in their leadership development? Include them in decision-making? Provide pastoral care? Be clear on what you are offering and not offering.

One important distinction you'll want to think through is "core vs. crowd." In any ministry, there is a core of faithful followers and a crowd of the curious or uncommitted. We see this dynamic playing out in Jesus' ministry. He invested much time in his twelve disciples, and even more with Peter, James, and John. He was focused on shaping and developing this community and passing on his DNA through it. Jesus still ministered to the crowds with great compassion, but they did not receive the time, focus, or relational investment that the Twelve did. At times, Jesus even offended the multitudes, turning them away when they were unwilling to accept his teachings (John 6:59–71).

Many church plants today tend to follow an "either/or" methodology. They focus entirely on public ministry (the crowd) with little, if any, emphasis on developing disciples and leaders; or, they negate the crowd completely to focus only on making disciples (the core). Jesus modeled a "both/and" approach to ministry, encompassing the needs of the crowd as well as the development of his core disciples.

As discussed earlier, these two categories are mutually interdependent. One cannot be a growing committed disciple without reaching out to the crowds and developing new disciples. And one cannot be truly devoted to the crowds without providing a path of discipleship and growth toward maturity. Jesus' ability to do "both/and" is critical to the church planting process. He gave the crowds what they needed, but he gave his disciples more.

If there are people who seem like they should be a part of the team, take time now to clarify precisely what they're committing to. What will they need to do? For how long? What can they expect from you in terms of support? What precisely will their roles be? How will they know if it's working?

Once you have commitment, you can move on from gathering your core team to leading your core team. However, recognize that you may continue to add core team members along the way as God draws people to the ministry—especially those from the ministry focus group.

Setting direction for your team
Once you have a team, you'll need to lead them. That means setting direction, getting people on the same page, and supporting them as you do ministry together. Yet nothing establishes your DNA as a team better than practicing prayer and intercession together. Take time to pray together and to share what's going on in your lives. It will help you relate more effectively as a leadership community.

Jesus lived and traveled with his disciples. He did ministry with them and explained the kingdom of God to them. Together, they functioned as a leadership community that ministered to others. Relationship and interaction in a whole-life format is essential for forming and training your leadership community. This goes beyond just a standard meeting or training session. It's life-on-life. Here are some of the ways Jesus led his community of disciples:

- He modeled the Father by showing them his nature and demonstrating his love and compassion.
- He showed them how to live in relationship with God and in relationship with each other.
- He demonstrated how to relate to those who were culturally and ideologically different.
- He brought God's kingdom to life for them through his works.
- He practiced a way of teaching and ministry that was vastly different from that of the religious culture of the day.

Again, remember the disciples weren't perfect. Even up to Jesus' crucifixion—and beyond—many of them demonstrated serious character issues, lack of obedience, and lapses of judgment. As a team, keep your focus on the mission of church planting rather than getting sidetracked with perfecting the team. Focusing too intensely on personal relationships between team members will most likely derail the church planting effort. Rather, see the team as a working group with complementary gifts and abilities and put energy into accomplishing the task—in spite of all of our imperfections.

Developing ownership
I always love the part in a church plant when the people on the core team begin switching verbally from "you" to "we." They do it almost unconsciously when they arrive at the place of ownership: "What should we do about . . . ?" "One strength we have is. . . ." This simple usage change indicates that a person has made the shift from seeing the church plant as something they're helping with to something that they're truly a part of.

Ownership involves mutuality: They have given you commitment, and you have given them responsibility. Giving your core team real ownership requires some letting go on the part of the planter. You'll need to let your people use their giftedness and initiative. You are not the only leader. You've brought them onto the team because you trust them and their vision aligns. So give them the freedom both to serve and to lead. Once you have a trusted team, allow them to speak into the vision, values, and approach. They may have valuable insights and ideas you hadn't thought of.

Provide ways for the team to interact:
- Have them share how they're experiencing God, and how that affects what they do.

- Talk about competing narratives in society that prevent them and others from fully engaging the kingdom of God.
- Have each team member write an article or tell a story of what the church will look like five years from now.

These kinds of activities will help your team take true ownership of the church plant. As a leader of leaders, you must learn how to work with people who are strong where you are weak. Knowing when and how to defer, and when and how to pass the baton, comes from a realistic self-understanding and an understanding of your core team. You'll need to master the skill of deferring to others and following appropriately, yet without abdicating leadership.

Direction can often be focused by the questions you raise—questions that get people to think about and process the right things. For example, "What are some ways we could serve the community?" focuses the agenda and provides leadership.

Achieving and maintaining that delicate balance is a difficult task, but one strategy that can be helpful is an attitude of learning. Not only are those on your core team learning, but you are learning as well. You can learn from them, just as they are learning from you. And in an attitude of mutual ongoing learning, you can lead them forward in the mission of establishing this new church.

To increase ownership by team members, allow them to try things and sometimes fail. Help them reflect on those experiences and learn from them, never shaming them but praising their courage and their resilience when they get up and try a different approach. It can be challenging for many of us to take the required hands-off approach, but the long-term development potential is well worth it.

Building community
Your core team is also a community. In many cases, it will function as a *de facto* small group, so you'll want to be intentional about building community. Engage in different types of activities together: praying, serving, studying, sharing, playing.

I have found it helpful to take an overnight retreat periodically. These can be a combination of light training, reminding them of the vision, and building relationships on the team. Getting away from the pressures of everyday life can make space for deeper relationships. Be sure to build in unstructured time as well.

Your common vision will be the initial basis for community within the core team, but you should also discover other interests and activities that you have in common.

Don't assume that people in different stages of life will not have things in common. A single person may actually have more in common with a married person than with another single in the group. An older person can be a valuable asset to those in earlier stages of life. Children should also be invited to become an active part in the community that's forming.

Not everyone on the core team will be best friends, but you should be able to enjoy each other's company. A healthy community life will draw in others. Discover activities you enjoy doing together such as going camping, playing in the park, attending a ball game in the community, or going out to eat. Focus on activities where you can dialogue while you play.

Another way to foster community is to spend time at each other's homes, helping with needed chores. Working together may be the key for some people to feel a part of the group. Not everyone does well with small talk—some need a clear task. Game-playing can also help people become more comfortable in the group.

While you want to foster relationships within the team, don't allow the group to become too exclusive. The longer a group remains together without newcomers, the more susceptible it is to becoming a clique. Danger signs that you have a clique include inside jokes and references, a strong sense of shared history, and a wariness of outsiders. Authentic Christian community remains open to newcomers. It is inclusive of those who are different and expands the circle to incorporate them rather than selecting only those who already fit the mold.

Use these interdependent relationships to support each other in outreach. Remember that you're building the DNA of the church. If you want inclusivity and service to be integral parts of church life, now is the time to set that in place. Community itself can be a great spur for growth.

We spend a lot of time working with those on our team—and that's difficult if we don't like or know each other. Spending time building community is well worth the investment. It's not just a nice-to-have—it's the foundation upon which all the necessary teamwork of church planting is built.

Development through coaching

As a church planter, one of the most important things you can do is to coach those on your team. Coaching is the "how" for developing others. Start coaching your team now, to get it into the church's DNA. As the church plant grows, you won't be able to coach everyone, but in the early stages you may be able.

Do it now so your core team members see the benefits, and begin using the same strategies to help others grow. If you consistently ask team members questions like, "What are you hearing from God?" "What's going well?" and "Where do you sense God wants you to grow?" and they find that kind of engagement helpful, they'll naturally begin to ask others those questions.

At some point, you'll need to develop more coaches in an official capacity, but for now be very intentional about getting coaching basics into the DNA of the church. This end is primarily accomplished by asking good questions, listening, and then providing encouragement to move
forward.

Here are some basic tips for developing new leaders on your team:

- *Notice teachable moments.* When are people most motivated to learn? When they need to know something, right now—when they need to guide a study, lead a meeting, practice a new skill. Look for those opportunities and provide teachable moments.
- *Help people reflect on their experiences.* People learn best by reflecting on their experiences and considering what worked well and what didn't. Encourage people to set aside time for reflection. It will increase their learning dramatically.
- *Ask the right questions.* Whenever possible, ask questions rather than make statements—and design your questions to guide people toward learning. Make your questions open-ended, so people can highlight various options and choose from among them. Good questions make people stop and think, and they are empowering.
- *Reinforce the positive.* Most people don't respond well to criticism. It's hard to hear and we end up feeling worse about ourselves. Instead, try to focus on what was done well and highlight that. You'll build people's confidence at the same time you reinforce doing things well.
- *Provide formative feedback.* Nonetheless, part of facilitating learning is helping people see what they can do better next time. Highlight a new skill they might try incorporating. Help them see a good direction for the future. Even when providing corrective feedback, keep it as positive as possible.

The basic process for development is: orient, involve, equip. *Orient* people to the ministry tasks you want them to do. For example, "Lead this small group tonight. First facilitate sharing, then pray together, then go through the Scripture study." *Involve* them: Let them try it and figure it out as they go, preferably while you're there and lending support. Then *equip*: Have a coaching conversation about how it went. What worked well? What didn't? What did you learn? What needs to change? What's next?

You'll definitely need this DNA of coaching as the church plant grows—and you'll be grateful in the future if you take the time to invest in it now. A church can only grow as large as its leadership base. As the church begins to expand, cultivating and developing leaders will be one of your primary responsibilities, and you'll need more coaches to do that. A strong leadership base results in healthy disciples, groups, and churches.

Tips for team-building

Stay on mission together. Each person is on the team for a reason. Build a common community by focusing on your mission. You all care about the same end goal—the one you're working toward. That's true even if team members are very different from each other in personality and gifting—in fact, that's good. A good team has different kinds of people, all working together for a common purpose.

Pray together. Spend intentional time together in prayer. Pray for the church plant, and for each other individually. Everyone needs support, and can take comfort in the fact that others know what's going on in their lives and are praying for them.

Have fun together. It's not all about work. Have some fun together, too. Host a team party. Have a game night. Put together a camping trip. Fun social events are often where people really get to know one another and build strong bonds—even with those people they may not have expected to enjoy.

Work well together. Assume the best of one another. Follow basic rules of engagement—such as talking with someone if you have a problem with them, rather than talking about them to others or letting the problem fester. Create an environment of openness and affirmation. If you're leading a team, these are the values you need to build into the DNA and encourage long-term.

Clarify roles. Everyone on your team will have different roles—just as they do on a sports team. If everyone is the goalie, it doesn't work. Clarify each person's responsibilities—then, based on giftedness, clarify what unique contributions each person makes to the whole. That contribution may or may not be specifically within their ministry area, but could still benefit others on the team. Clarify how the team is going to work together, in a way that maximizes each person's effectiveness.

Team transitions

Every team has transitions. Recognize that the people on your core team at the beginning may not be with you forever, and that's fine. Sometimes God brings people to us for just a season; hold them loosely.

Conversely, the people God wants on your team may not necessarily be the ones you'd choose yourself. Again, it's more like a sports team, with each person playing a different but independent role in moving toward a common goal.

Whoever God brings to your team through mutual discernment and shared vision, invest in those people. Build a healthy culture in which they can grow and develop. Create an environment of shared internal team values that allow you to live on mission together as a cohesive community. Coach them toward their fullest potential—even if God calls them to something else in the future.

How do you find potential team members?

Jesus prayed for workers for the harvest: *"Then he said to his disciples, 'The harvest is plentiful, but the laborers are few; therefore ask the Lord of the harvest to send out laborers into his harvest'"* (Matthew 9:37–38). Let's look at the context of this passage.

What did Jesus do directly before he said this? He traveled, taught, shared the good news, healed, and cared about the people: *"Then Jesus went about all the cities and villages, teaching in their synagogues, and proclaiming the good news of the kingdom, and curing every disease and every sickness. When he saw the crowds, he had compassion for them, because they were harassed and helpless, like sheep without a shepherd"* (Matthew 9:35–36).

And what did Jesus do immediately after praying for the harvest? He sent out the apostles to go live among the people, stay with them, build relationships, network, heal, and share the good news (Matthew 10:1–15). Let's look at this entire flow:

> Go, teach, share, heal, serve, care
> Pray
> Go, engage, build relationships, heal, share

We should do the same. Here are some modern-day tips:
- Get involved in serving the community.
- Build relationships with people.
- Identify real needs.
- Ask people who else we should be talking with.
- Get appointments with those people, and get to know them.
- Share the vision in conversation.
- Share the vision through public speaking opportunities.
- Ask other Christian leaders where we should be looking, and who might be interested.
- Explore relationships.
- Explore the networks of relationships of other team members.

Most of all, pray. We know this is God's will. Therefore, we ask him for workers for the harvest.

Journey Guide for Chapter 6
Building Your Core Team

No church plant should be without a team. A
healthy and effective core team will provide
relational support, diverse perspectives and skills,
and a unified vision for moving forward. Teams also allow church plants to function
as the body of Christ from the very beginning by developing giftedness, delegating
responsibilities, building ownership, and praying for one another and the ministry.
Choices made in the selection and development of team members are crucial for
long-term health. Consider the following checklist and reflection questions as you
go about the process of building the best core team possible for your church plant.

Checklist: for the road ahead

☐ Requirements for potential team members have been identified.

☐ Mutual discernment has been prayed for in selecting team members.

☐ Regular communication with intercessors has been taking place.

☐ Possible initial leadership team members have been identified, including
various roles, gifts, and representation of people groups being reached.

☐ Potential team members have been invited, and expectations and length
of commitment have been communicated.

☐ The church planting team has been solidified, and its identity developed.

☐ Ownership has been developed among team members.

☐ Healthy community has been built among team members.

☐ Coaching and leadership development have been incorporated.

☐ Vision and values have been consistently and creatively reinforced
during team gatherings.

Discipleship focus: Spiritual Responsiveness

Building your core team is a fun and exciting time. However, it is also a time to set
aside personal preference in favor of allowing the Holy Spirit to build the best team
for ministry God is calling you to. Take time to engage in listening prayer as you
work through these questions and consider how you will respond to the Holy Spirit
in the building of your team.

Inward focused:

1. How do you see the difference between faith and certainty?

2. When is obedience hardest for you? When is obedience easiest?

Outward focus:

    1. In what ways is God calling you to engage with your community outside of your comfort zone?

    2. What steps are you going to take to respond with obedience?

    3. Who might be good to partner with in this calling?

Strategic questions: for you and your coach

- In light of your gifts and skills, what specific roles need to be supplied by your core team members? What are some of the most important qualities you need to see in your core team members?
- Who might fit the roles needed on your team? How and when will you contact them?
- How can you share your values and vision with potential team members in a way that helps them take personal ownership? How can you determine whether team members have sufficiently embraced the values and vision?
- What commitment level do you expect of your team members? Be specific.
- Describe the kind of community you would like to see functioning within your team.
- What creative ways will you use, to help the team continue to engage with the values and vision?
- How can you invest in coaching and developing your core team members? What coaching skills do you possess? What skills do you need to develop further?

Discussion questions: For you and your team

- What do you see as the essential components of healthy community? List as many as you can.
- What are we doing to promote this type of community among us? What ground rules/support/commitment do we need, in order to best work together?
- What are some ways we can create a culture of ongoing learning within our team? What types of development do you need personally, right now?
- What is your understanding of coaching? How have you experienced it?
- What steps are you sensing God may be calling us toward as a community?

Guided prayer: for you personally

The gifts he gave were that some would be apostles, some prophets, some evangelists, some pastors and teachers, 12 to equip the saints for the work of ministry, for building up the body of Christ, 13 until all of us come to the unity of the faith and of the knowledge of the Son of God, to maturity, to the measure of the full stature of Christ. (Ephesians 4:11–13)

- God, please show me who you are calling to be a part of this church planting team. Help me keep an open mind, even if the people are not those I would expect.
- Help me cast a clear vision for this church plant and make expectations clear, as we work together toward mutual discernment.
- Lord, how can I build a sense of community and shared vision on the team?
- How can I best develop and invest in the people you've placed on my team? What will be required of me?

Guided prayer: for use with your team

Pray together with your team through each of these themes:

- God, please help each of us to clearly see our contribution to this new church plant.
- Help us listen to your Holy Spirit for direction and treat one another with respect.
- Please help us build a strong community as we work together on mission.
- Allow us each to develop and grow in the ways you have in mind for us.
- Even now, please draw the people you want to reach into our lives and help us faithfully reflect you to them.

Guided prayer: for your intercessors

Begin forming a formal intercessory team as soon as you begin the planting process. Communicate with them at least once a month. Be sure to personalize your updates by adding not just ministry concerns but personal concerns as well, so that the intercessory team can pray for you and your family.

Please pray that God would:

- help me cast a clear vision to potential team members and communicate clearly with them.
- draw those to this team that he wants to be a part of it.
- help me build community and a sense of shared ownership with all those he brings to the core team.

• establish a healthy DNA on our team as we move forward.

• continue to draw us to him in prayer.

Action guide: a place for planning your next steps

1.

2.

3.

Chapter 7:
Knowing Who You're Reaching

The scope of the mission Jesus gave us is vast: From his directive to make disciples of all nations to the fruit of that labor in the multitude before the throne from every tongue, tribe, and nation . . . the harvest fields are vast and diverse.

> *Go therefore and make disciples of all nations, baptizing them in the name of the Father and of the Son and of the Holy Spirit,* [20] *and teaching them to obey everything that I have commanded you. And remember, I am with you always, to the end of the age."*
> *(Matthew 28:19–20)*

> *After this I looked, and there was a great multitude that no one could count, from every nation, from all tribes and peoples and languages, standing before the throne and before the Lamb, robed in white, with palm branches in their hands.* [10] *They cried out in a loud voice, saying,*
> *"Salvation belongs to our God who is seated on the throne, and to the Lamb!"*
> *(Revelation 7:9–10)*

We sometimes think of these as "missionary verses," but I see them as primary directives to make disciples—and as a result, starting churches. This is a kingdom-wide job. It will take all different kinds of churches to reach every tongue, tribe, and nation. How many different people groups are there just in your own city or town? In your country? Some are called to planting overseas, but others are called to plant right where they are. There are potential disciples to be made everywhere.

This chapter focuses on discerning God's voice about who to reach with your particular church plant, and about learning as much about that people group as possible. Many planters are hesitant to name a ministry focus group, for fear they'll narrow their focus too much and miss the people God brings their way. In fact, the opposite is true. The identification of a ministry focus maximizes effectiveness.

Discovering the unique attitudes and perspectives of a specific group provides clues about how to reach them. Even when others who don't fit the profile begin attending, maintaining cultural relevance to a ministry focus group will pay off in more effective, focused ministry. Trying to reach everybody is a great way to reach nobody in particular.

Some are called to a specific neighborhood, some to a people group, some to a particular subculture. Whatever the calling, it must flow from what we are hearing from God. That requires patience, listening, and an openness to shifting our emphasis when needed. Sometimes church plants begin with a focus that is too broad; we must be open to hearing from the Holy Spirit and looking at what he is already doing in a community or region.

Take time to pray together as a team about who you'll reach. Who is around you? What are you hearing from God? How can you serve?

Selecting a ministry focus group
The selection of ministry focus groups generally falls into one of three categories: current effectiveness, opportunities, and potential.

Where are you effective? If there is already an existing core team or ministry base (such as a mother church), consider what you're already good at. The same is true of an individual planter. Who are you already reaching naturally? Who do you understand culturally? The likelihood is that if you already know and understand a group in some ways, you'll be more effective at reaching it. You may not be called to reach the people you're already engaging with, but it's an important starting point to see where God is already blessing your endeavors.

Where are the opportunities? What people groups are particularly receptive? Where do people seem more open to the gospel? In many cases, people who have recently relocated or are going through season-of-life transitions demonstrate greater receptivity. Other times, opportunities are discovered during the course of serving and engaging with people.

Where do you have the potential to expand? Who isn't being reached currently? What people groups are underserved? Often you can find these communities within easy driving distance. Again, engaging in prayer to discern where God is leading you and your team specifically is crucial to the discernment process.

Demographic research: academic
To help bring the group you'll be reaching into focus, you'll need to engage in some demographic research. Survey the harvest fields before you begin harvesting. What is the scope of the task? What do you need to be aware of? What barriers or challenges are you likely to run into? There is no substitute for spending some time researching the ministry focus group you'll be reaching. If you're not a researcher by nature or gifting, don't hesitate to draw on team members who are. This area of ministry is ripe for sharing.

Equip yourself with ways to understand the culture, and how it differs from your own. Research the country, area, language, history, people group, etc. In planting the first church in a region, think strategically about where a church could have the most impact. Paul planted his churches along trade routes and in centers of influence.

In surveying an area for church planting, several factors should be recognized:
- natural boundaries such as major highways, rivers, mountains
- major population centers
- industry, trade, commerce, farming
- economic levels
- education levels
- ethnic groups, size, and language
- age and family size
- dominant religions
- lack of existing faith options

Start with the information you can readily find, but don't stop there. What are the people like? What do they do in their free time? How do they spend their money? (Answers to questions like these provide important insight into values.) Do they live in single-family homes with large yards or multifamily dwellings like apartments? In what ways do people invest in their kids? Is there extended family involvement? What are their fears? Problems? Hopes?

Demographic research: conversational
To fully answer some of your questions, you'll need to move beyond academic research into relational and conversational research. Ultimately, getting to know the people in your ministry focus group and building relationships with them is the best research. That's how you'll really get to know the people and their culture. Once you know people personally, you can begin to understand them at a much deeper level through listening and asking questions.

Interact with the community. Observe the people God is calling you to reach—by sitting and watching, walking, driving. God can give you discernment and wisdom to know what your style of ministry needs to be, and your strategy emerges from there. As you get to know the people God is calling you to reach, listen for attitudes, interests, and needs. These are the clues you need to discover what God is calling you to do.

Seek to understand the culture by discussing these questions with your team:
- What is God already doing here? How has he been accomplishing that?
- What are the spiritual challenges and tensions that are taking place right now?
- Where are the issues of justice that need to be addressed?
- How do people relate socially?
- How is power structured in the community (both officially and unofficially)?
- What needs do you perceive?

Relate to the people. As you observe and listen and interact, you will collect soft data. When led by the Spirit of God, this information can help you understand what style you need to have, so that you can relate appropriately to people. Even the apostle Paul changed his dress, his diet, and his forms of communication to be able to more reach people:

> For though I am free with respect to all, I have made myself a slave to all, so that I might win more of them. [20] To the Jews I became as a Jew, in order to win Jews. To those under the law I became as one under the law (though I myself am not under the law) so that I might win those under the law. [21] To those outside the law I became as one outside the law (though I am not free from God's law but am under Christ's law) so that I might win those outside the law. [22] To the weak I became weak, so that I might win the weak. I have become all things to all people, that I might by all means save some. [23] I do it all for the sake of the gospel, so that I may share in its blessings. (1 Corinthians 9:19–23)

When God became incarnate and lived among us, he took on Jewish culture and form. He grew up in Galilee and learned a trade. All of that is a demonstration of "incarnational" ministry: a sense of becoming part of the group you're reaching. It's a matter of being truly able to see through the eyes of another and becoming a part of that group—even if we are being grafted in.

As planters, we really need to consider ourselves missionaries. We are in a post-Christian era, and need to bond with the culture group we are reaching. There has always been a significant difference in effectiveness between missionaries who live and spend time among the people vs. those who live on the compound and spend time with other missionaries. Interact with your people, live among them, get to know them. It will help shape you and your ministry in unexpected ways, as your heart bonds to them.

Often taking this posture requires crossing barriers. Sometimes those are cultural barriers, as when the apostles were sent to the Gentiles, to *"Judea and Samaria and to the ends of the earth" (Acts 1:8)*. Doing that is difficult because we often don't know what to do, aren't sure what the "rules" are, don't speak the language (either literally or culturally), and fear rejection. It's scary for most of us to cross to the other side of the street. It's uncomfortable. We don't want to treat others as completely foreign from ourselves—after all, they are people too, made in the image of God. But we also don't want to gloss over real differences that we need to understand and respect. We will certainly make mistakes, but the important thing is to try, and to be open to learning.

Even within our own culture, we need to be able to see through other people's eyes in order to reach them and serve them well. Consider someone in your own family or a spouse. Even if they're not of a different culture, chances are you sometimes have a hard time understanding their point of view. We need to be able to put ourselves in someone else's shoes and understand what matters to them and how they think.

This effort not only helps us love others well, but helps us to not become calcified in our own views and perspectives—becoming inflexible like the Pharisees. It's good for us to stretch our minds and try to see through other people's eyes, and often we can learn a great deal. Several activities listed at the end of this chapter can help you delve into understanding the people you're trying to reach—in ways both informational and relational.

Cross-cultural church planting

As we live in an increasingly secular, postmodern culture, our disciplemaking is increasingly cross-cultural. Generally speaking, planters can most effectively reach those who are similar to them. Planters with similarities to the culture they're reaching in these areas have an advantage—both in understanding the culture and in natural bridges for reaching people:

- size of families
- educational and economic levels
- social class
- rural or urban
- type of government/politics
- race, color, or language
- core values and assumptions

Having any of these categories in common can help you make important and appropriate connections with the people you're trying to reach. Yet in an increasingly globalized culture, it's more common than ever before to have regular interaction with people from different parts of the world. Cross-cultural relationships are not easy to avoid, even if we wished to. Navigating them well is a twenty-first-century skill.

To the degree you're different from your ministry focus group, you'll need to work additionally hard to overcome some barriers. Below is a partial list of cultural issues that may become problematic when planting cross-culturally:

- Time orientation ↔ event orientation
- Either/or thinking ↔ holistic thinking
- Crisis orientation ↔ non-crisis orientation
- Task orientation ↔ person orientation
- Status focus ↔ achievement focus
- Concealment of vulnerability ↔ willingness to expose vulnerability

Each culture will act on these value continuums in a different way. When someone from a time-oriented culture enters an event-oriented culture, adjustments in thinking and action will need to be made in order to relate effectively to others.

Cross-cultural church multiplication is difficult, yet sometimes that's what God calls us to do. Consider all of the harvest and be open to hearing God's call to reach out to different ministry focus groups. That may mean committing to address blockages and preconceived ideas existing within congregations. Ethnocentrism—the viewing of one's own culture as central and primary—is usually unconscious, and it's hard for people to become aware of their own cultural biases. The apostle Peter didn't recognize his own biases without the help of God and others (Acts 10; Galatians 2:11–14). Certain people groups or geographical areas that have been either consciously or unconsciously avoided may need to be reconsidered. In some cases when a particular target group has been unfairly overlooked, self-evaluation and repentance are an appropriate starting point.

Cultural differences are just that—differences. It's not a matter of better or worse, godly or ungodly. God calls his church to reach all areas and all people groups, not just those we're comfortable with. In some cases, we will be most effective reaching those who are like us. In other cases, God has called us to step out in faith and plant churches cross-culturally, to reach a broader spectrum of people. Much listening prayer will be required to discern his voice.

If you are called to cross-cultural church planting, you'll need to be especially careful that in sharing the gospel you are not inadvertently promoting your culture as well. Historically, that's been one of the biggest mistakes in missions. Instead of trying to change people's cultures to make them fit in better with established churches, we need to establish more churches that are culturally relevant. We need a church for every culture.

> People do not need to change their culture to become followers of Jesus.

This idea is a biblical one. Jesus came to a specific group of people—politically oppressed Jews of the first century—and tailored his message in such a way that they could hear it. He then commanded us to carry that message to every nation and people group.

We need to present the gospel in such a way that unbelievers can hear it from within their own cultures. Then they will be empowered to create churches consonant with how they live—churches that feel like home. People do not need to change their culture to become followers of Jesus. Rather, Jesus emerges within that culture.

Three basic rules of thumb for cross-cultural church planting:
- Practice humility.
- Communicate respect.
- Build relationships.

What is good news to them?
So what does it look like for Jesus to emerge within a culture? One helpful question to ask is, "What is good news to them?" Discovering what good news means to the people around you provides important insight into how to reach them and how to serve the community in meaningful ways. A church planter in Salt Lake City tells people that "through Jesus Christ they can realize their full potential; they don't

have to fit into anybody else's mold." In a predominantly Mormon culture, that's not just good news—that's great news!

A companion question is, "What would God's kingdom look like here?" If the seed of the gospel were planted and watered, what would grow in this particular ground? As the new church emerges, it should take on the context of whatever environment it is in. We are allowing the church plant to incarnate within the cultural setting. Plant the seed, and it will grow within the cultural context where it's planted.

What do you think Jesus might have said and done had he been born in inner-city Los Angeles, midtown Manhattan, rural Ethiopia, Bangkok, or Calcutta? He would be the same divine Son of God, but take on the likeness, culture, and language of the people there.

A starting point for determining what the good news looks like in a given context is to look at how God has prepared this people group for the gospel. What redemptive analogy connects to their culture? (Examples might include the sacrificial lamb, the raised serpent, the bread of life, the sower, the soldier, running the race, the parent-child relationship, the altar to an unknown god, or living water.) The more you understand the culture and its values and hopes for redemption, the better you can match your vision and strategy to the people group you're reaching. You'll meet real needs—the things that are meaningful to them.

The good news of the kingdom is expressed in culturally appropriate context and stories. It's often helpful to begin with memorable and easily understood stories of redemption, such as the prodigal son. Stories that speak to people, where they are, are more likely to hit the mark and more readily passed on to others. People can see what Jesus looks like living incarnationally among them.

Taking a learning posture

To take this approach effectively, you'll need to begin with—and maintain—a learning posture. Listen to community leaders. Hear their stories, discover their core values, find out what matters to them.

- How do they adopt new ideas?
- How do leaders emerge?
- What are the qualifying characteristics of leaders?
- How are decisions made?
- What needs are their present beliefs filling?
- What needs are not being met?
- Are there seasons of the year which influence receptivity?

- What preconceived notions do they have of Jesus?
- What has been their experience with church?

Make sure those on your team are taking a learning posture as well, rather than coming in ready to tell people what to do. Adopting the attitude of a lifelong learning keeps us in a state of humility—especially leaders. Be open to new ideas. Challenge yourself. Reflect on ideas you may initially disagree with. Consider their merits and why others might think this way.

We don't know what we don't know. And we certainly shouldn't assume we know everything. With each relationship we enter into, we should ask: "What can I learn from this person? What might God want to teach me?" The other person need not be a follower of Jesus, educated, or even an adult. We can learn from everyone. Learning and teaching are not mutually exclusive. Rather, they are each more effective when they run in parallel.

Develop the people you're reaching—they're the future leaders

God has called us to *"Judea and Samaria and to the ends of the earth" (Acts 1:8)*. No matter what people group you're reaching—those like yourself (Judea), those with some similarities and some differences (Samaria), or those wholly different from yourself (the ends of the earth)—you need to develop leaders out of that people group. Only indigenous leaders can carry church planting forth to the next stage of development and expansion.

Dr. D. T. Niles of Sri Lanka put it like this: "The gospel is like a seed, and you have to sow it…. Now, when missionaries came to our lands they brought not only the seed of the gospel, but their own plant of Christianity, flower pot included! So, what we have to do is to break the flowerpot, take out the seed of the Gospel, sow it in our own cultural soil, and let our own version of Christianity grow."[3]

Don't be surprised if those to whom you pass the seed of the gospel break the flowerpot—they *need* to do it. No matter how much you may like your flowerpot, it is not the gospel. The gospel must have space to flourish in native soil.

That holds true not only when we cross cultures, but when we cross generations. The new generation of leaders you develop will do things differently. So when you pass the baton, hold it loosely so the next runner can pick it up and keep running the race.

[3]Quoted in Mattias Neve, "A Quote about Planting the Gospel," To the Ends of the Earth, https://mattiasneve.wordpress.com/2008/11/28/a-good-quote-about-planting-the-gospel.

Even as you begin the early stages of church planting, begin laying the foundation for an exit strategy. If your plant is successful, by definition it will outlive you; others will need to lead. Disciple and develop new leaders to whom you can eventually hand off the baton of leadership. Transition needs to be part of the strategy from the very beginning.

You don't need to identify a successor right away, of course, but develop people broadly and see who God brings. Of the people who are serving and involved, you can often identify future potential leaders to develop. They are the ones whose opinions are heeded by the group. They are the ones who influence others. They are the ones who demonstrate faithfulness, availability, servanthood, and teachability.

From this pool of people, prayerfully choose some to invest in. Give them tasks and responsibilities that will stretch and challenge them, but that are also within their area of interest and ability. Together, with their input and ideas, you can then move forward toward the reality of God's kingdom.

We see so much biblical precedent for this development of leaders from within the people group of the next generation:

> Moses to Joshua: *Moses spoke to the Lord, saying, * [16] *"Let the Lord, the God of the spirits of all flesh, appoint someone over the congregation* [17] *who shall go out before them and come in before them, who shall lead them out and bring them in, so that the congregation of the Lord may not be like sheep without a shepherd."* [18] *So the Lord said to Moses, "Take Joshua son of Nun, a man in whom is the spirit, and lay your hand upon him;* [19] *have him stand before Eleazar the priest and all the congregation, and commission him in their sight. (Numbers 27:15–19)*

> Elijah to Elisha: *When they had crossed, Elijah said to Elisha, "Tell me what I may do for you, before I am taken from you." Elisha said, "Please let me inherit a double share of your spirit." …* [14] *He took the mantle of Elijah that had fallen from him, and struck the water, saying, "Where is the Lord, the God of Elijah?" When he had struck the water, the water was parted to the one side and to the other, and Elisha went over.* [15] *When the company of prophets who were at Jericho saw him at a distance, they declared, "The spirit of Elijah rests on Elisha." (2 Kings 2:9, 14–15)*

> Jesus to the twelve disciples: *You are witnesses of these things.* [49] *And see, I am sending upon you what my Father promised; so stay here in the city until you have been clothed with power from on high."* [50] *Then he led them out as*

far as Bethany, and, lifting up his hands, he blessed them. [51] While he was blessing them, he withdrew from them and was carried up into heaven. (Luke 24:48–51)

Paul to Timothy: *I am giving you these instructions, Timothy, my child, in accordance with the prophecies made earlier about you, so that by following them you may fight the good fight, [19] having faith and a good conscience. (1 Timothy 1:18–19b)*

The church you are planting will need to be passed down and led through many future generations. If no new leaders are developed, the leadership of the church will die out completely in one generation. Every new generation must pass on the mantle of leadership for it to continue. Remember, the ultimate kingdom goal is not just to plant one new church, but to plant churches that plant churches that plant churches: a legacy of multiplication.

Journey Guide for Chapter 7
Knowing Who You're Reaching

JOURNEY GUIDE

No one local church can reach everyone. That's
the nature of ministry: we need all kinds of
ministries reaching all kinds of people. With that
reality mind, planters and their teams need to learn as much as they can about the
people they are trying to reach and the culture they are working within. This can be
done through developing relationships, listening, and researching. Ministry strategy
then can be informed by learning what may be most effective with this particular
ministry focus group. Consider who you are really trying to reach—and how you
can best get to know them—by working through the journey guide below.

Checklist: for the road ahead

☐ Faithful prayer has been engaged in to help identify potential ministry
focus groups.

☐ The harvest fields have been surveyed, and compassion developed.

☐ Through research and relationships, the needs and values of the
ministry focus group have been identified.

☐ Cultural values and understanding have increased, and culturally
appropriate reproducible methods have been used.

☐ Relevant cross-cultural challenges have been addressed.

☐ A culturally appropriate church planting strategy has been developed, in
harmony with the ministry focus group.

☐ Strategy has been evaluated and revised as the plant proceeds and new
learnings are gathered.

☐ New leaders from the ministry focus group have been developed.

☐ A vision for church multiplication and the development of a new
generation of leaders has been communicated and adopted.

Discipleship focus: Community Transformation
Part of being a disciple of Jesus is transforming the community around you. That is
done not only through your church plant, but through you personally. Take some
time to consider your own life of discipleship in this arena.

Inward focus:

1. How is God changing your heart toward your community and
opening your eyes to their needs?

2. How can you mirror the love of God to the broader community
around you?

3. When people look at your life from the outside, what do they see?

Outward focus:

1. How can you serve in ways that bring widespread change to the larger community?
2. What effects would you like to see result from your ministry? Describe the vision.

Strategic questions: for you and your coach

- What are you hearing from God about those you are called to reach? Describe a sample person from your ministry focus group; an ideal amalgam of the kind of person you are trying to reach.
- What relationships do you already have within your ministry focus group? How could you develop more?
- How can you demonstrate humility and a posture of learning as you interact with this group?
- What would truly be good news for this group?
- What cross-cultural challenges do you see for yourself engaging with this group? How can you best address those challenges?
- How could you go about developing leaders from within this group?
- How are you praying for this ministry focus group?

Discussion questions: for you and your team

For this chapter, we have enough discussion questions for three separate team meetings, each with a different focus. This issue of identifying a ministry focus group and engaging in culture is worth returning to multiple times with your team. Two of the sets of questions were referenced within the chapter itself.

For identifying a ministry focus group:

- What other cultures are near you? (Think broadly: socially, ethnically, economically, by age group.)
- How might you go about entering into these cultures?
- Who could you get to know? How?
- What mistakes might you make?
- What contributions might you make?
- What might you learn?
- What might you have to repent of?
- How can you best show respect?
- What action steps are you sensing God would have you take in seeing through another's eyes?

For understanding a ministry focus group:

- What is God already doing here? How has he been accomplishing that?
- What are the spiritual challenges and tensions taking place right now in the community?
- What issues of justice need to be addressed?
- How do people relate socially? Where do they naturally gather?
- How is power structured in the community (both officially and unofficially)?
- What needs do you perceive?
- What hopes or desires do the people have?

For creating strategy within a ministry focus group:

- How does this ministry focus group adopt new ideas?
- How do leaders usually emerge from within it?
- What are the qualifying characteristics of leaders?
- How are decisions made?
- What needs are their present beliefs filling?
- What needs are not being met?
- Are there seasons of the year which will influence receptivity?
- What preconceived notions do they have of Christianity?
- What has been their experience with Christianity?
- What exploratory steps might we take?

Guided prayer: for you personally
"But you will receive power when the Holy Spirit has come upon you; and you will be my witnesses in Jerusalem, in all Judea and Samaria, and to the ends of the earth." (Acts 1:8)

- God, where is my Judea? My Samaria? My ends of the earth?
- In what ways am I willing to be all things to all people, that I may save some (1 Corinthians 9:22)? In what ways am I unwilling?
- What would be good news to these people, like living water to the Samaritan woman at the well (John 4:1–15)?
- Please humble me, and make me a learner who shows respect to other cultures.
- Lord, please open my eyes to the work you are already doing in this ministry focus group and the leaders you already have there waiting to be developed.

Guided prayer: for use with your team

Pray together with your team through each of these themes:

- Lord, please open our eyes to the needs of the people we seek to reach.
- Break our hearts over what breaks your heart.
- Help us to be humble learners of the people around us.
- Provide the courage needed to go to the other side of the street, to meet people where they are.
- Give us the strength and humility to serve.

Guided prayer: for your intercessors

Please pray that we would:

- discern God's leading regarding the ministry focus group we are being called to reach.
- understand the cultural differences and uniqueness of our ministry focus group, and ways that might impact our ministry to them.
- treat those we are reaching with the respect and equality due to fellow image-bearers, regardless of differences in race, culture, education, language, or socioeconomic level.
- be able to put ourselves in the shoes of those we are serving, understand their perspective, and learn from them.

Action guide: a place for planning your next steps

1.

2.

3.

Chapter 8:
Designing Effective Ministry

By wisdom a house is built, and by understanding it is established; ⁴ by knowledge the rooms are filled with all precious and pleasant riches. ⁵ Wise warriors are mightier than strong ones, and those who have knowledge than those who have strength; ⁶ for by wise guidance you can wage your war, and in abundance of counselors there is victory.
(Proverbs 24:3–6)

Like the house described in this passage, building a healthy, functional church is no small feat. It requires all of these same qualities: wisdom, understanding, knowledge, guidance, and many advisers. Solid planning on the front end can make the difference between unchanneled momentum that fades away and a lasting church that blesses the surrounding community for years to come.

Within some Christian circles, planning is viewed with suspicion, or even considered unspiritual: "God's plans are higher than ours—he is in control and is powerful enough to accomplish his will. He is the one who brings renewal and revival—not us." Certainly that is true. Yet it's only one side of the story. The question remains: Will we cooperate with what God is doing? Are we positioned to take full advantage of the opportunities he provides? Proactive planning and intentional awareness allow us to say yes to those questions.

No matter where you are along the development path, you can significantly increase your effectiveness by being intentional, deliberate, and focused. What kind of church do you want? That's an important question to ask and there's no one right answer. Even though it may shift and change as you go, it's best to start out by aiming for something, rather than moving forward with no sense of what type of church you want to plant.

There are many different models, approaches, and options. You're probably familiar with some of them: seeker-sensitive, multisite, house church, megachurch, multiplication movements, etc. There's nothing inherently good or bad about any of these models. The incarnational, missional life of Jesus can be expressed regardless of the form or size of a church. They're simply different ways of accomplishing the same ends: the Great Commandment and the Great Commission.

However, these models represent different organizing principles for getting there. If your organizing principle is a classic congregation, that colors how you go about it. You need a pastor, a service, somewhere to meet, etc. If your organizing principle is small groups, you may take a different approach: You need group leaders, a plan or structure to follow, homes to meet in, etc. Where you're trying to go determines how you should go about getting there.

Although there's an almost infinite variety of structures, I sometimes think of three major types of stores as a shorthand for different categories of churches: megastores, general stores, and farmers markets.

Some churches are like megastores. There's everything under the sun there. Lots of options. They may not have really niche, artsy items, but you can get all the expected essentials there. If you show up at a megastore with a big long list of diverse but basic items—dish soap, a new toaster, soy milk, cinnamon-flavored cereal, lipstick, and a pair of shoes—you can reasonably expect it all to be there. That's the point of a megastore. The employees aren't going to know your name, but you don't expect them to. Churches modeled along these lines provide a lot of helpful services and a lot of different inroads: singles groups, expansive small-group options, hip youth ministries, large-scale service projects, Vacation Bible Schools, counseling centers, etc.

Other congregations are more like general stores: They have all of the basics—bread, milk, fruit—but there's not a huge selection. However, they also usually carry specialty items—things you can't get anywhere else, like locally made jam or regional specialties that are favorites among their clientele. General store customers are often extremely loyal, but they know better than to go in with a lengthy grocery list and expect to find everything. That's not the kind of store this is. In the same way, some churches provide good pastoral care, the people feel known and supported, and there's a sense of belonging. The people are loyal and often stay at the church for a long time. Yet people don't go into a small congregation expecting professional-level music and a huge children's program. It's not that kind of church.

Yet other churches are more like farmer's markets: Each stand represents a separate vendor. They each stand alone, but they're interconnected. They all show up at the same time on the same day because they know they're stronger together when there's connectedness. The beet salesman will do better business because the guy selling orchard-grown fruit is next to him. And if they don't have corn that day, you're not going to complain; you'll just look around to see what they do have. The advantage of the farmer's market is not completeness—it's freshness. You may not know how to make a peach pie, but if you see lots of fresh peaches on sale you might try to figure out a way to make use of them. A church using this organizing principle often doesn't look like what people expect churches to look like at all—there may be no building, no large Sunday gathering, no full-time paid pastor. Rather, it may consist of an interconnected group of house churches or disciplemaking groups.

The real question for a church planter and team is, what kind of church model and structure will best accomplish your mission and goal? Which will be most likely to reach the people you want to reach? The form and approach can change to suit your goals; just think strategically about what that might look like in your case.

The dangers of copying a model
The fact that other churches have already done the heavy lifting of designing and building models leads to an obvious question: Why not just do what they did? Copy it.

The reality is, what works there might not work here. In church planting, context is everything. Even in cases where some of the main structural points may be the same, tweaks and changes and adjustments will need to be made to suit the location, the ministry focus community, the financial realities, the giftedness of the leaders available . . . any number of variables.

It is also important to take into consideration whether the model you are about to use is based on a specific cultural or historical paradigm. Some models work well in one setting but not in another. Even if you've seen a good model up close, it's not a given that it will function exactly the same in your situation.

The reason? It's more a matter of biology than engineering. All models contain a genetic code, and you cannot superimpose a new genetic code upon an existing organism without altering or doing damage to the organism. If a church plant adopts a model without thinking through these ramifications, it runs the risk of altering or damaging the DNA God has already placed within the community.

One size does not fit all. Jesus used the idea of a wineskin (Luke 5:37–39). A new church plant requires not only a new wineskin, but a new and *unique* wineskin.

Finding a model that fits your values and your people

Design a model that will work for your people. You may borrow certain ideas, but the overall structure needs to be tailored to your unique ministry context. That means taking two areas into account: your values and your people. Those two elements will have a significant impact on models, strategies, and structures.

An effective strategy must harmonize with the values and the ministry focus group. If it doesn't, something like foreign tissue rejection occurs. The body has something foreign placed within and it responds by saying, in effect, "This doesn't fit here. This isn't part of us. Let's get rid of it."

Let's say a ministry focus group is poor, with limited education. How would it be if you came in and tried to impose a professional structure with a lot of paid staff, slick presentations, and a la carte programs/classes with fees? No amount of saying, "Scholarships are available" is going to make people get on board with that approach. People want to feel like they fit in their own church and that they can be full participants just as they are. Evaluate how well all aspects of a model fit within a specific cultural setting, and make adaptations as needed.

Don't lock in your organizational approach until you have something to organize. There's not much purpose in creating an elaborate service project structure if no one's even currently serving in simple ways. You can have ideas about how you'll structure serving as it grows, but you'll need to practice it first. If your structures are not enhancing existing life, they can actually restrain new life from forming.

One last important point is to create a structure that can be easily replicated. A good rule of thumb there is to start small. One person discipling another person can be easily replicated. A whole complex system with classes, resources, and a schedule cannot. Start small and grow from there. If you build reproducibility into the smaller pieces, you'll be able to replicate the larger pieces too as the ministry grows.

Many ministries and churches rely on the genius and/or expertise of their key leaders for success. That's a mistake. The effectiveness and scope of their ministry is limited by this dependency. How many times have you seen a church fall apart when the great speaker leaves? If the main leader or teacher of a church plant leaves, how much of the church remains? How you answer this question has a significant correlation with church health. Keep things simple, so most people with basic giftings in line with that role can do the job. If you want your ministry to outlive you, make it reproducible.

How will we worship? Services and gatherings

In considering an effective structure for your church, you'll need to think through three areas: worship, serving, and discipleship. Any church must cover these three basic areas. Although you'll certainly tweak and make changes as you go, think through the big picture now.

How will your church worship? Do you envision a large service? Small gatherings in homes? How will the sacraments be practiced? What type of music will be involved? We'll explore this topic later in chapter 15, so there's no need to go into great detail here. The purpose here is to think through, in broad strokes, what worship could or should look like in your context.

The clearer you are on your central purposes for worship, the more likely you are to accomplish them. Rather than feeling pressured into meeting popular demand, prayerfully and strategically consider what the needs of the church are at this stage and how worship can best accomplish those ends. Collect input from those who represent the people you'll be reaching. If you ask the right questions and listen patiently, they often have brilliant ideas about what worship means to people, and how worship can bring about spiritual transformation and the spread of the gospel.

How will we serve?

One of the essential elements of effective missional ministry is an outward focus on serving others. No matter what type or structure of church you have, you'll need to find a way to serve. Keep compassion in the forefront of your vision and strive to develop it. Compassion for others isn't limited to just Christians or just non-Christians, to just spiritual needs or just physical needs. We are called to serve all.

We do not serve with an agenda (i.e., you can have the soup if you listen to the sermon) and we do not pressure people to agree with our beliefs. We serve because Jesus told us to serve, and modeled such service. As we live like Jesus did, following in his footsteps, some will be open to his spiritual message and curious about it. Although we don't force that message, we don't hold it back either. Meeting needs often offers an emotional bridge into the lives of those in the ministry focus group, but that is not a right. It is a privilege to be granted by those you're serving.

So how do we serve? Although particular methods and means may change over the years as God provides various opportunities, you'll want some form of structure in place from the beginning, to facilitate service. Through what channels would someone in your church become engaged with serving? Through small groups? Through encouragement to listen to the Holy Spirit? Membership class? A challenge via the sermon? Community-wide service days? Coaches?

Consider some big-picture questions first to brainstorm options: What are our long-term goals? What could be done now? What might that lead to in the future? What could we stop doing to free up time and energy? Who could oversee our serving engagements? How? What help might he or she need? How would new people become engaged in serving?

List as many options as you can—then list some more. Put down any that come to mind, even if they seem unworkable or impractical. Sometimes combinations of two different ideas can come together to create some good options.

After brainstorming, prioritize your potential courses of action. Which options seem most important? Which seem most doable? Which could be foundational to the other options, so we could build on it? Which could provide the most leverage for future change? What are our people hearing from God? What is he placing on their hearts?

The ways we serve will likely change over time as God leads, and will look different from one stage of the church's life cycle to the next. Maybe you don't currently have the building space to create a huge food pantry, but your people could volunteer at an existing local food pantry. Maybe you don't have the resources to put on a big parenting seminar for the community, but you could still offer a parenting group in someone's living room that's open to the community. The DNA is the same—it just looks different during different seasons.

The central concern now is to put some structure into place to facilitate serving others. That way, as you discern needs in the community, you'll be in a position to act on them. The early church did the same:

> Now during those days, when the disciples were increasing in number, the Hellenists complained against the Hebrews because their widows were being neglected in the daily distribution of food. [2] And the twelve called together the whole community of the disciples and said, "It is not right that we should neglect the word of God in order to wait on tables. [3] Therefore, friends, select from among yourselves seven men of good standing, full of the Spirit and of wisdom, whom we may appoint to this task, [4] while we, for our part, will

devote ourselves to prayer and to serving the word." [5] *What they said pleased the whole community, and they chose Stephen, a man full of faith and the Holy Spirit, together with Philip, Prochorus, Nicanor, Timon, Parmenas, and Nicolaus, a proselyte of Antioch.* [6] *They had these men stand before the apostles, who prayed and laid their hands on them. (Acts 6:1–6)*

How will we grow?

A third area we will need to create structure for is growth as disciples. How will we go about accomplishing the core of our mission: making disciples?

> *And he said to them, "Follow me, and I will make you fish for people."* [20] *Immediately they left their nets and followed him. (Matthew 4:19–20)*

A disciple is one who follows Jesus. Therefore, my working definition of disciplemaking is: helping people take one step closer to Jesus from wherever they are. They may be very far from Jesus, or they may have been following him for years. They may know much about Jesus or very little. Everyone needs help taking one step closer to Jesus from wherever they are. When someone connects with your church plant, they are probably already somewhere on that journey. How can you meet them where they are, and help them take one step closer to Jesus?

> . Everyone needs help taking one step closer to Jesus from wherever they are.

What you need is a disciplemaking process of some sort. You'll find much more on this topic in the chapter on disciplemaking, but here are the basic pieces:

1. *A clear sense of what a disciple is.* If you want to accomplish something, you need to know what you're aiming for. Consider what you want a disciple to be—and to do.
2. *Environments to find people to disciple.* Too often we look only inside churches—and even then, only among those who sign up for a discipleship program. Think more broadly. Consider environments outside the church. Where do you, and others in your church, have relationships with people? And inside the church, think of ways to get everyone involved in both making disciples and growing as disciples themselves.
3. *Relationships to facilitate disciplemaking.* Find ways to connect people with one another. That could be done within small groups, in peer

groups of three or four, or in one-on-one relationships. Discipleship is not something to be embarked on alone; relationships are essential.

4. *A process to facilitate disciplemaking.* Next, you'll need to answer the "how"—how will you go about making and growing disciples? You'll need some type of structure or vehicle. What kind of reproducible process will you use? Do you have coaching guides, books, a practice of Scripture reading and prayer? You may want to develop two or three different options. They should be systematic enough to be reproducible, but flexible enough that people don't feel forced into a mold.

5. *A recognition that living as disciples means discipling others.* Everyone will need to recognize that no matter where they are on the path of discipleship, they can help someone else along it as well. Don't create an environment where people feel they need to be experts to disciple others.

6. *A path for people to get from one step to another.* Once someone is in a healthy environment, how will you connect them to others? Then, once someone is connected to a person or a small group of people, how will you provide them with a process or means of discipleship? How will you move them into the role of discipling others?

Again, this is only a very basic overview to help you start thinking through initial steps toward developing a disciplemaking process in your church plant. Chapter 12 will take you into much more depth where you can fine-tune your process, but you need to start laying the structural groundwork now. For example, if you eventually want to create peer discipling groups of three or four who work through a series of coaching guides with Scripture, begin practicing that now among your core team. Adding it in after the fact, when you decide you need "more emphasis on discipleship," will be much more challenging. Put the foundation in place now.

Drawing a ministry flowchart
It's time to write your first draft. It will not be perfect and it will change, but you need to start somewhere. What's your initial thinking on how to structure your church? Just draw the broad strokes of what that will look like. Here are a few possible examples:

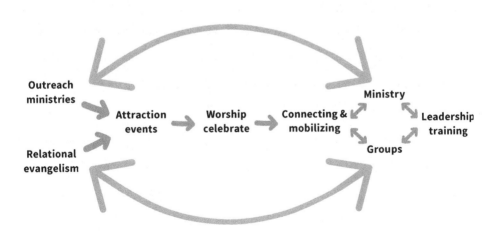

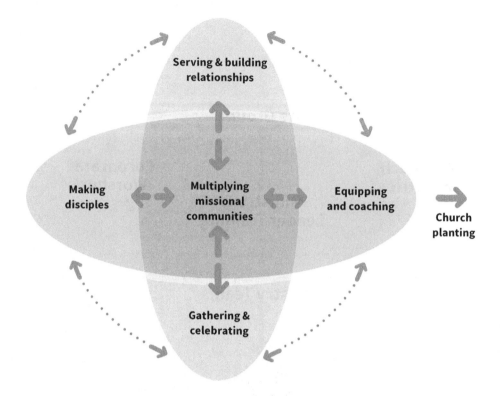

Include elements in your ministry flowchart that answer these questions:
- How do new people get connected from where they are?
- What does the people-flow look like as individuals go from just discovering this church to becoming fully involved?
- What are the connections between various ministry areas of the church, and how do they fit together?
- How does the process of disciplemaking fit into the people-flow?
- How do people get involved in serving?
- How are leaders connected with one another?

What is the value of a ministry flowchart at this stage? It helps you understand how you'll function, which then helps you begin to see how your organization will emerge. A good ministry flowchart will help give you a general idea now of where you want to go, so you have something clear to work toward.

Yet, be sure to keep your flowchart in rough draft form; don't lock it in too soon. It can feel awkward to change it later if you do. Plus, you want to allow freedom for the people God brings your way to help shape the organization, and that may very well look different than what's in your head right now.

Governance and bylaws

You'll also need to select some type of local church governing structure early on for the church. Various terms are used by different groups: pastors, elders, overseers. In the Bible, these three terms are all used interchangeably. I find that the generic expression "board" for your collective governing body tends to be the most neutral option, so that's what I'll use here.

The function of the board is governance and accountability. The pastor leads, the staff manages, and the people do the ministry. Set things up so you're clear on who makes what decisions and who has authority over what areas. Clarity on these points from the beginning can avoid a great deal of conflict later on.

The bylaws need to clarify essential areas, such as who is responsible, and what procedures will be followed, for:

- setting up provisional leadership.
- receiving and dismissing members.
- disciplinary policy and procedures.
- selecting a governing board.
- hiring and firing pastor and/or staff.
- setting goals and budget.
- buying and selling property.
- church affiliation.
- amending the constitution and bylaws.
- dissolving the organization.

Early on the initial core team, and possibly a few others, has given oversight to the church. Now it's time to establish a more permanent governing structure that will best serve your church in the years to come.

However, that does not mean that you need people permanently in those spots right now. There is great value in delaying the formation of a permanent church board until you have sufficient strength, DNA, numbers, etc. A provisional board will allow you to make important changes as new potential board members come into the church. The point is, if you prematurely solidify your leadership, your plant may not be mature enough to get the right people in to help you long term. Establish the right pattern, then find the people over time. Even then, I highly recommend term limits; they will allow for review and easier transitions as needed.

For your board, you will need spiritually mature individuals who have a calling and capacity to see the big picture and work with you closely on the direction of the church. Selection of leaders is not about fair representation but about giftedness and calling. Spend time in prayer, as Jesus did before he selected his disciples. Consider how to involve the congregation in the selection process; this decision will depend on your church polity.

Evaluate your provisional leadership structure and those who make up the team. Sometimes planters will involve experienced leaders from outside the church plant to provide wisdom and accountability. This strategy allows greater focus to disciple emerging leaders and avoids prematurely appointing new Christians to the board.

Prayerfully consider those who are on the team or who you are considering for the team:

- Have they proven themselves committed and faithful to the call?
- Are their gifts and skills adequate for the job?
- Are their gifts and skills needed now in this position?
- Are there others you believe God is calling?
- Are there gifts/callings that are missing on the team?

Selecting board members:
1. Whom do you feel God may be calling to serve in a governing capacity for the church?
2. What qualifications are needed?
3. How will you approach them about the possibility of serving as provisional board members?
4. What kind of commitment will you ask of them (responsibilities, time frame, length of service)?
5. What orientation and training will you provide?

Commitment and membership
Some churches have formal membership; others don't. However, almost all churches have some way of identifying and tracking regular attenders who are a committed part of the congregation. Membership should focus less on numbers and more on the processes you have in place for helping people stay faithful to their commitments, refresh their vision, and live into their values.

Another practical advantage of membership, from a planning perspective, is that it allows you to project into the future and budget accordingly. You can project income, expenses, and attendance trends based in part on membership statistics.

What does it mean to be committed to a local congregation? How do you frame that in terms of behavior? How and when do you facilitate conversations around commitments with people who are visiting or attending your church? That can be akin to a defining-the-relationship talk in dating—clarifying the level of commitment and expectations around how to engage with one another.

Consider your position on membership. What is it for? What does it define for you as church? Does it give the right to vote, and in what situations? Are children considered members?

Consider your requirements for membership. Once you've established them, you can create a process for getting there—member classes, doctrinal confirmations, baptisms, signing of a covenant, public commitment to the church, or some combination of these. Some churches require an annual recommitment to membership, which keeps you current in your understanding of who is committed. Be careful not to go overboard on requiring too much, or erring on the other side by only asking for minimal assent. What you do and what you require should be in alignment with the values you're trying to instill.

Remember, there is no need to build all of your own systems from scratch. Why re-invent the wheel? There are plenty of tools out there that can help you with tasks around tracking, organizing, and managing. Go online and find something that works for you. A search for "church management software" will yield many options, and new innovations are always coming.

Church discipline

Consider whether and how you practice church discipline. If you do, in what types of cases and for what issues? Are you a peacemaker? Can you confront, restore, resolve? To what degree will you get involved with disputes, and in what circumstances? With who? What if a leader has a significant moral failure?

The best time to make decisions about all of these questions is before they become an issue. Have a clear plan in place, with general principles for commonplace scenarios. Talk with other planters and pastors about issues that have arisen and how they've handled them. Ask how they've set up their church discipline policies. Having processes ready in advance is helpful, so that when an issue arises no one can say it's personal.

Legal incorporation

Once you have a provisional leadership structure, you'll need to become legally incorporated. This is similar to starting a business, but you'll be registered as a church. Precisely how to do that depends on national and state laws, but I highly recommend checking with an attorney to make sure it's done in accordance with local requirements.

In the US, becoming incorporated as a church involves registering as a nonprofit organization and receiving 501c3 status. This status provides you with a tax ID number, which you'll need in order to receipt donations and allow people to give money on a tax-free basis. Similar principles may apply internationally, but with different terminology.

As for timing, you can become incorporated early on or along the way. Wait until you're sure about denominational affiliation, though. You don't want to incorporate before then, because you'll want a tax ID number associated with the denomination. However, if you will not be part of a denomination, you'll need to incorporate earlier, so you can receive donations.

Financial structure

A full and legal financial structure is a must for any church that accepts offerings or donations of any kind. Make sure you have each of these pieces in place, assuming they are in accordance with your church's structure and your country's government:

- accounting system
- bank account
- tax ID number
- payroll tax
- worker's compensation
- insurance
- properly designated housing allowance
- ordination or licensing of clergy
- a clear budget aligned with your priorities
- proper receipting of gifts
- recordkeeping
- accountability

Churches are notorious for not taking these items seriously. They think because they are churches, they don't have to do this. Legally, that's not true.

For new churches without a large denominational affiliation, connecting with an accounting service specifically designed for churches can be a good option. Often the kinds of items above can be outsourced to experts who know how to establish a new church legally and set up appropriate tax structures. Do an online search to find one. These groups often provide virtual services to help you get set up right.

Planning and adjusting as you go
The apostle Paul adjusted his strategy throughout the course of his missionary journeys, changing his approach over time. (Read and meditate on the book of Acts sometime, reflecting specifically on this aspect.) You too should continuously look at what is going on and adjust accordingly. Planning should be an ongoing spiritual process. Follow this cyclical process: plan, act, evaluate, and adjust.

Think through the material in this chapter carefully. Hold the strategy lightly and pray over it. Learn how to adjust and be flexible. Your planning should be an ongoing process, as you think through principles and watch to see what works most effectively in your specific context.

Journey Guide for Chapter 8
Designing Effective Ministry

JOURNEY GUIDE

Building a healthy, functional church is no small
feat. Solid planning on the front end can make
the difference between unchanneled momentum
that fades away and a lasting church that blesses the community for many years
to come. New church plants can significantly increase their effectiveness by being
intentional and focused. They'll need to think through models and structures for
effective ministry that will support worship, serving, outreach, and discipleship. If
you want to plan ahead now about how best to transition into the desired future,
you can work through the journey guide below.

Checklist: for the road ahead
- ☐ A timeline for accomplishing the goals below has been created.
- ☐ Existing structural models have been evaluated, and adaptations
  considered.
- ☐ Strategy for facilitating worship has been designed.
- ☐ Strategy for facilitating serving has been designed.
- ☐ Strategy for facilitating discipleship growth has been designed.
- ☐ A path of assimilation has been created.
- ☐ A rough draft of a ministry flowchart has been drawn.
- ☐ The pros and cons of denomination/network affiliation have been
  weighed, and a determination has been made.
- ☐ Local governance structure has been designed.
- ☐ Decision-making authority has been clarified.
- ☐ Potential conflicts/disciplinary issues have been considered and planned
  for.
- ☐ A provisional leadership group has been established.
- ☐ The church has been legally incorporated.
- ☐ Strategy and structure have been evaluated and revised as you've
  proceeded and learned more.

Discipleship focus: Take Inventory
In the midst of planning, don't forget to take stock of your own spirituality as well.
It's easy to get lost in the weeds of the ministry.
  Inward focus:
    1. Take a personal barometer reading. On a scale from 1-10 (1 being
    terrible, 10 being wonderful), how are you feeling…

- In general?
- In your relationship with the Lord?
- In your family relationships?
- In your ministry relationships?

2. Spend time in silent prayer.
3. Celebrate what's going well.
4. Ponder what's not going well.

Outward focus:

1. Who else might be able to give you some perspective on these areas?
2. What action steps do you sense God may be calling you to take?

Strategic questions: for you and your coach

- On a scale of 1–10, with your inclination to grow without planning a 1 and your inclination to plan without adjustment being a 10, how would you rate yourself? What steps will you take to find the right balance?
- What church models are you most drawn to and why? How might you draw together some of the strongest points of different models?
- How is your church structure shaped by the culture and location of your community? In what ways does your church structure need to resist the culture?
- What do you view as the primary purpose of your worship service? What are some secondary purposes?
- How will you help people become involved in serving?
- How will you help people grow in their discipleship? How will you help them begin to disciple others?
- What is your plan for assimilating people into the life of the church? What relationships and communication help people move from one level of involvement to the next?
- What strategies do you have to establish provisional leadership in your new church? How will you develop leaders for your board? What should that selection process look like?
- How can you take your planning process for the structure of your church to the next phase? How can you build in flexibility for needed changes?

Discussion questions: For you and your team

- What ideas can we generate for facilitating worship?
- What ideas can we generate for facilitating serving?
- What ideas can we generate for facilitating discipleship growth?

- What elements of our unique values and DNA need to be reflected in our church structure? Who can help us create an effective structure for our church?
- What safeguards do we need? What pitfalls do we want to avoid?
- What action steps are you sensing God might have us take next?

Guided prayer: for you personally

In the same way, you who are younger must accept the authority of the elders. And all of you must clothe yourselves with humility in your dealings with one another, for "God opposes the proud, but gives grace to the humble." [6] Humble yourselves therefore under the mighty hand of God, so that he may exalt you in due time. (1 Peter 5:5–6)

- God, search my heart for a spirit of arrogance or independence.
- Whose authority should I be willing to submit to? Whose should I not?
- Who can I trust to help me and my church when we face difficult times?
- Please make this not my church, but yours.

Guided prayer: for use with your team

Pray together with your team through each of these themes:

- Lord, please help us open our ears to what you have to say to us.
- Help us be wise, yet humble as we design a church that will last.
- Allow us to be good stewards of all you have given us.
- Please grant us wisdom and judgement.

Guided prayer: for your intercessors

Please pray that we would:

- be sensitive to the Holy Spirit, as we listen for God's direction about how best to structure this new church he is building.
- be humble to God's authority, recognizing our need for him and for others to help us.
- have wisdom to make good decisions and ensure a fair decision-making process.
- provide us with the people, spiritual gifts, and other resources we need in order to create a good foundation upon which to move forward.
- have the flexibility needed to adjust as we find problems with our plans and structure.

Action guide: a place for planning your next steps

1.

2.

3.

Chapter 9:
Establishing Financial Support

So how much money does it cost to plant a church? Obviously, the actual number varies widely—from zero to millions, depending on the church and the culture. Yet whatever the case, the reality of money needs to be taken into account. Although it would be nice if money had no bearing on our decisions or options as leaders, this is rarely the case in church planting. We live in a world where money does matter—even in ministry. And like everything else in God's world, we are called to steward it well.

Just as lack of money sometimes means making hard choices about what we can and cannot do, it also opens doors for creativity and innovation. And while a bounty of money for church planting can open doors of opportunity that may not otherwise exist, it also creates the temptation for misuse, waste, or dependency. In either case, we must make wise choices as leaders and invest in what will truly bring about kingdom results.

Money is often an uncomfortable subject for planters and laypeople alike. I'd like to help you make an important perspective shift. To many planters, raising funds makes us feel like we're begging on a street corner for money. I used to feel that way sometimes, but was able to make a mental shift when I realized that raising funds is actually an opportunity to disciple people—I'm helping them process the strategic investments they're making financially in God's kingdom. I'm presenting them with an opportunity to think through the principles that govern their giving. What are they giving and why? How are they investing their money? What kind of return are they looking for?

These are helpful questions for them to ask, whether or not they invest in your ministry. The process helps people reflect on their priorities and on what they really value. Where your treasure is, there your heart will be also.

In many ways, this is similar to investing into a business opportunity. If I'm vested in this, so to speak, and I think it's a good deal, I'll let friends know. Then they'll think about it, talk it over with their spouses, and if it lines up with what they want, they'll invest, too.

Be clear about the return on the investment. If you're raising support, you ought to be able to demonstrate results. Missions support is not Christian welfare— it's making a strategic investment to advance God's kingdom. What are you aiming for? Changed lives? How will you measure that? What has already been accomplished? People give based on your track record. If you can't articulate the return on people's investment, spend some more time thinking through your ministry strategy and goals.

Also, remember this: If God has called you and asked you to raise support, he obviously has people out there that he is prompting to make this investment. What you're doing is going through a discovery process to find out who those people are. Some will be intercessors, who'll want to make a very strategic investment in the ministry.

People who give are not doing planters a favor or supporting a pet project; they are participating in God's plan for his church, according to the particular way he has called them. Some people will be called to give to church planting in a way similar to how others are called to give to other causes. The practice of generosity is an opportunity for growth and obedience in the lives of all believers. That's an important perspective shift: It's about discipleship.

> If God has called you and asked you to raise support, he obviously has people out there that he is prompting to make this investment.

Making a living

Much of the discomfort over raising money for church planting is that in many cases, some of the funds raised will go to provide a salary for the church planter. Every planter must wrestle with the question of how to make a living and how to provide for his or her family.

There is often a philosophical question among church leaders about who should receive financial support. Church leadership must be understood as a calling rather than a career. While one might be able to make a living at leading in God's kingdom, he or she must be willing to lead, whether there is a paycheck or not. Jesus delineated between a true shepherd who would give his life for the sheep and a hireling who would not.

Financial support in the New Testament was meant to release the proven leader to invest greater time and energy into their calling. They were investing in provenness, not potential. As a leader demonstrates gifts that create fruitful ministry and leaders, the support base will grow naturally. Such leaders can raise support (i.e., missionaries), or it can be developed within the emerging network of churches. Think of your ministry as a lifestyle, rather than a job description with regular office hours.

In the New Testament, it appears that apostles were the only ones who received financial support for their calling. Elders and teachers are to receive financial reward but in the first-century context, it is probably not meant to be the equivalent of a full-time salary and benefits. In some cases, like Paul and Barnabas in 1 Corinthians 9, we see leaders rejecting financial support for philosophical reasons. Much depends on the specific situation and the culture being served.

Think through your own theological beliefs about raising support. Here are a few practical means for planters to make a living:
- Denominational, or sending church support
- Donations raised for support as missionaries
- Bivocational work. Those in ministry can be "tentmakers" like Paul, where they work regular jobs to pay their bills, or are partially supported by the church and partially by their job.
- Increased support as the network expands. The leader's support will increase naturally as the ministry demand also increases.
- Spouse's income. Sometimes a spouse's income can release the other to serve with greater freedom. Obviously, both partners would need to feel equally called to church planting.

Often, it's a combination of multiple options that enable someone to serve in ministry. Creative solutions can be key. Brainstorm to broaden your options, and consider pros and cons.

Whatever your financial plan, do your research and know what you're aiming for. If you're part of a denomination that provides funding for planters, contact them about options. However, most groups don't offer full funding, so work through the questions below to help you think through your particular situation:

- What financial resources will you need for your first year?
- What sources of income do you currently have in place?
- What is your plan for securing any additional financing needed?
- List the pros and cons of each of the options below:
    - Bivocational work
    - Church or denominational sponsorship
    - Raising financial support

Bivocational ministry

Many church planters will at least start out bivocational. This route is an excellent option if you have a job that is flexible enough to allow adequate time for evangelism and recruitment of a core team. Many jobs today allow for a great deal of flexibility, as well as putting you in touch with a wide variety of people. See chapter 2 for further discussion of what bivocational ministry can look like.

Church or denominational support

Funding through a sending church or a denomination can be ideal, as it frees up a good deal of your time to focus on church planting rather than either another job or fundraising. Yet be sure to be clear on what the expectations are in return for support. Do you report to someone? Follow certain denominational procedures? Meet certain benchmarks for progress along the way? None of these are bad things, but you need to know in advance what the expectations are. Don't be afraid to have a frank discussion about it—and get all decisions in writing—so everyone is clear beforehand.

A word of advice on outside funding, though: Avoid long-term subsidies. They create dependency, and can result in a focus on getting subsidies extended rather than reaching people. Subsidies are best done over a period of about three years, with decreasing support from the sponsoring group over that time. All church plants should aim for financial independence within a few years, even if that means that the planter needs to be bivocational.

Raising funds

Raising your own funds is the traditional missionary model. Other followers of Jesus who are not part of your church give money for you to go out and reach the unreached. Whether those unreached are within your own country or not is beside the point. There is plenty of mission field at home, wherever you may be. If you're serving as a catalyst to start and multiply churches, this type of support would be ongoing. For founding pastors, it would be short-term—until the church is able to pick up the ongoing financial responsibilities, thereby releasing the raised funds for new church planting endeavors.

An important benefit of fundraising is that your financial support is spread out over many people. While you can lose a job or your denomination can let you go, the likelihood of all of your supporters dropping their support at once is extremely low. Fundraising can provide a higher level of financial security through diversification. Yet many people are uncertain how to do it, so we'll provide some basic pointers here.

Fundraising 101

First and foremost, rather than asking for charitable donations, the perspective of the planter must be focused on inviting others into the opportunity of kingdom investment.

Why do people give? I learned this a long time ago, when I was being trained to raise missionary support. Here are the reasons people give:

- They have a relationship with you.
- They believe in the vision.
- There's a strategy (plan) to accomplish the vision.
- You have a track record of results.

The more personal the approach, the better the result. As mentioned earlier, it's like offering friends the opportunity to get in on a good business investment. It's also an opportunity to disciple them in stewardship, by helping them discern the principles that govern their giving. Here's the basic process of fundraising:

- *Make a list of people and organizations that may want to give.* Think through denominations or associations, Christian businesspeople, pastors, and missions committees.
- *Send each of them a brief, personalized email.* Highlight a few basics about your church plant and express a desire to sit down with them to share the vision—including how they can make a strategic investment in turning that vision into reality. Let them know you'll be calling in a few days to set an appointment.
- *Follow up, to set an appointment.* Work around their schedule and meet at a location that's convenient for them.
- *At the appointment*:
  - Share the vision (preferably with stories).
  - Clarify the opportunity.
  - Present the strategy.
  - Present the financial need (be specific: e.g., $80k over two years).
  - Ask, "Is this the kind of ministry opportunity you'd like to invest in?"

- Wait in silence (this is important, and more difficult than it sounds).
- Receive a response.
- Set a time for follow-up.
- Leave a strategy paper or written proposal so they can read more.
- *Follow up when and how you said you would.* This can be done with a future conversation or with a letter. A letter should include a response card for a commitment with an envelope, a receipt with a tear-off for the next gift, instructions for how to establish online giving, and—for potentially big donors—a challenge to begin with a significant gift to help you get started.
- *Ongoing contact.* Send a personal thank-you note promptly! Then establish a system for communicating monthly with ongoing supporters. Each communication should include updates on progress, stories about specific people who've been impacted by your ministry, and intercessory requests.

Some advance planning is necessary for following this process effectively. Before you begin raising support, you'll need to develop a proposal for the church plant. This proposal will include vision, planning, budgeting, and a timeline. Having a proposal in place will give potential supporters clarity about what you're planning. We've devoted chapter 10 entirely to writing your planting proposal.

Personal preparation and accountability matter too. Planters who have undergone an assessment process, retained a coach, and set clear, measurable goals for success are seen as better investments by potential partners and donors.

Keys to effective fundraising:
- Local churches and organizations are more than channels for financial support; they are partners with a constructive joint role to be played.
- Vision is validated by action. Any focus on the big picture must be translated to specific concrete reality, in terms of changed lives.
- Effective ministry includes sharing the gospel by both words and deeds. Don't neglect either sharing the message of Jesus or serving people wherever they're at.

- Good stewardship must be clearly demonstrated both in terms of ministry outcomes and financial management. Avoid vague or unsubstantiated claims; be transparent and specific.
- Concrete ways are provided through which supporters can be meaningfully involved through contribution of money, time, and prayer—serving as true partners.

Giving from within the church plant

Remember that money isn't your major goal—your major goal is reaching people and making disciples. Additional resources will be found in the harvest as you grow the new church. Part of planting a healthy church, on the road to becoming self-sustaining, is cultivating an attitude of stewardship in those you're ministering alongside. Each person who becomes a part of a church plant should be encouraged to steward well what they have, using their personal money appropriately, saving, and giving generously. That's an important part of discipleship.

> *Of course, there is great gain in godliness combined with contentment; [7] for we brought nothing into the world, so that we can take nothing out of it; [8] but if we have food and clothing, we will be content with these. [9] But those who want to be rich fall into temptation and are trapped by many senseless and harmful desires that plunge people into ruin and destruction. [10] For the love of money is a root of all kinds of evil, and in their eagerness to be rich some have wandered away from the faith and pierced themselves with many pains.*
>
> . . .
>
> *[17] As for those who in the present age are rich, command them not to be haughty, or to set their hopes on the uncertainty of riches, but rather on God who richly provides us with everything for our enjoyment. [18] They are to do good, to be rich in good works, generous, and ready to share, [19] thus storing up for themselves the treasure of a good foundation for the future, so that they may take hold of the life that really is life. (1 Timothy 6:6–10, 17–19)*

So how do we as planters talk about money? How and when do we start teaching on stewardship and giving? Many planters are afraid to talk about money at all, for fear that people new to Christianity will think that's what ministry is all about—just trying to get people's money. And of course, done wrong, that can certainly be the impression people get.

It needs to be about a spirit of generosity—not just giving to the church because the church needs money. Generosity needs to become a part of people's spiritual lives as they grow. Jesus talked extensively about money. It's one of the main barriers that can hold people back from God. So by all means, be bold in teaching on stewardship, generosity, and giving. Your role as a planter is to free people from being enslaved to money—letting go of a tight grip on money *so that they may take hold of the life that is truly life* (1 Timothy 6:19).

Start with your core team, within the first six months of gathering, and then address it at least annually. By addressing the issue regularly, those who are added to your number will learn that financial stewardship is simply a part of a life of discipleship. It can take a long time to help unchurched people work through these issues, as the issue of money is often fraught with shame and fear, but don't give up establishing generosity as a norm of basic discipleship.

Addressing people's financial pressures can be not only a part of disciplemaking, but also a great opportunity for outreach and serving the community. Many people seek to learn how to handle their money well in a way that aligns with their values.

> **Key principles for teaching about money:**
> - *Give all you can.* Begin with a heart of generosity—a heart that reflects God's heart. Everything belongs to God, and he has only entrusted us with it for a time. We are managers, and he will come back to see how we have invested his money. So the first principle is generous giving: Give as God has blessed you, and give back to God first.
> - *Save all you can.* After we have given our firstfruits back to God, set some aside to save. We never know what crises may come our way, and we should do our best to be prepared.
> - *Spend wisely.* We should spend wisely and with joy and gladness. Think about the money we use for our home, food, family, and clothing. We need to distinguish between needs and wants, cover the needs first—then we may be able to cover some of the wants. A budget laid out in advance will help us immensely with stretching our money to cover what needs to be covered.

- *Adjust as needed.* There's always a need to monitor and make changes. If our financial management isn't going well, we have three basic choices: We can reallocate our spending so it is more in line with our values, increase our income, or reduce our expenses. Depending on the situation, we decide which option is the most appropriate for us right now.
- *Be content.* And in all things, we must be content. It's easy to be discontent with what we have, always wanting more. But by focusing on what we do have—what God has entrusted to us and how we can use it for his kingdom—we can gain a better, more accurate perspective. Contentment is not related to how much we have, but an attitude of the heart: thankfulness.

In addition to 1 Timothy 6 above, some important passages about money include Deuteronomy 8:17–18; Matthew 25:14–30; Mark 12:41–44; and Luke 12:13–21.

Teaching people to give also creates a sense of ownership. When planting efforts are subsidized with outside money to the point where local believers do not feel the need to give, the plant has developed an unhealthy sense of dependency and lack of ownership.

Financial transparency

The same principles that apply to individuals in your church plant—generosity, saving, and giving—apply to the planter and the church as well. Leaders are responsible for administering the church's finances appropriately. This means being honest, transparent, and making decisions in line with kingdom values. What is truly important in the kingdom of God? That is what we should invest in. We also need to invest appropriately. What types of spending will yield fruit and get the results we are looking for?

Motives are always important to examine when it comes to money as well. We need to be generous, yet wise. We need to avoid greed and self-aggrandizement. We need to live as though we are not permanent residents of this world—because we aren't. We are entrusted with what we have for a time, and God knows whether we are investing it well or poorly.

One of the most important things is to have multiple people involved with church finances. If one person has too much control, the temptation can be great. Don't put any of your leaders, including yourself, in that position. Create transparent systems, so that everyone knows how the church's money is being used. This involves advance planning, but it is essential for managing finances effectively. Misuse of church funds—either intentionally or through carelessness—is one of the easiest ways to destroy a church.

Here are some practical ways to practice financial transparency:

- Accounting: Create a clear and transparent system for monitoring and tracking the money. An accountant or someone with basic accounting skills can record income and expenses, and compare that to the budget. A clear paper trail is essential.
- Safeguarding: This includes practices like keeping receipts and making sure the same person doesn't do the books and sign the checks. It means creating a system of checks and balances that protects your church against any accusations of misuse of money. When the offering is collected, have more than one person involved. Make sure your systems are in line with whatever legal requirements exist in your area.
- Communication: Periodically tell the congregation (whether they've asked or not) how the money is being used. This doesn't necessarily mean divulging individual salaries, but providing overall amounts of staffing, giving, facilities, etc. Make the information clear and readily accessible. Helping people understand what decisions are being made and by whom goes a long way toward financial transparency.

Budgeting

As soon as you have money coming in and money going out, you'll need to make a budget. Don't think you'll do it at a later stage when there's more money; you need a clear, written budget from the very beginning. If you're raising support and connected to an organization, they will handle your salary. However, if you're independent, you need to have a team that's involved in putting together a budget and giving approval to spending. For example, the planter cannot set his or her own salary, as that has legal and ethical ramifications. You'll need a team to help create a system for how financial decisions are made.

It may sound counterintuitive, but don't start by setting a budget. First, figure out what you're trying to accomplish, then what that will cost. That means bringing all your ministry area proposals together and—as a team—prioritizing what's most important. Consider the worth of the goals themselves. Is the amount of investment (time, money, personnel) worth the potential return? Don't just allocate money to certain ministry areas (worship, office space, outreach) without thinking about how it will be used—have a clear goal for what is supposed to be accomplished with the money. Also remember that some important items may not be expensive; much of the important work of outreach, service, and disciplemaking can be accomplished with very little funding. In this way you can create a budget that reflects and aligns with your goals.

When writing an initial budget, most people tend not to include anything related to a benefits package (medical, disability, retirement, etc.), thinking they will come back and add those items later when they have more funds. The reality is, most don't come back to revisit those items if they're not already in place. Put these in as line items now, even if you put a zero next to them. If you don't, no one will ever ask why there isn't anything going to those areas. The same is true of other long-term goals, such as building needs. If your church planting model is such that you will need to either rent or buy meeting space at some point, write those line items into the budget. Whatever you envision the long-term plan being, put corresponding line items into the budget now.

Finally, you'll need to consider cash flow management. This can be a simple spreadsheet that tracks your receipts and expenses monthly, helps keep you on top of cash flow, and provides early warning signals before you hit a crisis. Picture your cash flow like a water tank: Even if you know water is coming soon, it needs to be there before you can use it. Plan for the income to hit the account before the bills are due, otherwise you can technically be within budget but still broke. Weigh carefully the timing of major expenditures and make sure you have enough in the account ahead of time to cover them. A good team or administrative assistant can help you track cash flow to avoid unexpected surprises.

In your church planting budget, aim for sustainability, just as you would with your personal budget. Long-term, you can't spend more than you bring in (unless you are being subsidized by a wealthier sister church, which can't and shouldn't be counted on forever), so plan your ministry expenses accordingly and grow them as your organization grows and your people grow.

Generosity

In all things, we are called to generosity. Even as we may be struggling financially or raising funds ourselves, we are still called to be generous to others. A good rule of thumb is to aim to give 10 percent of whatever you are bringing in to missions outside of your own organization. Those could be overseas missions, other church planting missions, or local ministries that serve the poor. The early apostles set this example for us when they made plans to reach out to different people groups:

> And when James and Cephas and John, who were acknowledged pillars, recognized the grace that had been given to me, they gave to Barnabas and me the right hand of fellowship, agreeing that we should go to the Gentiles and they to the circumcised.
> [10] They asked only one thing, that we remember the poor, which was actually what I was eager to do. (Galatians 2:9–10)

Biblical stewardship for church planters is not just about raising enough money for your church plant. It's also about practicing generosity, helping other churches that are also just getting started, helping the last and the least. Just as many individual believers are called to give financially, so are newly planted churches. Yet, that can be extremely challenging. Much faith is required to be generous when you don't know how your own operating expenses are going to be covered.

One young church found itself in the position of sending out their key associate pastor with fifty people and their tithes, plus another $100,000, at the same time that they were buying a new building for themselves. The senior pastor remembers sitting down at a board meeting and going over the numbers. He told me the story:

> We still had the mortgage on the old building, we were losing fifty people and their tithes, and we were increasing our monthly need with the new building. The bottom line was a $6,000 per month increase in expenditure without any visible means to pay for it, and we were giving away that much in tithes and offerings. It didn't make sense on paper—it looked like suicide on paper. I remember looking up at the members of the board after running the numbers and asking, "Does this make sense?" Their basic response was, "No, it doesn't make sense. But we feel called to do it and we believe God's going to help us."
>
> That was a huge step for our church in terms of our commitment to multiplication. I still don't know how this happened, but over the next few months, our income actually went up, even though we lost all those people. We never missed a beat. We just kept on going and the church continued to grow. It was phenomenal to see how God took care of us. On top of that, the church we planted, planted another church almost immediately in the same community. The commitment to church planting had become part of the genetic code and was passed down to the next generation.

God sometimes calls us to dramatic steps of faith in giving and other times he calls us simply to steady, incremental giving. Sometimes generosity means taking financial risks, sometimes the risk of giving away people, and always the risk of shifting your focus from your own congregation to the wider work that God is doing. It will feel difficult to go from being focused on your own church plant to being more outwardly focused on the needs of other ministries, but it's clearly a biblical direction. Paul urged the church at Corinth to be prepared to give to the poorer church in Jerusalem—a work outside of their own local church ministry and even outside of their own culture:

> Now it is not necessary for me to write you about the ministry to the saints, [2] for I know your eagerness, which is the subject of my boasting about you to the people of Macedonia, saying that Achaia has been ready since last year; and your zeal has stirred up most of them. [3] But I am sending the brothers in order that our boasting about you may not prove to have been empty in this case, so that you may be ready, as I said you would be; [4] otherwise, if some Macedonians come with me and find that you are not ready, we would be humiliated—to say nothing of you—in this undertaking. [5] So I thought it necessary to urge the brothers to go on ahead to you, and arrange in advance for this bountiful gift that you have promised, so that it may be ready as a voluntary gift and not as an extortion.
>
> [6] The point is this: the one who sows sparingly will also reap sparingly, and the one who sows bountifully will also reap bountifully. [7] Each of you must give as you have made up your mind, not reluctantly or under compulsion, for God loves a cheerful giver. [8] And God is able to provide you with every blessing in abundance, so that by always having enough of everything, you may share abundantly in every good work. [9] As it is written,
>
> > "He scatters abroad, he gives to the poor;
> > his righteousness endures forever."
>
> [10] He who supplies seed to the sower and bread for food will supply and multiply your seed for sowing and increase the harvest of your righteousness. [11] You will be enriched in every way for your great generosity, which will produce thanksgiving to God through us; [12] for the rendering of this ministry not only supplies the needs of the saints but also overflows with many thanksgivings to God. [13] Through the testing of this ministry you glorify God by your obedience to the confession of the gospel of Christ and by the generosity of your sharing with them and with all others. (2 Corinthians 9:1–13)

Prayer

Remember as you are pursuing funding for your church plant that you are also looking to develop prayer support at the same time. There may be some people who are not currently in a position to give financially right now but would be glad to support the planting effort through consistent, focused prayer. A solid team of intercessors is one of the most foundational building blocks of support for any ministry endeavor.

Below are some tips to help you get on track for creating and communicating with an intercessory team:

- The people you ask to pray don't need to be a part of your plant. In many cases, it can be helpful if they're not.

- Invite people who have a passion for prayer and who share your vision.

- Gather a variety of different people on your team: different gifts, skills, personalities, and vocations.

- Ask for a limited but specific commitment, such as six months or a year.

- Communicate regularly with your intercessors.

- Ensure that communication is two-way. Ask your intercessors what they're hearing from God.

- Keep—and regularly share—a list not only of prayer needs and but also of answered prayers.

- Share not just ministry concerns but personal concerns, so that the intercessory team can pray for you and your family.

- Find ways to thank and celebrate your intercessors.

Financial issues may not be the favorite topic of most church planters, but taking the time to lay the foundation now for the wise stewardship of your new church will yield many dividends in the years to come: *"But as for what was sown on good soil, this is the one who hears the word and understands it, who indeed bears fruit and yields, in one case a hundredfold, in another sixty, and in another thirty"* (Matthew 13:23).

Journey Guide for Chapter 9
Establishing Financial Support

In most cases, church planting involves some
type of fundraising. This chapter provides
direction on how to determine the needs and
how to select among the options for supporting the ministry financially, such
as being bivocational, raising funds, and receiving denominational or network
funding. It also encourages embracing healthy principles and thinking around
money, giving, and discipleship. How will you finance this new church plant?
Consider all of your options by walking through the journey guide below.

Checklist: for the road ahead

☐ Options for financial support (including bivocational work,
denominational support, and fundraising) have been brainstorming and
evaluated.

☐ Groundwork has been laid for giving from within the church plant as it
grows.

☐ Fundraising strategy has been developed.

☐ A team to help with financial oversight has been formed.

☐ Initial financial support has been secured.

☐ Transparent financial practices have been put into place.

☐ A budget has been developed, in line with priorities and goals.

☐ Long-term goals have been taken into consideration.

☐ A practice of generosity has been established.

☐ Prayer support has been raised, along with financial support.

Discipleship focus: Generous Living
Consider how you approach financial giving in your own life of discipleship.
Inward focus:

1. What is your internal attitude when you think about financial
giving?

2. In what ways are you generous with your resources? In what
ways are you not?

3. What principles do you follow for practicing wisdom in giving?

Outward focus:

1. Where do you feel God is calling you to be more generous with
your time and resources?

Strategic questions: for you and your coach
- What financial resources, or options for raising finances, are currently at your disposal?
- What are the pros and cons of bivocational work? denominational or network support? fundraising?
- Who can help you establish financial oversight and practices for your church plant? What additional safeguards might you need?
- When can you sit down to create a budget for your church plant?
- If you've already created a budget, to what degree does it reflect your specific ministry goals?
- What are some creative ways your church plant can invest the money you have to make the most impact?
- How can you encourage those you lead to handle their money both wisely and generously? How are you leading by example?

Discussion questions: For you and your team
- What would it look like for us to steward our financial resources well, as a church plant?
- What are some ways you've seen that done well?
- What are some mistakes we need to avoid?
- How can we live generously as a church?
- What Scripture passages inform how we think about money?

Guided prayer: for you personally
"Whoever is faithful in a very little is faithful also in much; and whoever is dishonest in a very little is dishonest also in much." (Luke 16:10)
- God, please show me how you want to support this church plant.
- Help me to be open to all options and consider them prayerfully.
- Please provide your guidance and discernment as I develop financial support, and help me to see it as a part of discipleship.
- Lord, teach me to trust you.

Guided prayer: for use with your team
"One man gives freely, yet gains even more; another withholds unduly, but comes to poverty. A generous man will prosper; he who refreshes others will himself be refreshed." (Proverbs 11:24–25, NIV)

Allow time for others to pray, after praying aloud through each of these themes:
- God, please help us steward well all of the opportunities and resources you've entrusted to us.

- Please allow your spirit of generosity to flow through us and out to others.
- Help us to remember the poor.
- Please make clear to us the connection between money and discipleship.
- Give us wisdom as we make decisions about how to handle the topic of money in our church.

Guided prayer: for your intercessors

Please pray that God would:

- provide the financial funding for us to do what he has called us to do.
- help us see the opportunities before us, even if they are not what we expected.
- give us the strength to be faithful in the face of fear or greed or scarcity— that we would rely on him in all seasons.
- help us to recognize that we are only stewards for a short time in this life.
- continue to direct our church plant in the way he would have us go.

Action guide: a place for planning your next steps

1.

2.

3.

Chapter 10:
Developing Your Proposal

Depending on the cultural context in which you are planting, you may not need this chapter. Especially in the developing world, many churches are planted, grow and reproduce without any written proposal at all. Certainly there was a plan, direction, and a sense of vision. Certainly there was leadership and intentionality. But sometimes outside support or permissions are not needed to do what you need to do.

That said, in many contexts and for many planters, creating a solid, written proposal is an important step toward getting approval, funding, permission, and blessing from denominational groups and networks. Most denominations or networks will require a substantive church planting proposal before partnering with you. Donors, community partners, intercessors, and potential team members will also be interested in the strategy and timeline laid out in your proposal. A good proposal answers the question, "What is your plan for starting this church?"

Even if you're not raising funds or working with a sending organization, a proposal can help you create and stick to a clear course of action. A secondary benefit is to give you and your team greater clarity about how you're going to go about achieving the vision. In essence, a proposal is an elaboration on your values, vision, and mission statements in a way that includes the answer to the "how" question. Taking the time to think through and write down a comprehensive strategy can provide a great deal of focus as you move forward.

> A proposal can help you create and stick to a clear course of action.

There is one caveat: You won't have a full and accurate plan in advance. Circumstances will change your plans as they arise, and you'll absolutely need to keep listening to the Holy Spirit for direction. Recognize that your proposal will be a living document, changing as you learn more. Build in times to revise it now. However, you still need to start with a tentative plan in order to begin effectively moving forward.

What goes into a proposal?

Taking the time to create a thoughtfully prepared proposal ensures that some advance preparation and thinking has been done. Yet planters often need help creating acceptable proposals. The more specific an organization is regarding expectations and criteria, the more likely they are to receive satisfactory submissions. Requirements vary from organization to organization, but good proposals generally include the following:

- Rationale for planting: Why here? Why now?
- Church planter: Who are you?
- Values, vision, and mission: What are you aiming for?
- Ministry focus group: Who are you reaching?
- Model of church/ ministry philosophy: What kind of church do you want to plant?
- Core team: Who will be working with you?
- Preliminary strategy for achieving goals: How will you go about planting this church?
- Ministry flowchart: What will the ministry process look like?
- Projected timeline: When do you expect to see progress?
- Support systems: What support and oversight will you need?
- Proposed budget: How much will it cost?
- How the reader can help: What are you asking of the reader, specifically?

We'll spend the rest of this chapter walking through each of these areas in more detail. Essentially, your church planting proposal will bring together all the preliminary work you've done in conceptualizing your new church. Thus, you'll need to refer back to previous work you've done in areas such as vision, values, planter assessment, and demographic research.

Rationale for planting

Your introduction should answer the question, "Why start this church?" Why are you planting in this particular place, at this particular time, with these particular people? You don't need to get into all of your demographic research at this point; focus more on your sense of calling. Demonstrate the need for this ministry and briefly share your calling, passion, and vision.

Church planter

Describe your personal sense of the gifts, skills and abilities that God has given you for this endeavor. Church planters are not one-size-fits-all. Each individual comes with different experiences, passions, and gifts. Each leader will bring something unique to the table. Consider your own abilities. How has God uniquely gifted you for this ministry situation?

Include the giftedness and contribution of your spouse as well, if you have one. His or her sense of calling and involvement should be clarified, as spouses often work as a team and bring complementary abilities to the table.

Write a bit about your passion and calling: What do you care about? What makes you excited to get up in the morning? Your passions are an important aspect of your planting proposal. Pay attention to your heart. Given your gifts, the world's needs, and your passion and calling, where do they all intersect? That place is your unique contribution.

Values, vision, and mission

List these items, along with any clarification or expansion that may be necessary. Return to your core values and vision statement, reviewing the material you created with the exercises in chapter 1. This section is your chance to clearly and concisely articulate the core values, vision, and mission for your church plant. Write out these statements, and then expand on them as needed.

You'll also want to include any specific theological statements or statements of faith you hold to in this section. This information is often particularly important to denominations and networks as they assess compatibility.

Ministry focus group

Describe the kind of people you feel God is calling you to reach with this church plant, along with some of the felt needs you've identified. Who is the ministry focus group that will be served? Describe these people, including basic demographic information and experiential evidence to support your research.

Model of church/ministry philosophy

This section provides you with an opportunity to showcase the uniqueness of your church plant. It answers the question, "What kind of church are you seeking to establish?" If you're planting a network of house churches, here's where to describe what you envision that model looking like. If you have a philosophy of ministry that emphasizes social justice, write about it here. In this section, cover any plans you have around models, structures, and philosophy of ministry.

Core team
This section answers the question of who will be working alongside you and in what capacity. Describe the roles and functions required on your team, and include a profile of those team members who are already committed and/or in place. Understanding team assignments and how the team will work together is helpful for readers evaluating your proposal.

Preliminary strategy for achieving goals
Your planting strategy is at the heart of your planting proposal. It is your best estimation of what it will take to achieve the vision that God has given you. Your plan should include critical milestones that you will reach in the next two to five years. A preliminary strategy for reaching the target group and achieving initial goals should be laid out as clearly as possible. Be sure to develop a strategic plan, with goals and action steps that can be put on a timeline, as that will be a later step in the proposal-writing process. Here are some items for consideration:
- Your evangelism and gathering strategy
- How you will recruit people for your initial leadership team
- Steps you'll take to increase your contacts with unchurched people, and how you will follow up
- Any service projects or felt needs you'll be addressing in your ministry focus group
- Ways you'll go about discipling people
- Systems you'll need to create (e.g., assimilation, children's involvement, leadership development, small groups, governing structures, worship leading, future staffing)

Identify any key decisions that still need to be made, along with your timeline for making them, to show that you have covered all the bases in your strategic planning.

Ministry flowchart
A flowchart can visually depict how your ministries and systems network together to move people from unchurched all the way into leadership. In many ways, the ministry flowchart is a visual version of your strategic plan, but it usually focuses in more on people-flow.

Projected timeline
Another important visual element of your proposal is a timeline. The milestones and goals you listed under the strategy section should be placed on a timeline that will map your course forward. For each milestone, consider who will be involved, what steps will be taken to reach that milestone, and the resources it will take to accomplish. You might consider drawing an overall five-year timeline, along with a more detailed timeline for your first year.

Support systems
No matter how gifted or competent the planter may be, starting a church cannot be done by one individual alone. In this section, list any additional support systems you will rely on, such as intercessory support, peer networks, coaching, and accountability.

Proposed budget
Here you'll need to describe how you will financially support your family and the church plant. Include a budget for the first two years. Include any cash flow projections and necessary startup financing. Define your budget strategy and describe volunteer involvement.

Facility needs often require a significant portion of the budget. Depending on your model and on how fast you grow, those needs can vary widely. Consider meeting spaces for groups, teams, office space, and worship. Clarify what facilities will be needed as you begin your gathering and worship, whatever form that may take. You'll also need to decide when more facilities will be needed to support your strategy.

How the reader can help
This final portion is the "ask," made directly to the reader. Be specific and be clear. Don't ask for prayer when you're actually trying to ask for money. If the proposal is intended to raise money, don't hedge or imply—be upfront about the request and the amount (e.g., $2,000 per month, $15,000 in startup costs, a monthly pledge of $200 from each household). Remember that you'll want to adapt this section depending on who you are writing to. It will help you to be more specific and accurate if you have done your homework in the budgeting section.

Aside from finances, include additional ways the reader can help, such as:
- Prayer needs
- Volunteer needs
- Networking requests

- Potential contacts
- Equipment needs

Again, be specific. If you're asking for volunteers, how many and what kind? For how long? Clarify expectations similarly with material resources, prayer support, affiliation, blessing, or encouragement.

In some cases, you may wish to include the direct "ask" in a cover letter, rather than at the end of the proposal. This is particularly likely if you will be mailing letters.

Evaluating your proposal
When you've finished writing a first draft of your proposal, go back and test it for accuracy. Is it complete? What else needs to be added? Is it compatible with your ministry focus group? Is it realistic? Does the timetable seem doable?

Before you make your proposal public, you may want to test it with family, friends, and your coach. Allow them to ask probing questions to test the completeness of your thinking. Especially if you are raising financial support, having a well-thought-through plan will inspire confidence in your venture.

Here are some additional points to consider as you create your proposal:
Make it readable. Make sure those who review it are able to understand it without additional verbal explanation from you. Ask them to summarize what they read, and see if they're tracking with you. Ask for help especially from people you know who are good at writing; they can often help you with the editing process.

Make it personal. Share about who you are. You don't need to share your entire story, but give them a sense of who you are as a person and what motivates you. Who are your family members, and what will their involvement look like? Mention those you'll be partnering with, and the strengths they bring to the team. Don't be afraid to include photos; giving your readers visuals can personalize your proposal in ways words alone cannot.

Make it true. Don't exaggerate your past experience, or your present reality. If you imply that there are current sixty people involved, and someone goes to check it out and sees only twenty, you lose credibility. Confidence is good, but be sure not to overinflate the progress you've made so far.

Make it concise. Don't make your proposal too long. If you do, no one will read it. Three to five pages, plus your budget and timeline, is probably sufficient. Only go longer than five pages if you have a situation that's especially interesting or unusual.

Make it realistic. Especially when it comes to funding, don't over or underestimate. If you're unsure, have a coach or others in the field check your numbers to see if they look like they're in the ballpark. Also be sure not to overestimate your expected progress and how quickly you project being able to get to that point. In your ask section, find out how much the group normally gives and keep your request reasonable.

Moving forward

Consider who will be reading your proposal, and be sure to tailor it for each audience, making it as relevant as possible for each group. Like a resume, your proposal should be customized for different uses. For instance, a proposal geared toward denominational leaders should look different from those aimed at prayer supporters. Although your budget numbers won't change, you'll want to provide more detail on the budget for denominational leaders or large donors, as they'll be asking questions and considering investments that others won't. For intercessors or potential team members, you may want to create an abbreviated version of the proposal.

Be especially sure to tailor the "ask" section at the end, as you are likely hoping for different types of support or help from different groups of people.

No plan for the future will be perfectly accurate. Regardless of how careful you are in putting together this proposal, adjustments will need to be made along the way. During the early stages of your church plant, set aside time at least quarterly to come back to your proposal and consider how it may need to be adapted. Check your benchmarks for progress—how are those coming and how might your goals need to be adjusted? Same for your budget: Both expenses and income will likely be different from your projections, so be sure to update your proposal regularly to reflect reality. Having set times scheduled in advance for reevaluation and refocusing will help you stay on track with what God is doing.

Journey Guide for Chapter 10
Developing Your Proposal

JOURNEY GUIDE

Even if a planter is not raising funds or working with a sending organization, a strong and well thought out proposal can help him or her create and stick to a clear course of action. A secondary benefit is providing the planter and team greater clarity about how they're going to go about achieving the vision. In essence, a proposal is an elaboration on values, vision, and mission statements in a way that includes the answer to the "how" question. Taking the time to think through and write down a comprehensive strategy can provide a great deal of focus as the planting process moves forward. You can use the following checklist and questions to ensure all of the basics are covered.

Checklist: for the road ahead
- Previous work or writing you've done has been collected for each of the areas below:
  - ☐ Rationale for planting
  - ☐ Church planter
  - ☐ Values, vision, and mission
  - ☐ Ministry focus group
  - ☐ Model of church/ ministry philosophy
  - ☐ Core team
  - ☐ Preliminary strategy for achieving goals
  - ☐ Ministry flowchart
  - ☐ Projected timeline
  - ☐ Support systems
  - ☐ Proposed budget
  - ☐ How the reader can help
  - ☐ A complete proposal, including each of the areas above, has been put together and geared toward your denomination or network.
  - ☐ The proposal has been evaluated for completeness, accuracy, and readability.
  - ☐ Feedback from coaches, ministry partners, team members, or others has been invited.
  - ☐ Different audiences and uses for the proposal have been considered, and adaptations have been made.
  - ☐ At least one short version has been created.
  - ☐ These proposals have been used as tools for fundraising, recruiting team members, and raising other types of awareness and support.

Discipleship focus: Authentic Relationships

As you are working on writing your proposal, don't forget about the people around you. They are why you're doing this in the first place. Take some time to reflect on your relationships and how you are seeing others.

Inward focused:

1. When have you recognized God in someone else? What has that looked like?
2. How can you more intentionally seek to see the image of God in people?
2. When have you felt unaccepted, like you don't belong?

Outward focused:

1. Who do you know right now who needs to believe that the image of God resides in them?
2. What steps can you take to create a safe and welcoming environment that fosters authentic relationship building?

Strategic questions: for you and your coach

- What are the major milestones you want to accomplish in the next two to five years? What will it take to accomplish them?
- If you are working within a denomination or network, what steps do you need to take to obtain their official approval? What specific standards and guidelines for proposals do they require?
- Brainstorm a list of people you might want to show your proposal to. What sorts of feedback would be helpful to you?
- How could you use this proposal to recruit core team members and increase their sense of ownership?
- How could you write the proposal so that it could be used effectively for raising financial support? What are some parallels between a planting proposal and a good business plan?
- In what ways might your intercessors find the church planting proposal helpful?
- With each audience, how can you make your "ask" clear?

Discussion questions: For you and your team

Before writing your proposal, gather with your team to collect their input on the important areas by asking these questions. Take notes on their responses and be sure to incorporate some of their ideas into your written proposal. After you've written a first draft, come back to your team a second time and ask for their feedback.

- What words or phrases best represent our values? Our vision? Our mission?
- How would you describe the people we are reaching? What are some tangible ways our church plant will benefit them?
- How do each of you envision your particular role on this team? What is your contribution?
- How will this church look different from other churches? What motivates us and helps us move forward?
- What are some goals you see us accomplishing in our first year? In our next three years?
- What needs do we have? How can people best pray for us?

Guided prayer: for you personally

Without counsel, plans go wrong, but with many advisers they succeed. (Proverbs 15:22)

- God, please guide me toward writing a church planting proposal that accurately reflects your heart for this endeavor.
- Help me represent myself neither too highly nor too lowly (Romans 12:3).
- Please bring people into my life who can speak wisely into these plans, and open my heart to hearing from them with a spirit of openness.
- Lord, lead me in connecting with the people you want to see this proposal.

Guided prayer: for use with your team

Pray together with your team through each of these themes:

- Lord, please guide us as we lay plans for this new church plant.
- Help us to see opportunities and open doors.
- Give us the courage to reach out and extend ourselves beyond our comfort zones.
- Continue to grow us in our own walks of discipleship, and challenge us to greater growth.
- Bring to mind those you would have us connect with about this new church plant.

Guided prayer: for your intercessors

Please pray that we would:

- envision more clearly what God has for us to do.
- be both humble in our own abilities and filled with faith in what God is calling us to do.

- take notice of people God is bringing into our path and consider how we could work together.
- raise the funds necessary for this next phase of the church plant.
- stay on track with what God is calling us to do and be able to represent it accurately.

Action guide: a place for planning your next steps

1.

2.

3.

Get Going:
Living Out the Mission

Part 3 outlines the mechanics of what you need to be doing ministry-wise as you're getting started. Chapters 11–15, taken together, create a dynamic of missional living. They operate simultaneously; you don't stop doing one to move to the next.

Chapter 15 is only relevant for certain models and structures of churches. If you are planting a cell church or a network of house churches with no centralized worship gathering, or planting in a restricted country, you may skip this chapter, as much of it will not be applicable. You can still live out all the essential functions of the body of Christ without having a public worship gathering.

Chapter 11: Casting Vision
Chapter 12: Engaging Culture
Chapter 13: Making Disciples
Chapter 14: Multiplying Disciplemaking Communities
Chapter 15: Launching Public Worship

Chapter 11:
Casting Vision

We opened this book by talking about developing vision. Now we come back to fine-tune, reaffirm, and cast this vision outward to others.

One of the biggest ongoing challenges of starting and leading a church is keeping the vision in front of people. We may have great ideas, but if we can't communicate them to others, they'll *stay* ideas. It's easy to lose sight in the midst of day-in, day-out logistics, problems, and tasks—but in church and ministry, there are *very* few things we can do completely by ourselves. When we cast the vision, others decide whether it's something God is calling them to be a part of. It may or may not be, but if we don't cast the vision, they'll never have the chance to decide.

Casting vision beyond your existing team can help you accomplish many critical ministry tasks:
- Recruiting new team members
- Connecting with service opportunities in the community
- Networking with new contacts and interested parties
- Discovering new sources of assistance
- Raising funds
- Creating a referral and support network
- Increasing prayer support
- Creating increased visibility in the community

Know your goal for vision-casting
Consider your specific goals for casting vision, including differing goals for different groups of people. As it was with your proposal, how you cast vision for potential future team members will be different than how you cast vision with potential service partner organizations in the community. With business leaders, you may be looking to raise funding. With people in the neighborhood, you may be wanting to increase awareness and involvement in certain opportunities you are offering.

Reflect on each group separately, considering what kinds of responses you're looking for and what ways you're currently communicating with them. Then consider additional ways you could be communicating the vision to each group.

Group of people	Goals of communication	Ways you are communicating	Additional ways to cast vision
Potential core team members			
Leaders and volunteers			
Opinion leaders (influential people without official position)			
Potential intercessors			
Potential donors			
Resource providers			
Partner organizations			
Those you are serving			
The community at large			
Others			

For each of these groups, be sure to connect with the "why" of church planting, not just the "what." (Simon Sinek gave an excellent TED talk on the difference between inspiring people and presenting something that feels like the same old thing. Although not specifically about church planting, it's applicable and definitely worth a watch.[4]) You can also see a lot of great examples of vision-casting in the Bible. Read about Moses addressing the Israelites before they enter into the Promised Land (Deuteronomy 30:11–20), Peter addressing the crowd at Pentecost (Acts 2:14–24, 36–39), and Paul addressing the Greeks in Athens (Acts 17:16–34). In each case, look at how the leader considered his audience and desired outcomes, and how he then decided to go about casting vision in light of those elements.

Formalizing the vision, values, and mission with your team

Before you can properly begin casting the vision, you'll need to be very clear on what the vision *is*. Although you've likely reflected on and articulated your vision in the very early stages of your church plant, you'll want to revisit it at this time, for a few reasons.

First of all, things change as you move forward. Don't allow your earlier work on vision limit your later creativity. You'll get new ideas as you go, and new information will come to light as you engage in ministry. Vision is a bit like an old Polaroid picture, where the image doesn't appear all at once. At first it's a bit blurry and out of focus, then you look again and see how it's changed and sharpened. Likewise, changing and sharpening your vision as you go isn't failure; it's a healthy response to God's leading.

Second, your team may have changed since you first began thinking about the vision for your church plant, and you'll need to ensure ownership among the current team. Who are the key influencers on your team who need to be included in shaping the vision? Vision can empower people only to the degree they embrace it. Involving people in the envisioning process helps them feel they have a hand in creating the vision and turning it into action. People are most committed to what they help develop.

> People are most committed to what they help develop.

[4]Simon Sinek, "How Great Leaders Inspire Action," TED.com, www.ted.com/talks/simon_sinek_how_great_leaders_inspire_action.

Include these items in your vision statement:
- Who are we going to serve?
- What will this church look like?
- What will be the result of our disciplemaking process?
- What are we actually producing and multiplying?
- Where will we see evidence of transformation?
- What are we expecting to see God accomplish?

It's important to work through a collaborative process with your team that results in a written statement. The resulting document will give you clarity and direction as you move forward.

> I will stand at my watchpost,
> and station myself on the rampart;
> I will keep watch to see what he will say to me,
> and what he will answer concerning my complaint.
> ² Then the Lord answered me and said:
> Write the vision;
> make it plain on tablets,
> so that a runner may read it. (Habakkuk 2:1–2)

Casting vision well: tips and principles

The job of a church planter is to be very clear and very consistent about the vision you're leading toward. Use these general tips and principles to ensure you're doing that:
- Make sure to cast the vision in an appealing light. This is something everyone should want and hunger for, so be clear, precise, and motivating.
- Make it specific. Paint a picture others can see. Include details and behaviors. What would it look like if the vision became a reality?
- People are motivated by vision, not by need. Seeing only the needs can become overwhelming and paralyzing unless there is a compelling vision that tells them they can make a difference.
- Speak in ways people can hear. Make it easy for people to engage with and understand the vision. Consider their cultural context. Share it in bite-sized pieces they can digest.
- As much as possible, engage in a two-way flow of communication with those you're casting vision toward. Make it a dialogue.
- Use multiple methods of communication and multiple venues: online, in-person, video, etc. Find out what communicates best to those you're trying to reach.

- Say it over and over. Vision cannot be presented once then left alone, assuming people have it. People can lose sight of the vision in less than a month. Reiterate and re-present it often.

Methods of vision-casting

Once the vision is clear in your mind and your team is fully on board, begin to look for ways to cast the vision more broadly. Be creative; be artistic; encourage experimentation.

The list of ways to cast vision could be infinitely long. We'll start here, but see how many additional ideas you can add by brainstorming together with your team:

- Talk about it in conversation.
- Model it.
- Tell stories about it.
- Memorize the vision statement.
- Include it in sermons.
- Connect it to a Bible story or passage.
- Discuss it in small groups.
- Live it out in small groups.
- Pray for the vision alongside others.
- Make a banner or mural.
- Blog about it.
- Ask people questions about the vision and get their thoughts on it.
- Make a video about it.
- Cast it via social media.

Note: The Internet is now a primary way people look for churches if they have some memory or consciousness of churches in their past. If you're not already engaged in social media, now is the time to start thinking about it.

Sharing the values and vision of the church must be done repeatedly and creatively. Many times, people in your congregation who are gifted in the creative arts or technology will be your best resources for helping you find ways to communicate that vision.

The "elevator speech"

Often, unexpected ways to cast vision will arise. To be prepared for those times, everyone on your team should be prepared with what is commonly called an "elevator speech"—a description of the church plant and its vision that can be shared in under two minutes, the approximate length of an elevator ride. Take turns in your team gatherings to give everyone a chance to try it out in their own words. It is key to remain brief, clear, and compelling. The description should be easy for people to remember and pass along.

Certainly there will be times that call for a fuller description, but it can be helpful to have a short version readily on hand, as opportunity arises. Elevator speeches can be helpful for gauging people's level of interest. Do they ask follow-up questions? How closely do they pay attention? What level of engagement do you sense? An elevator speech is the verbal equivalent of a flyer. It doesn't contain everything—just enough of the basics to help a person know whether this is something they're interested in or not.

As the planter, you'll also want to have a written one-or-two-page overview and description of the church plant. Something brief on paper can be helpful as you meet with potential team members, donors, community partners, or other interested parties.

The value of story

Stories are one of the most powerful ways to share vision. We live in a story culture. Images and metaphors are powerful. Creating a picture in someone's mind through the use of words will capture their imagination and commitment in a way that a three-point sermon rarely will. A vision paints a clear picture of a desired future.

Whenever possible, share stories people can visualize, feel, and relate to. They connect with people in a way that other methods do not. To be able to do this, you'll need to keep close to those you're ministering to. Stay actively involved in direct ministry. As the church plant grows and you gain additional responsibilities, you can still do this with a lower time commitment, but you do need to remain a part of what's going on at a grassroots level.

Also listen for stories from your team members. If they speak in generalities, ask for specifics. For example, "Wow, we've really been seeing God at work." "How so? Tell me about it." Then listen for personal stories that you can share; write them down as soon as you hear them.

You can also use stories to reinforce positive behavior on your team. Whenever someone is doing something right—something in line with the vision—share that story with the team. It illustrates how the vision can be lived out. Affirm even small steps in the right direction.

Stories serve an important function in keeping the vision fresh and current. Use new words. Memorizing the vision statement is good, but how else could you express it? What words seem to communicate well to others? People will be moved by stories that embody the vision more than they will by mere facts or need.

Intercession

Another essential piece of casting vision outside of your church plant is ensuring enough prayer support. Gathering and preparing a team of intercessors for your ministry is one of the earliest and most critical steps in planting a church. God did not create us to walk through the Christian life alone. We were made to function as part of a team. We each have blind spots, and others are able to perceive them more easily than we can on our own. We need one another. A ministry team is only as strong as the team that supports it, and a team of intercessors is the most foundational building block of support for any ministry endeavor.

Hopefully you've had at least an informal intercession team throughout the entire planting process. However, if you haven't yet formalized it, now is the time. Continue adding people and communicating with them. The end of every chapter suggests ways to communicate with intercessors about the topic discussed. Chapter 9 also includes a checklist to help you get on the right track building your intercession team. Prayer is essential in all of your planning and support as you plant a church. Don't try to do all of it yourself.

Broaden the vision

Although we've been talking specifically about the vision for your church plant, remember that ultimately the vision is not just about what you're doing locally, but about the church universal and how you fit into that broader reality of the kingdom of God.

Keep on praying, allowing God to expand and renew your vision. How does it contribute to the wider work God is doing beyond your own community? How are you envisioning beyond your own church? How can you help, serve, and support other local churches and ministries? It's not too soon to start thinking about that, even when you're still in the planting stage.

Remember the seashore vision I shared in the introduction? When I was at my most despondent as a struggling young church planter who had no idea what he was doing, I told God, "If you get me out of the mess that I'm in, help me learn how to plant a church, I promise that I will come back and help others learn how to plant churches." God answered that prayer, and I've been working with church planters in one way or another ever since. The vision of church planting is so much bigger than just one church.

Journey Guide for Chapter 11
Casting Vision

JOURNEY GUIDE

Vision has been considered from the very beginning of the book, but this chapter returns to the topic to fine-tune, reaffirm, and re-cast this vision outward to others. Not only does the planter need to understand and own the vision, but he or she needs to be able to cast that vision to others. That means creating a narrative that people can buy into, whether they are part of the planting team, part of the surrounding community, donors, or potential new participants in the ministry. The checklist and questions below are designed to walk you through an effective visioncasting process.

Checklist: for the road ahead
- ☐ The need for casting vision beyond your team has been recognized.
- ☐ Who you're casting vision to has been clarified.
- ☐ The vision has been sharpened and clarified among your team members.
- ☐ The vision has been prayed over together, and you've listened for God's leading.
- ☐ The message has been presented in a variety of ways, so different groups of people can easily hear and understand it.
- ☐ Two-way dialogue has been employed as you've cast vision.
- ☐ The vision has been cast regularly, consistently, and creatively in multiple venues, and you've paid attention to what approaches have been most effective.
- ☐ Brief overviews of the vision have been created in both oral and written form.
- ☐ Stories that illustrate and reinforce the vision have been listened for and communicated.
- ☐ Perspective has been regularly renewed and broadened beyond the local church.

Discipleship focus: Disciplemaking
When visioncasting for your church plant it is essential to always connect your vision to discipleship. Take time again now to rehearse these essentials and draw fresh connections between your vision and disciplesmaking.

Inward focus:
1. What do you understand to be the basic essentials of the gospel?
2. How do you balance your intellectual understanding of the essentials with experiential understanding?

Outward focus:

1. How can the decision to follow Jesus be made more plain to people?
2. Who do you know who needs to consider the essentials of the gospel?
3. How can you best invite that person to do so?

Strategic questions: for you and your coach

- What is your current understanding of your vision? How will you confirm your vision?
- How and when will you set aside time for cultivating God's vision for this church plant?
- How will others be involved in the process?
- Who do you need to cast vision to outside of your team? What response are you hoping for, from each of those groups? In what ways is your vision bigger than your own church plant?
- What ideas do you have for casting vision? How could you generate more ideas? How have people responded to the vision so far, and what does that tell you?
- Present the vision in two minutes or less (elevator speech).
- In what ways are you able to cast and recast the vision?
- What stories are happening in your ministry that illustrate the vision, even in small ways?

Discussion questions: For you and your team

- Describe your vision in thirty seconds or less. (Take turns allowing each member to do this.)
- How compelling is this vision? How specific is it?
- What stories illustrate this vision? What do you see God doing?
- What are some ways we could cast vision outside our team?
- What do you envision your role being in that?

Guided prayer: for you personally

Read aloud Hebrews 11, and consider the role of storytelling in vision-casting and motivation.

- God, please open my heart to what you may have for me and for this church, even if it's not what I expect.
- Help me to discern your voice in the feedback I receive from others.
- Allow me to speak boldly as I should, and wisely as I listen for your leading.

- Open my eyes to the opportunities around me. Who can I share the vision with?

Guided prayer: for use with your team

Pray together with your team through each of these themes:

- God, please give us direction about what you want this new church to look like.
- Give us glimpses even now of what it will look like as it grows to maturity.
- Bring to mind new ways to cast the vision you've given us.
- Help us see opportunities for what you might want to do and who you might want to reach.
- Give us the faith to broaden our perspective about what you may want to do through us and through our community.

Guided prayer: for your intercessors

Please pray:

- that all of our core team members would be on the same page regarding the vision for the church plant, and that there would be confirmation and ownership of this vision.
- that we would continue to be open to the voice of God as he directs us.
- that God would lead us to the people and organizations he wants us to connect with.
- that we would see his hand at work in the lives of those we are ministering to, and in our own lives as well.

Action guide: a place for planning your next steps

1.

2.

3.

Chapter 12:
Engaging Culture

A fictional missionary went to a tribe in central Africa, with a vision of baptizing his converts in the river. Although the people were initially open to hearing what he had to say, they were universally opposed to getting into that river. They especially didn't want their children anywhere near it. The missionary continued to insist on river baptisms, without having engaged with the people enough to understand the roadblock he was running up against.

Their concern? There were dangerous crocodiles in that river. Had he taken the time to get to know the people, ask questions, listen, and understand how they did things and why, he might have been willing to find an alternate baptism plan.

All effective ministry is built upon who we serve. This requires correct exegeting of that culture. We need to engage with those around us, listen, ask questions, and learn. Without that level of personal engagement, we will not be able to do effective ministry with those particular people.

Where do we start? By stepping in, listening, and building relationships. If you are also planting in a culture different from your own or in a generation different from your own, you'll need to do the additional work of understanding ways of thinking that may feel foreign from your own. This type of learning can best be done relationally, and will require humility and openness on your part.

Building relationships beyond the church
If your church plant is to be anything other than a clique of people who are already Christians, you'll need to reach out and build relationships with people beyond the church. That means working not only through your web of relationships, but through those you meet through them.

In the New Testament, this is known as the *oikos* concept. *Oikos*, literally "household," is the Greek word for a network of relationships. Throughout the early church we see countless examples of apostles reaching one person, and then through that one person, their entire household—spouses, children, servants, their whole community. Acts 16 provides two examples of this dynamic:

> A certain woman named Lydia, a worshiper of God, was listening to us; she was from the city of Thyatira and a dealer in purple cloth. The Lord opened her heart to listen eagerly to what was said by Paul. [15] When she and her household were baptized, she urged us, saying, "If you have judged me to be faithful to the Lord, come and stay at my home." And she prevailed upon us. (Acts 16:14–15)

> The jailer called for lights, and rushing in, he fell down trembling before Paul and Silas. [30] Then he brought them outside and said, "Sirs, what must I do to be saved?" [31] They answered, "Believe on the Lord Jesus, and you will be saved, you and your household." [32] They spoke the word of the Lord to him and to all who were in his house. [33] At the same hour of the night he took them and washed their wounds; then he and his entire family were baptized without delay. [34] He brought them up into the house and set food before them; and he and his entire household rejoiced that he had become a believer in God. (Acts 16:29–34)

Since most church planters believe that the spread of the gospel happens most effectively through relationships, they'll want to explore and expand their *oikos* relationships. There are many ways to go about this: plan events of interest to the community, participate in activities, invite people to do things, host people in your home, get involved in existing community activities. These are all great ways to broaden your network.

As you expand your relationships, you may run across a "person of peace"—a seeker who welcomes you into his or her *oikos* of relationships. In many cultures, getting to know and building trust with one person introduces you to a large network of relationships. Initial contacts are often bridges into whole social or family groups. One person of peace can lead you to a network of fifty people, each of whom also have an extended *oikos* of relationships. By exploring these relationships, you'll find others who are receptive to the gospel as well.

To plant a church, you have to start by cultivating relationships. Seek out places where those who don't know Jesus socialize and live. Bridge into a web of relationships with a group of people you long to reach and serve. Note that setting an example is important. If you, as the planter, are hesitant to build relationships outside the church, those you lead will be unlikely to prioritize doing so as well.

Outward-focused serving

A natural response to getting to know the community will be a desire to bless and serve it. As you get to know the people and talk with them, you'll hear about problems, needs, and challenges they're facing. If you're not hearing about these things, ask. Are the schools in trouble? What do families need? What types of crime is the community facing? What are people concerned about or afraid of? Put yourself in people's shoes and look outward.

After you have identified specific areas of need, take an inventory of your own resources. How has God blessed you and your team to meet these needs? Consider skills, abilities, spiritual gifts, financial or material resources, time, etc.—then consider how you and others connected to your church plant can serve.

One plant had identified a need in their community for helping families in the foster system. Their people volunteered to do home visits. For most of them, this activity was way outside of their comfort zone and they had only volunteer-level training— but they noticed that God seemed to be blessing all of their efforts. Serving effectively is often a matter of noticing what God is already doing and joining him there.

Another new church plant in a poor area found that when they did outreach events, kids would show up hungry. In response, they began a ministry called "supper church," where they would feed the people who came. That recognition of the needs in the community ultimately led to a food pantry ministry, as well as a busing ministry for those who had no transportation to church.

In other cases, needs may be less obvious or less physical. A church planter working in a largely Mormon community found that his ministry focus group often had felt needs similar to those of Christians. One of the most successful outreach events they did was hosting a parenting seminar. Working together with other Christian churches in the area, they built a coalition of resources and participation. They held the event on neutral territory at a local high school and it brought in 1,200 people. Because that planter cared about and understood the needs of his ministry focus group, a whole coalition of Christian churches were able to do meaningful work in that community.

Be sure not to serve with an agenda. Serve selflessly, the way that Jesus served. When people are curious, talk with them about Jesus. When they are not, serve anyway. Keep compassion for others in the forefront of your vision and service.

The two-pronged approach to effective outreach is building relationships and meeting needs. Beware of a cookie-cutter approach. Do your homework first by engaging in relationships. Talk to people—and listen, to ensure you understand the needs and that they can be met effectively by the methods you're considering.

Living among people incarnationally

In addition to outward-focused serving, there is great value simply in being present. How do you posture yourself? Do you have an open door? Do you have a mindset of servanthood and availability? Are you emptying yourself of your own desire to be served? Are you willing to be a consistent presence with people when they are hurting? These are ways we can live incarnationally.

As Tim Keller writes, "Jesus didn't commute from heaven every day. He moved in!"[4] He lived close to people—right with them—and we need to live close to people as well. We can't do it long-distance. It's hard to plant a church if you're commuting from twenty minutes away. We need to live among those we're trying to reach, identify with them, ask them questions, listen to their answers, and become part of them so that our interests are intertwined.

The simplest definition of being incarnational is being Jesus to those around us: serving like him, loving like him, being Jesus with flesh. It's no accident that Jesus was called Emmanuel: God with us. We are to be Jesus to those we are with.

Evangelism and spiritual conversations

During the early stages of your church plant, be sure not to lose sight of building relationships with those who don't know Jesus. That may sound obvious, but the people who are already involved in your church plant can quickly consume much of your energy. As the community aspect of the core group strengthens, the tendency will be to invest more heavily in forming good relationships with each other. The passion to spend time with and serve those who don't yet know Jesus may wane. Continually help the people on the core team focus outward. Plan activities that people can easily invite friends to, whether large group or smaller group activities.

We can begin by asking the Holy Spirit to lead us to those he is working in. As we develop relationships and serve others, we will encounter some who are spiritually open or seeking. There are some people out there who are looking for God, and he may be drawing them to himself via you and your church plant. How do you

---

[4]Timothy Keller, "Planting a Church in the City," Melchizedek School of Ministry, www.melchizedekschool.files.wordpress.com/2011/10/planting-a-church.pdf.

identify those spiritually open people? You need to talk with them. Often, asking people about their spiritual journey can put you in a posture of listening and learning. If you never discuss anything spiritual, you'll never know if they're responsive to the gospel.

As we live incarnationally, we have to be able to start spiritual conversations. We can't just hope and wait for someone to ask us, "Why are you doing what you're doing?" Yet if they do, what is our answer? "We do this because we love Jesus and want others to know Jesus. This is one way of demonstrating his love to people." In this way, we take a both/and approach. We serve *and* we share. It's a natural outworking of relationship with Jesus that we want to demonstrate him to others, so that they might know him, too. Yet usually the question isn't asked.

As we build relationships and serve others, what are we saying? We need to prepare for those conversations. Consider your own story. How has Jesus changed your life? Story is important as we share the gospel. It looks different for everyone, and opens up the opportunity to ask others what that story looks like for them. How have they experienced God? When have they sensed his presence? What would the kingdom of God look like if it came into their world?

In some cases, people will want to hear your story. In other cases, they won't and you'll find it more fruitful to delve into their stories and ask questions. Many people deeply desire to be listened to, and their own story is where you can seek to discover together where God has been working in their life. Be sensitive to the Spirit's leading, and be sure not to project your own story or situation onto others. Everyone experiences God in different ways.

Working with your core team, take turns giving everyone the chance to share a brief story of their own encounter with God. This need not be a dramatic conversion experience; it could be a time when they simply saw God at work or were aware of his presence in a new way. Also practice brainstorming spiritual questions to ask others. Finally, give each team member a chance to articulate the gospel in a minute or less. You may want to go around the group more than once to get people used to it and more comfortable with the ways they can express it in their own words. Each person needs to be able to communicate the essence of the gospel. It's not about a particular method, but about being able to communicate in a way that is simple, clear, and succinct.

Joe Aldrich called it "show and tell." For some people engaging the culture, it's all about what you say. For others, it's all about what you do. The reality is, it's both together. We show the gospel *and* we tell the gospel. For those who respond, this is what moves us more deeply into the disciplemaking process.

Bridge to discipleship

The joy of seeing a person enter into faith in Jesus is a time for celebration, but it is far from the end of the process. Intentional discipleship of some kind is essential. Involvement in relationships where new believers can taste Christian community and see the life of Jesus modeled through others is essential for their growth. Involvement in sacrificial service and sharing faith with others should be done straight away as well. If that's not part of the early stages of faith, it is often never incorporated.

We'll look at creating discipleship processes in the next chapter, but as a planter, you'll need to make sure there is a clear bridge between engaging culture and making disciples. You and your planting team need to be engaging in culture so that some will respond to the gospel message and engage their journey of discipleship. Conversely, as people engage their discipleship journeys, you'll want to ensure that they continue reaching out to others—it's important for their own growth and development.

Sometimes it is tempting for Christians to try to surround new believers with other believers, isolating them from their old network of friends and family. However, this network is the most natural place for new Christians to share their newfound faith and has great potential for bringing others to Christ. Provide support as they learn to be witnesses to what God is doing in their lives.

The outworking of engaging culture

Jesus called us to be fishers of people:

> As he walked by the Sea of Galilee, he saw two brothers, Simon, who is called Peter, and Andrew his brother, casting a net into the sea—for they were fishermen. [19] And he said to them, "Follow me, and I will make you fish for people." [20] Immediately they left their nets and followed him. [21] As he went from there, he saw two other brothers, James son of Zebedee and his brother John, in the boat with their father Zebedee, mending their nets, and he called them. [22] Immediately they left the boat and their father, and followed him. (Matthew 4:18–22)

Your church plant is an outworking of that vision. What do you need to do to see that become a reality? Who, how, and where we will serve must all intersect.

Together with your team, identify "fishing pools"—places to plug in and become part of the community, places to serve, places to live incarnationally, places to be available to people who are looking for God. Consider proximity and natural affinity, but don't rule out the leading of the Holy Spirit toward people and places out of your comfort zone.

What is God already doing, and how can you join him? Find partners you can serve alongside. They don't need to be part of your denomination; they don't even need to be Christian. You can work with anyone who is making a difference in the community. Remember that God has been at work here before you arrived—and that your church is not God's only outlet for his redemptive and transformative work.

Be present, be humble, be available. Live incarnationally and share the good news of Jesus in both words and deeds. Be faithful, and see what God does.

Journey Guide for Chapter 12
Engaging Culture

We need to understand the culture around us
and adapt our ministry to fit that context in
order for our efforts to bear maximum fruit.
Through engaging culture, we get to know people, ask them questions, listen to
them, and understand how and why they do things. Without that level of personal
engagement, planters and their teams won't be able to do effective ministry with
those particular people. Appropriate relational engagement is key. Listen to what the
Holy Spirit may be saying to you as you follow the journey guide below.

Checklist: for the road ahead
- ☐ Stories and understanding of the culture have been gathered through listening.
- ☐ Mutual relationships have been built and invested in.
- ☐ A network of relationships has been expanded.
- ☐ Points of need in the community have been identified.
- ☐ Outreach and relational engagement have been engaged and are ongoing.
- ☐ Team members are living incarnationally.
- ☐ Discernment of what God is doing and where he may be at work has been sought.
- ☐ Core team members have prepared for spiritual conversations, and spiritual dialogues have been respectfully engaged.
- ☐ Discipling options have been prepared.
- ☐ Prayer for additional ways to engage and serve the community have been considered.

Discipleship focus: Sacrificial Service
If you are going to lead a church that serves out of compassion, the roots of that
compassion will need to sink deep into your own life of discipleship.

Inward focused:
1. How would you describe the role of compassion in your life?
2. What practices might help you grow in compassion?
3. How have you seen God work in your life because of a step you took in serving others?

Outward focused:
1. Who do you consider the 'least of these' in your community?
2. Who do you consider neighbors in your community?
3. In what creative and practical ways can you serve these people?

Strategic questions: for you and your coach

- What types of activities is your ministry focus group involved in? In which of those activities could you participate?
- How will you encourage your team to interact with your ministry focus group? What are some other ways you and your team can serve this community?
- What steps will you personally take to begin developing relationships with people in your ministry focus group?
- How will you prepare your team members to deepen their relationships with those in the ministry focus group? How will you prepare them for engagement in spiritual conversations?
- How can you expand the network of relationships you have with unchurched people? Of the unchurched people you are relating to, who could be a "person of peace?" How will you explore that person's *oikos*?
- What are some ways you could take the relationships you've already established to a deeper level?
- What additional steps are you sensing God might have you take?

Discussion questions: For you and your team

- What relationships are you currently establishing in this community?
- What needs do you sense? How are you serving?
- How are you listening and growing in your understanding of the culture?
- How will you know when to engage people in spiritual dialogue? What are your concerns? What support or training do you need?
- How can you bridge the spiritually curious into discipleship?

Guided prayer: for you personally

Ask, and it will be given you; search, and you will find; knock, and the door will be opened for you. [8] For everyone who asks receives, and everyone who searches finds, and for everyone who knocks, the door will be opened. (Matthew 7:7–8)

- God, how can I engage relationally and authentically with people in the community?
- What barriers—either internal or external—do I face?
- In what ways can my life be an example for others on the core team?
- Please give me an open heart and a listening ear.
- Please guide me to those who are seeking you.

Guided prayer: for use with your team

Pray together with your team through each of these themes:

- God, who do you want us to connect with relationally?
- How do you want us to serve?
- Please bring across our paths those who are seeking you or open to you.
- Give us the courage to share the gospel in both words and deeds.
- Help us to treat all people with respect and dignity, regardless of their posture toward you.

Guided prayer: for your intercessors

Remember to communicate at least once a month with your intercessors. Update them on answers to prayer from the past, as well as specific new challenges in the future. Ensure that communication is not just one-way, but two-way—ask them periodically what they are hearing from God as they pray. Make it clear that you welcome any ideas they have for outreach, assimilation, and service, as well as anything they are sensing from God regarding the church plant.

Please pray:

- that the team and I would follow the leading of the Holy Spirit as we seek to engage relationally in the community.
- that we would discover ways to serve that truly benefit those we seek to reach.
- that we would be sensitive to the ways God is already at work.

And please pray Ephesians 6:18–20 (NIV) over us:

And pray in the Spirit on all occasions with all kinds of prayers and requests. With this in mind, be alert and always keep on praying for all the Lord's people. [19] Pray also for me, that whenever I speak, words may be given me so that I will fearlessly make known the mystery of the gospel, [20] for which I am an ambassador in chains. Pray that I may declare it fearlessly, as I should.

Action guide: a place for planning your next steps

1.

2.

3.

Chapter 13:
Making Disciples

It's absolutely essential that you create a clear bridge from outreach and evangelism to discipleship. Many people never make that leap, and it's up to us as planters to make the path as clear as possible.

Living as a disciple of Jesus is essentially about listening to the Holy Spirit and responding according to what you are hearing. It isn't primarily about knowledge, but obedience. Discipleship is done in the context of community, yet with everyone taking responsibility for their own growth. This chapter is all about ways to create and facilitate a discipleship process, as well as essential components of that process.

What is a disciple?
Discipleship begins with a call to action: *"'Come, follow me,' Jesus said, 'and I will send you out to fish for people.' At once they left their nets and followed him"* (Matthew 4:19–20, NIV). A disciple is one who responds to that call to follow Jesus. A disciple is one who loves God, loves others, and makes disciples—combining the Great Commandment with the Great Commission.

But let's drill deeper. What does that really mean? If you're going to make disciples, you need to know what disciples are. What do they look like in real life? How would you identify them if you saw them? What behaviors are involved?

What are the signs of growth?
Only after you are clear on the qualities and behaviors you're trying to develop can you build them into your discipleship process. My book *The Discipleship Difference* outlines what I consider to be the essential dimensions of discipleship. Here are the areas of discipleship growth that can be measured:
  • *Experiencing God*: Intentionally and consistently engaging with God in such a way that you open yourself to a deeper understanding of him and deeper relationship with him

- *Spiritual responsiveness*: Actively listening to the Holy Spirit, and taking action according to what you're hearing
- *Sacrificial service*: Doing good works even when it's costly, inconvenient or challenging
- *Generous living*: Faithfully stewarding what God has given you so you can contribute toward the advancement of the kingdom
- *Disciplemaking*: Living in obedience to the Great Commission of Jesus, which entails making more and better followers of Christ
- *Personal transformation*: Changing your attitudes and behaviors in positive ways as a result of your relationship with God and others
- *Authentic relationships*: Engaging with other people in ways that reflect the heart of God toward them
- *Community transformation*: Personal involvement with others to facilitate positive change where you live and beyond

Although no one will be perfect in all of these areas, all disciples should be growing in these areas. Sometimes a person will need to focus on just one area at a time, then later shift to a different one; but holistic, healthy discipleship involves each of these eight qualities. Without healthy DNA, our discipleship is flawed and we will reproduce new disciples with the same spiritual birth defects we carry.

I've done a lot of reflecting on disciplemaking processes, especially over the last five years. The following is my advice to planters who want to establish the making of disciples as an integral part of their churches from the very beginning.

Prioritize obedience over knowledge
It's one thing to know a lot about what Jesus taught. It's quite another thing to do it.

> Go therefore and make disciples of all nations, baptizing them in the name of the Father and of the Son and of the Holy Spirit, [20] and teaching them to obey everything that I have commanded you. And remember, I am with you always, to the end of the age." (Matthew 28:19–20)

When Jesus commanded us to make disciples, he made clear that it was about teaching people to *obey*, not teaching people to *know*. This distinction is at the very core of what it means to be a disciple. When Jesus says "teaching them to obey everything that I have commanded you," he is saying the journey of discipleship is one of obedience to the Holy Spirit as we listen, discern, and confirm what he is saying to us.

George Patterson, a missionary for many years in northern Honduras, emphasized practicing obedience to Jesus' commands above and before all else. He asked all new believers to memorize the following list of Christ's basic commands:

1. Repent and believe (Mark 1:15)
2. Be baptized, and continue in the new life it initiates (Matthew 28:19–20; Acts 2:38; Romans 6:1–11)
3. Love God and neighbor in a practical way (Matthew 22:37-40)
4. Celebrate the Lord's Supper (Luke 22:17–20)
5. Pray (Matthew 6:5–15)
6. Give (Matthew 6:19–21; Luke 6:38)
7. Disciple others (Matthew 28:19–20)[5]

When you look at this list, it seems rather simple, doesn't it? That's intentional. These commands will not be easy to live out regularly, but they are easy to understand. Obedience doesn't require intellectual depth and understanding of nuance. It requires a willingness to act based on what God is calling you to do. In that sense, it's much quicker and more direct than learning knowledge.

Discipleship starts with unbelievers.

Much of teaching to obey is simply about following up. Here's the basic mechanism:

1. Ask: "What are you sensing God wants you to do?"
2. Follow up the next time: "What happened when you obeyed?"
3. Discern what's next: "What are you sensing God wants you to do next?"[5]

This process is specific, behavioral, and immediate. It's also self-directed. The coach or discipler is not telling the disciple what to do; the disciple is listening to God for himself or herself and discerning God's direction. Then there's a constant cycle of checking in to see how that obedience is going and where God is leading next.

As we engage in our own discipleship journey, we also make disciples of others. And here's something that comes as a surprise to many: Discipleship starts with unbelievers.

Discipleship starts with unbelievers
Jesus didn't say, "Find those who are already following me and help them learn to

---

[5] Adapted from George Patterson, The Spontaneous Multiplication of Churches, Daniel Training Network, 603, cited at www.danieltrainingnetwork.org/wp-content/uploads/2013/03/SN10b_JohnH_BPOM_GeorgePatterson_TheSpontaneousMultiplicationOfChurches.pdf.

follow me better." He said *"make* disciples." That means going to the harvest fields and calling people to follow Jesus. It means meeting people wherever they are—and helping them move one step closer to Jesus from there.

I've been surprised how controversial this position is. Most people agree that Christian growth is on a continuum. Why shouldn't the process of becoming a disciple be as well? A person may start out far from Jesus or hostile to him. Later, she may be asking questions. Still later, she may be willing to engage in dialogue to hear what other people think. Each step takes people one step closer to Jesus from wherever they are.

When Jesus gave the command to make disciples, he was focusing the disciples' attention on people who were not yet his followers. He was thinking of people in the harvest. According to Jesus, disciplemaking starts with people who are not yet believers. However, we usually think of this as evangelism, not discipleship.

Today we too often artificially separate evangelism and discipleship in a way that doesn't seem to be reflected in the reality of the Scriptures—or in the reality of how people around us come to faith and grow in that faith.

I think of people my wife and I have reached out to. Some have responded by moving toward Jesus, while others remained indifferent or moved away from him. But for those who moved toward him, they began engaging with us in conversation and relationship as they tried to understand Jesus more fully.

At some point, they came to saving knowledge of Jesus and began to experience transformation as their faith in him grew. Yet, they couldn't always point to a fixed point in time when they became believers. They experienced it more as a gradual progression of faith.

We see a similar approach in Jesus' ministry. We do not see Jesus artificially separating evangelism and discipleship. He drew people toward him and engaged with them. They developed a progressive understanding of who Jesus was and their relationship to him.

Consider this exchange—not at the beginning of Jesus' ministry to his disciples, but at the Last Supper: The disciples said, *"Now we know that you know all things, and do not need to have anyone question you; by this we believe that you came from God." Jesus answered them, "Do you now believe?" (John 16:30–31).* And then, after the resurrection when Jesus appeared to the eleven remaining disciples, *"When they saw him, they worshiped him; but some doubted" (Matthew 28:17).* Their faith wasn't all at once, but progressive. Following Jesus, believing in him, growing in him, experiencing transformation, and calling others to follow Jesus was all part of one whole journey. And it wasn't always linear.

There is often a great deal of overlap in evangelism and discipleship. We reach out to others as we practice our discipleship. As we engage with others, we are transformed. And people move toward Jesus as they learn more about him.

Do we approach discipleship as a centered set or a bounded set? A bounded set means that either you're in or you're out. There's a boundary. Looking at the process of how people come to faith, many have viewed it as a bounded set: You're either in or you're out. That certainly reflects the reality of some conversion experiences, such as the apostle Paul's.

The other way to look at how people come to faith is a centered-set approach. In this case, there's more of a continuum, more of a process. The primary question is not whether you're in or you're out; it's, where are you in relationship to Jesus? Are you far away or close? And which direction are you moving—away from him or toward him?

What then is our role? To call people one step closer to Jesus . . . from wherever they are.

Everyone is a disciplemaker
Here's another common misconception about disciplemaking—that it's an optional, specialty type of involvement (e.g., some people are involved in worship team, some people are disciplers). Not true! Disciplemaking is for everyone. Even brand-new believers are called to help others grow in their relationship with God. Discipling others is not only for the fully mature—everyone should be discipling someone.

Now, it's true that not everyone is gifted in the same way. Some might be more effective at disciplemaking than others. But we are all called to participate in the same way that all believers are called to give, even those who do not have a particular spiritual gift for giving.

Therefore, we train everyone to be disciplemakers, not just a few who show exceptional promise. Disciplemaking is not an optional leadership program for the few—it's for everyone. In this way, we multiply disciplemakers far and wide, creating a culture that holds each other accountable to stay involved in disciplemaking. It becomes an expectation, a given.

What's the desired end product? It's not thousands of people attending your church, giving, or serving. The end product is lots and lots of disciplemakers.

For this approach to be functional and reproducible, you'll need to create a system of disciplemaking that's relational rather than knowledge-based, and easily passed on. You'll also need to train all of your people how to do it.

Take a relational approach

Disciplemaking is relational at its core. It's about action and obedience, not reading and study. Consider the first disciples. Many of them were illiterate. They had no formal education. They were not trained in the finer points of theology. Yet they were able to live as disciples. How? They were empowered by the Holy Spirit, relationally connected to one another, and willing to live in obedience to God.

> All who believed were together and had all things in common; [45] they would sell their possessions and goods and distribute the proceeds to all, as any had need. [46] Day by day, as they spent much time together in the temple, they broke bread at home and ate their food with glad and generous hearts, [47] praising God and having the goodwill of all the people. And day by day the Lord added to their number those who were being saved. (Acts 2:44–47)

Most Christians—new or old—will need an intentional discipleship relationship where they can learn more about Jesus and discuss their lives and struggles candidly. Even the small group setting may be too large for nurture and intimacy in some situations. As a planter, create small environments for everyone to be discipled in their walk with God. These can be one-on-one, or peer groups of three or four people. You may want to develop two or three different options.

Then train everyone in relational skills. In this context, that means helping people become like Barnabas: coming alongside by listening, asking good questions, and reflecting together on what they're hearing from God. It means learning not to interrupt others, learning not to guide them toward preset agendas, and learning not to tell others what they should be doing. Rather, it means helping others listen to the Holy Spirit for themselves and respond to God's agenda. A whole culture of that kind of relational approach will do wonders in your church. Even a one-day seminar on these basics—including practice exercises—can be incredibly helpful.

One note of caution in these relationships: It can be tempting for the person who has been a Christian longer to feel that they have all the answers and none of the struggles—or at least that they *should* have all of the answers and none of the struggles. This belief is not consonant with reality. We all have struggles, we all have questions, and we all have things to learn. The one who has been a Christian for ten years can learn a great deal from the one who became a Christian last week. Humility is essential.

Coaching skills can help immensely with a spirit of humility. By training your people to listen well, to ask open-ended questions, to avoid preset agendas, and to remain open to the leading of the Holy Spirit, you can remove much of the sense of pressure people often feel to know everything. Even though a person may have just come to faith yesterday, he or she has the Spirit of God inside and can listen and learn.

Make the method easy to pass on
Whatever type of system or approach you take, ensure that it's something easy to pass on. You need a simple, reproducible disciplemaking process. You can create your own process, or you can borrow one of the following options.

Focused discipleship conversations: Any discipling relationship must be intentional and developmental, with both an inward and outward focus: 1) helping people celebrate where they're at, 2) listening to God together to pinpoint where he may want them to grow, and 3) thinking about how they can disciple and serve others outside of themselves.

Guide for Discipling (Bob Logan and Charles R. Ridley): This set of guides is based on the eight discipleship qualities described earlier in this chapter. It can be used as a resource for focused discipleship conversations, or in a peer discipling group. People can read Scripture together, pray together, and ask one another questions about their growth (Hebrews 10:24–25).

Life Transformation Groups (LTGs): Another option designed for two to four people is the LTG. These groups meet weekly to challenge each other in the reading of Scripture and for accountability in life choices. The agenda is always the same: prayer, Bible reading between sessions, and asking one another accountability questions:
- Describe your interaction with God this week.
- How did you share Jesus with others?
- What temptations did you face this week? How did you respond?
- What did the Holy Spirit teach you through your Scripture reading this week?
- What next steps does God want you to take personally? With others?

Discovery Bible Study (Cru): This study has a simple structure with three basic parts. The first is connection, thanksgiving, and prayer. The second is reading and engagement with Scripture. The third is committing to living in obedience in response to what you're hearing and learning.

There are many, many others. Precisely which method you use doesn't matter, as long as it includes both an inward and an outward journey—a way of personal growth and a way of reaching out to others. Choose one that is simple enough to be reproducible, but flexible enough that people don't feel forced into a mold.

Avoid the temptation to scatter your efforts. To be effective, just start with one—or maybe two—approaches that work. When you have too many options and too many activities, it's easy to overwhelm a newcomer or a new believer. They may try to attend everything rather than focusing in on one thing that will facilitate growth and outreach.

Also, while curriculum can be helpful initially, there are also risks to becoming curriculum-dependent. It can feel intimidating to laypeople if it's too complex to pass on. It can also be viewed as a course or class that, once completed, is never revisited. You'll need something transferable, ongoing, and relational. You also need something flexible enough to allow people to listen to the Holy Spirit—sometimes people need to address issues in a different sequence than traditional curriculum allows.

Listening to the Holy Spirit and responding in loving obedience—that is the essence of discipleship. We tend to give people more direction when they're younger in the faith and less when they're more mature, but we want to encourage people to take responsibility for their own growth at all times. We are not "gurus"—everyone is on this journey together.

A good disciplemaking process focuses more on facilitating the reproduction of the message than about teaching specific information. The responsibility goes beyond one generation:

> You then, my child, be strong in the grace that is in Christ Jesus; ² and what
> you have heard from me through many witnesses entrust to faithful people
> who will be able to teach others as well. (2 Timothy 2:1–2)

Consider what type of simple and reproducible method you might use to create a disciplemaking pathway that moves people from not knowing Jesus to following and helping others follow Jesus.

Address the right barriers

Along the way, you will face barriers. That's a simple reality for a fallen world. Our discipleship efforts will seldom go according to plan. When people veer off track, it's up to us to consider how to address the obstacles that stand in the way.

Let's say you are discipling someone and they seem to be running into barriers. It's often helpful to begin with a general discipleship audit. Ask them, "What's working?" "What's not working?" and, "Where are you sensing God wants you to grow?" Take the time to listen to their answers and help them determine the source of the blockage.

In my work with Dr. Charles Ridley, we've identified four common obstacles—each requiring a different approach. When faced with God's call to loving obedience, people usually run into one of these four barriers:

Cognitive	"I don't know what to do."	Example: "[W]e have not even heard that there is a Holy Spirit" (Acts 19:1–7).
Behavioral	"I don't know how to do it."	Example: "How can I [understand], unless someone guides me?" (Acts 8:26–40).
Emotional	"I'm afraid to do it."	Example: "I do not know him" (Luke 22:54–62).
Volitional	"I don't want to do it."	Example: "[H]e went away grieving, for he had many possessions." (Matthew 19:16–22).

When discipling a person, you can work together to determine their barriers to growth. To some degree, this identification depends on the level of a person's self-awareness, but you can ask questions to help them recognize where they are. From there, obviously you'll deal differently with a person who doesn't know how to do something than you would with someone who is unwilling to do it. Make sure you're addressing the right problem.

Establish new believers into the church

Of course, a foundational step for all discipleship is establishing believers in a local church. In different traditions, this can mean baptism, membership, or confirmation. Whatever your route, you'll need a clear way to help people become clearly established as part of the body of Christ. This connection will provide the support necessary for ongoing growth and development.

Here's a story of one of my favorite methods of establishing new believers—done in a way that's thoroughly interwoven with ongoing discipleship. This story comes to me from Honduras, via the ministry of Humberto Del Arca: When a new believer began to follow Christ, the church baptizes that person immediately. The church follows the approach described in Acts: They believed, were baptized, and were added to the church. This practice is different than in most Latin American countries, where lengthy catechism or sanctification came before baptism. After new converts' baptisms, while they were still dripping wet (these were Baptists, after all), the follow-up began.

First, the baptizer read from Romans 6: You died with Christ, were buried with Christ, were raised with Christ—the power of God that raised Jesus from the dead frees us from sin. Then the baptizer asked the first follow-up question: What sinful habit do you have that you need the power of the resurrected Jesus to change? This was not a rhetorical question. An answer was expected, then and there.

The new believer had already experienced the transforming power of Jesus in justification; now they needed to experience it in sanctification. And since they now had the Holy Spirit, it was assumed that they had the capacity to listen to God for themselves. Once an answer was given, the baptizer then asked them how to move forward in that area (again, not a rhetorical question) and gave them a passage of Scripture relevant to the stated issue. The new believer then had a plan of action on the number-one issue in their personal and character development, along with scriptural input.

The second part of the follow-up (still dripping-wet), began with a citation from Acts 1: You are now a witness to the resurrected Christ. No training is necessary for a new believer to be a witness; it is simply a matter of testimony to what they have experienced, telling others what's happened to them. The new believer is already eminently qualified to be a witness. Then the baptizer asks: "Who do you know that needs the transforming power of Jesus?" The new believer thinks of a spouse, brother, neighbor, etc., and they are then asked what they could do to help that person experience the transforming power of Jesus. That course of action is then linked to a passage of Scripture they can reflect on.

So right at the moment of coming to faith, the new follower of Christ is put on two tracks: growing personally, and serving and reaching out to others. They report back each week to the person who baptized them on what they've done and what's next. The baptizer has no other agenda or plan, but relies on the Holy Spirit to grow this new follower of Christ, trusting that he is at work in their lives. As they tell others about their experience with Jesus and someone responds to that message, the original baptizer will ask, "So what needs to happen next?"

"Well, I suppose they need to be baptized." "Yes. You know how to do that. And then what?" And the cycle continues, as they take others through the process they have already been through.

Out of this basic process, new believers emerge, new leaders emerge, and new churches emerge.

Do you see the ways this story not only plugs people directly into the body of Christ, but also teaches them how to listen to the Holy Spirit for themselves? How to repent? How to reach out? How to make disciples of others by doing precisely what was done with them? In cultures such as this, where Christianity can be practiced openly, baptism can be a time of witness. Holding a baptism in a public place allows others to come and observe this public commitment to Jesus and his church.

Raise leaders only from disciples
The process of discipleship—whatever it may look like in your specific context—is the beginning stage of leadership development. It's also an essential precursor to leadership. I strongly recommend developing leaders only from those who are already active and demonstrating lives of discipleship. One of the challenges many pastors end up with, after the church has been planted, is recognizing that you have leaders who aren't actively engaged in discipleship or disciplemaking. As a planter, you are in the unique position of being able to prevent that common problem.

All leaders, no matter how gifted or how naturally talented, must continue to walk in the Holy Spirit, rely on him, and continue in their personal spiritual formation. This is not a matter of perfection, but of being actively in the process of becoming more like Jesus. Discipleship is the foundation of all leadership. If we are not first and foremost disciples of Jesus, we have no business leading. That's true for planters, for pastors, and all the other leaders that pastors and planters go on to develop.

There are many ways to continue in your spiritual formation: prayer, meditating on God's Word, meeting with a spiritual director, listening to the Holy Spirit alongside a coach, gathering together with peers for fellowship and accountability, continuing to serve with humility in ways that are not always considered "leadership."

If senior leadership isn't actively engaged in discipleship and disciplemaking (two sides of the same coin), it's highly unlikely their church will be making disciples. The basic function of a church isn't theological education, serving its constituents, building community, or getting things done—it's making disciples. That's why it exists. So ensure that all of the potential leaders you are developing have a firm foundation of discipleship on which to build.

Journey Guide for Chapter 13
Making Disciples

JOURNEY GUIDE

As part of church planting, we need to prioritize discipleship and cast vision for the kind of discipleship that begins in the harvest and multiplies outward from there. True discipleship is founded on authentic relationships with God and others and is the core purpose of church planting. Use the checklist and questions below to consider the role and function of discipleship in your church plant from every possible angle.

Checklist: for the road ahead

- ☐ Discipleship attributes and behaviors have been confirmed.
- ☐ Obedience has been prioritized over knowledge.
- ☐ Discipleship engagement has been established as foundational to any subsequent leadership development.
- ☐ Discipleship has begun among unbelievers, and a clear bridge has been created between evangelism and discipleship.
- ☐ All people have been trained in basic disciplemaking skills.
- ☐ Relational environments have been established for all forms of discipleship.
- ☐ A simple and reproducible method of discipleship has been designed or selected.
- ☐ A plan for addressing barriers has been put into place.
- ☐ A route for establishing new believers in the local church has been created.

Discipleship focus: Authentic Relationships

Inward focus:

Take time to reflect on the connection between authentic relationships and discipleship.

1. What are some of the ways people have invested in you over the course of your life? What impact did that have?
2. What are some of the ways God has invested in you?
3. With whom are you in an authentic and accountable relationship?

Outward focus:

1. Who, outside your family and ministry circle, is God calling you to invest in?
2. In what ways can you build that relationship(s)?

Strategic questions: for you and your coach
- What do you want a disciple to look like in your context? How would you know if you saw one?
- What methods of discipleship are you familiar with?
- Where could you learn about more options?
- What methods of discipleship fit the qualifications of being simple, action-oriented, and easily reproducible? Which process will you use?
- How are you modeling intentional discipleship?
- How can you encourage everyone to be involved in discipling others? What minimum training or preparation will they need?
- How will you go about establishing new believers into the church?

Discussion questions: For you and your team
- What discipleship methods are you familiar with?
- What has worked well with each of those? What has not worked well?
- What qualities does an effective discipleship method need to include?
- How can we encourage everyone to be involved in discipling others?
- What barriers will need to be addressed to accomplish that level of involvement?

Guided prayer: for you personally
If I speak in the tongues of mortals and of angels, but do not have love, I am a noisy gong or a clanging cymbal. ²And if I have prophetic powers, and understand all mysteries and all knowledge, and if I have all faith, so as to remove mountains, but do not have love, I am nothing. ³If I give away all my possessions, and if I hand over my body so that I may boast, but do not have love, I gain nothing. (1 Corinthians 13:1–3)
- God, how am I currently growing as a disciple?
- What do I need to address next in my own walk with you?
- How might you be able to use me as a conduit for increasing discipleship?
- How can I cast vision for system-wide discipleship and discipling?
- How can I be a part of supporting others as they learn?

Guided prayer: for use with your team
Pray together with your team through each of these themes:
- God, please help us to live in obedience to your commandment: *"Go therefore and make disciples of all nations, baptizing them in the name of the Father and of the Son and of the Holy Spirit" (Matthew 28:19).*
- In the words of the Apostle John, *"Little children, let us love, not in word or speech, but in truth and action" (1 John 3:18).*

- Jesus said to his disciples, *"By this everyone will know that you are my disciples, if you have love for one another"* (John 13:35).
- In the words of the Apostle James, *"But be doers of the word, and not merely hearers who deceive themselves"* (James 1:22).
- Let us follow the example of Jesus: *"When he saw the crowds, he had compassion for them, because they were harassed and helpless, like sheep without a shepherd. Then he said to his disciples, 'The harvest is plentiful, but the laborers are few; therefore ask the Lord of the harvest to send out laborers into his harvest'"* (Matthew 9:36–38).

Guided prayer: for your intercessors

Please pray:

- for me personally, that I would actively engage both in living as a disciple and in making disciples.
- that God would bring us a disciplemaking method well-suited for the community we serve.
- that all of the people in our church plant would be raised up as disciplemakers.
- that we would continue to reach out in a spirit of service and inclusion as God brings people across our paths who need a relationship with him.

Action guide: a place for planning your next steps

1.

2.

3.

Chapter 14:
Multiplying Disciplemaking Communities

After making disciples, it's time to fold them into the body of Christ. That doesn't mean asking them to cut off relationships with their previous communities. On the contrary, new believers should be engaging there to make more disciples, as well as to love and serve others outside the church. But as believers, they are now part of the church as well. One of the best ways to relationally support new believers in their faith is by including them in smaller gatherings, of maybe five to twenty people.

In its earliest form, the church met in house churches—by definition, small enough groups of people to fit inside a modest house. The church still meets that way throughout the world today, in many places. Smaller groups of people allow people to know each other and be known, pray together, learn together, and encourage and challenge one another on toward love and good deeds. These smaller communities form the core of Christian community.

Some churches call these small groups, community groups, life groups, or cell groups. In my mind, it doesn't really matter what you call them, as long as the term works for the people you're reaching. For the purposes of this chapter, I'll be calling them disciplemaking communities. I like that term because it indicates both the inward community aspect of support and encouragement, but also the outward focus of reaching out to and serving others. It's a way of keeping the missional in community—and the community in missional.

No matter what type, structure, or model of church you're planting, people will come in all different ways: front door, back door, side door. Some simply start attending services. Others come because of a relationship they have with someone in the church. Hopefully many are new believers reached through sacrificial service and authentic relationships. Some may have just moved into the area.

In all cases, the goal is to find a culturally appropriate way to identify those people, welcome them, and invite them into a disciplemaking community. If they are simply attending services, that's not enough. They need to be involved in a smaller, more intentional community of growth, service, and discipleship.

Small groups aren't just a side dish—they're the main entrée. They're not just a matter of what we attend (small groups, services), but a matter of who we— the church—are. We're family, we're missionaries, we're community, we're disciplemakers, and we're servants. Solid spiritual growth, both individually and corporately, can take place only through authentic, loving relationships. In most churches, disciplemaking communities serve as the primary vehicle for this growth.

> Small groups aren't just a side dish—they're the main entrée.

The purposes of disciplemaking communities

So what are some of the things disciplemaking communities are to do? They develop authentic community and provide pastoral care. They help identify spiritual gifts and provide outlets for serving. They foster spiritual growth and loving obedience. They do a lot of things—so I've boiled it down to three main functions:

- authentic relationships
- sacrificial service
- spiritual transformation

Authentic relationships

Disciplemaking community forms as believers experience a common life together in Christ. Groups provide fertile ground for the formation of interdependent relationships. People often feel like they're joining a family, and choose to live out their commitment to serve each other in practical ways throughout the week. Small group community creates a place where people can be nurtured in their faith, challenged to use their gifts, encouraged to reach out to others, and mentored into leadership—all within the context of relationship.

One common misunderstanding is that all pastoral care should come from the paid-staff pastor. Most pastoral care needs can actually be better addressed through the members of a loving, disciplemaking community. The leaders of those disciplemaking communities are on the front lines of pastoral care. It is their responsibility and privilege to care for those in their groups. However, the group as a whole should also strive to address pastoral care issues for a hurting member.

Some situations will also require professional counseling or input from other congregational leaders.

Sacrificial service
Disciplemaking communities can provide a nonthreatening, relational atmosphere in which people can discover and begin using the gifts God has given them. Each person has been gifted and called by God in a unique way. When people participate in ministry in ways that complement their giftedness, they receive joy from their service. They'll be less likely to burn out and their ministry will be more effective. Disciplemaking communities encourage people to serve within their areas of giftedness whenever possible.

Ideally, disciplemaking communities also serve together. They may all go together one week to serve at a shelter, put together toy and clothing packages for kids in need around Christmas time, or gather with refugees to help with language learning. There are an almost infinite number of ways to serve, but many of these can be done together by the disciplemaking community. We forget that we can be missional in community—either as a full group or in groups of two or three. Jesus modeled that for us in Mark 6 when he sent his disciples out two by two.

Spiritual transformation
Although all aspects of a church should foster spiritual growth, this is one of the primary functions of a disciplemaking community. In the context of loving community, people are challenged to grow as the group discusses how to apply the Word of God to their lives. Personal sharing and accountability also helps the small group to be a place of ongoing spiritual growth.

The disciplemaking community is not separate from the basic disciplemaking method used by the church. In fact, it is most often its central context. Disciplemaking community gathering times can include worship, prayer, communion, Bible study, and a "teaching to obey" mechanism: 1) asking, "What do you sense God calling you to do?" 2) following up afterward, "What happened when you obeyed?" 3) moving toward what's next, "What do you sense God is calling you to next?"

How to spend the time
Obviously, with so many significant functions, disciplemaking communities need to consider how to balance their time, to give emphasis where it's needed at the time. It's unlikely that in an hour meeting per week, a disciplemaking community can effectively dedicate twenty minutes to authentic relationships, twenty minutes

to sacrificial service, and twenty minutes to spiritual transformation. One week may be spent almost solely focused on Bible study, but that means allowing time the following week for relational engagement and deeper-level sharing. It also means setting aside focused time for serving together.

Over the course of a month or two, the time dedicated to each of these three main areas should be roughly equal. One church builds this balance into their schedule, dedicating the fourth Sunday of every month to outward-focused serving instead of gathering in disciplemaking communities that week.

Most disciplemaking communities gather once a week for approximately two hours, but this schedule can shift according to the needs of the people and the culture. It's not so much about how many meetings and for how long, but more about the practices and habits we develop in that community. What does the normal rhythm of life look like as people engage culture and go about their daily business? If you all live on the same few blocks and see each other at school, work, the grocery store, and in each other's homes, official gathering may not need to be as frequent or formal. If the only time you see each other is at disciplemaking community gatherings, you'll need those gatherings to be more frequent, more extended, and more meaningful. The question is what is needed to really build and invest in those relationships.

That leads us to the deeper issue of rhythms of life. Although you need to know how to structure formal meeting times, you also need to help people create a structure for their day-to-day lives that allows them to most fully live as disciples. What are the essential core rhythms? What constitutes not just a meeting but a life together on mission? What are the fewest number of connections we need to maintain our focus and live the life Jesus wants us to live? To help us stimulate one another on to love and good deeds? This is the 24/7 nature of life as a disciple—and life as a community of disciples on mission together.

General principles for effective facilitation
Much has been written on how to facilitate disciplemaking communities effectively, but for any planter wanting to develop them well, a few basics are worth mentioning.

First, we need to recognize that it's not just about teaching. People learn best through dialogue, action, and considering questions. Let people ponder, let them make guesses and consider ideas, even if it's outside the bounds of your particular theology. Interactive processing is how people learn best. Never say something you can get others to come up with.

A good facilitator provides structure. He or she convenes the gathering, introduces times of sharing, discussion, Bible study, service, or prayer. He or she ensures that everyone has a chance to talk and participate, and that everyone's contributions are listened to and respected even if there is disagreement.

Facilitators also foster action. Is someone in the group sick or in crisis? How can you serve them? How can the group serve the surrounding community? What can you pray for or do together? The facilitator takes the initiative to lead others toward action. It's this life-on-life living out of the Christian faith that helps us experience it in tangible ways.

Children in disciplemaking communities
One question that frequently arises in disciplemaking communities is how to handle children. We want to incorporate children and teens into the life of the church, but at the same time we want to facilitate a level of sharing and engagement that is not always appropriate with a six-year-old present.

For this reason, I recommend a hybrid approach. Have children present for all of the parts you reasonably can, but provide alternate settings when it's truly needed. Here are a few options for younger children during adult sharing times:
- Hire a babysitter.
- Hire a couple of responsible teens from within the church. Younger kids often look up to these teens and enjoy engaging with them.
- Take turns among adults teaching the children in another space.
- Swap child care with another disciplemaking community that meets at a different time.

During other parts of the disciplemaking gathering, when kids are welcome, you may wish to allow them to disengage at times. You can provide an alternate activity such as coloring in the next room. This allows them to feel free to come and go as their attention span allows. Some churches even run their corporate worship services this way, with children coming in and out freely or sleeping on pews.

Overall, integration into church life has proven more powerful than segregation based on age. Involving children can often lead to some of the most profound questions and thoughts. Don't be afraid to allow them to hear personal stories of challenges or difficulties. By allowing them in on these conversations, the children will witness the life-changing power of Jesus. Value their spiritual contributions to the life of the church, and let them see that they are valued.

In some cases, parents will push for starting a traditional worship service, so their children have a class to go to. Often this is simply because it's their only default for what to do with kids in church. For better or worse, it's in many cases the cultural norm. But don't let the issue of children pressure you into starting a service too soon. There are many ways you can relationally engage and disciple children without a full Sunday School program. Focus also on resourcing and training the parents to disciple their children throughout the week. The church should take an equipping role rather than the role of primary discipler of children.

Starting the first disciplemaking community
During the prenatal development phase of the church planting life cycle, when you form the first disciplemaking community, the church is beginning to emerge. While the disciplemaking community may still have a lot of growing up to do and the adult church may eventually look much different than it does at the beginning, it will still share the same basic DNA. For that reason, you'll want to put a lot of effort into making sure this first community is a healthy prototype from which to birth future groups.

A key to starting the first disciplemaking community is getting the right people. Look for people who:
- have grasped and share the vision of the church.
- demonstrate the values of the church in their lives.
- have proven themselves faithful.
- have influence in their relational networks.

Some church planters recommend starting the first disciplemaking community without including everyone from the original launch team. One church started with two groups: one group had just a few launch team members and some newcomers, while the other was comprised entirely of launch team members. The first group multiplied three times in a relatively short period of time, but the group made up of all launch team members has never multiplied. The group dynamics were such that new people just didn't feel comfortable there.

The idea is for the first disciplemaking communities you start to multiply and grow, as others come to faith from the network of relationships. Given that desired end, you'll want to host disciplemaking communities not in your own home (as the planter), but in homes that are part of the community. That location makes it easier and more comfortable for those who aren't followers of Jesus to visit and take part.

Moving toward the same goal of eventual multiplication, you'll also want to pay attention to potential new leaders within the disciplemaking communities and invest in developing them.

Developing new leaders

Here are the basic steps to raising up new disciplemaking community leaders:
- Identify potential leaders.
- Offer ministry opportunities.
- Identify giftedness and passion.
- Train new leaders.
- Encourage toward ongoing challenges.
- Provide ongoing support.

Choose new potential leaders carefully, giving them opportunities to try out elements of leadership. Practice distributive leadership. Even if you are the facilitator of the first disciplemaking community, you don't need to do everything. Try distributing the various components—prayer time, sharing time, Scripture discussion, service component—among potential future leaders. Whatever you normally do in a gathering can be facilitated through shared leadership. In this way, you give others a chance to prove themselves faithful and teachable.

After you've made careful and prayerful selections, prepare your new leaders well. *How* you train your first leaders is as important as *what* you train them. If you want to train them to lead disciplemaking communities, then train them in the context of a disciplemaking community. This group can act as both a leadership training group and a first group. Participants should begin to experience all the essential aspects of how that type of gathering works. Everything you do should be simple enough to be reproducible by others.

As people step out and try new leadership skills, provide them with support, encouragement, and intentional feedback. Check in regularly to see how they're feeling and whether it seems they're on the right track. Without someone being intentional about their development, most new leaders will default to whatever they're already most comfortable with: "just" a Bible study, or "just" a relational gathering, or "just" a service project.

Consider the basic skills and understandings people will need to lead a disciplemaking community. These might include:
- the values and vision of your church.
- pastoral care in the small group.
- building community.

- evangelism through service and outreach.
- skills for facilitating a group meeting.
- developing and empowering additional new leaders.
- a vision for multiplication.

As your new leaders continue to develop, ask God to show them who their own apprentices might be. The most obvious choices may not be the best choices. If possible, encourage them each to begin developing more than one new potential leader. (Chapter 16 will directly address developing leaders of all kinds.)

Multiplying new groups

One of the most important rules in church planting is to begin multiplying disciplemaking community groups before launching public worship services. The questions are when and how. In some cases, the starting of new training groups can even provide a greenhouse from which you can launch new disciplemaking communities.

The optimal group size for multiplication is ten to twelve people. When you've grown larger than twelve at most of your gatherings, it's time to start thinking about releasing new leaders and multiplying. Counterintuitively, if you wait until the group is averaging twenty-five to thirty people, it becomes much harder to multiply—you've created an expectation that hosts need to have a large home and leaders need to have a high level of capacity. Although this number can work if you have a large meeting space, you'll also need to institute subgroups.

You'll want to check for healthy DNA before you start multiplying. Looking at the earlier sections of this chapter, what practices are in place? What values are at work? What functions are being lived out? Once you have the right DNA in place, then it's time to start multiplying.

Next comes the issue of *how* to multiply. The multiplication of the first group is often the hardest. Good relationships have formed, a sense of unity and common purpose has been forged, and people are often reluctant to leave the nest that has provided safety and stability. Therefore, you'll need to continue to raise the vision of reproduction for the expansion of the kingdom of God, while assuring people that God will meet their needs in the process.

If you've been able to develop two new teams of leaders through this first group experience, you'll be able to multiply the group three ways. By having three groups instead of two, it will feel less like a "split" and you'll have a more solid base for growth. There will be a greater sense of camaraderie when you meet with all the leaders—and if one group doesn't survive, you still have two groups to absorb the people.

Ways Groups Multiply
- In a larger group, the leader and the apprentice each take members to start new groups.
- The leader leaves to pioneer a new group.
- The apprentice leaves to pioneer a new group.
- A new group starts to reach a different people group.
- A new group starts to reach a different neighborhood.
- Multiplication occurs along geographical considerations.
- The mother group continues to meet, as individuals start their own groups at different times and locations.

How will you decide who goes in which group? You may simply let each person decide which leader they'd like to be with, or you may want to be more strategic. Prayer should be an integral part of the process. Things to consider in a multiplication include:
- relational networks.
- maturity of believers.
- giftedness, passions, and calling.
- geographic location.
- mentoring/discipling relationships.
- potential apprentices.

Take your groups through a clear reproducible process. Have leaders share their sense of urgency for multiplication with the group and ask the group to be in prayer. Give time for members to voice reservations and excitement about the prospect of multiplication. For several weeks, following a joint worship time, divide into two groups for discussion/sharing/prayer, with the apprentice leader giving direction to one group.

Your objective is to help your new leaders and their apprentices establish their own groups. As they take on the full weight of leadership, they will need more intensive coaching through the next month or two. You may want to consider weekly leadership meetings during this season, since there are few competing ministries at this stage of the church plant.

Two things are needed for groups to continue to multiply—more members and more leaders. If your groups are not multiplying, evaluate which areas are lacking. Most often, the main blockage to reproduction is lack of new leaders. When a group gets too large due to lack of leaders, attendance will slip and people will be less likely to invite others.

The outflow of disciplemaking communities

The point of disciplemaking communities isn't the communities themselves. It's about what happens in and through them: engaging the culture, fostering spiritual transformation, serving others, building authentic relationships, making disciples, developing new leaders. This is the outflow. It's not about the groups—it's about the disciples. Gathering is contributing to the disciplemaking process, not an end in itself.

That said, healthy multiplying disciplemaking communities are the catalyst that launches public worship services for some churches. These groups embody the DNA before public worship begins, which is essential.

Depending on your model and structure of ministry, you may not plan to hold larger public worship services. If that's the case, you can skip the next chapter. But for those working within a model that is moving toward public worship services, that's the next step after forming healthy, multiplying disciplemaking communities.

Journey Guide for Chapter 14
Multiplying Disciplemaking Communities

Smaller, more intentional communities of
some kind often form the core structure for
disciplemaking. Whether a church plant uses
small groups, life groups, Bible studies, missional communities, or any other group
structure, in all cases, the goal is to create groups that accomplish these three ends:
authentic relationships, sacrificial service, and spiritual transformation. Consider
the best way to create smaller communities within your church plant by walking
through the checklist and questions below alongside your coach and team.

Checklist: for the road ahead

☐ Your philosophy of disciplemaking community groups has been
  processed and clarified.

☐ Specific purposes for disciplemaking communities have been identified.

☐ Frequency and length that disciplemaking communities gather has been
  determined.

☐ How the time will be spent has been clarified.

☐ Healthy and balanced DNA for your first disciplemaking community
  has been established.

☐ Options for including children have been considered.

☐ Good facilitation practices have been modeled.

☐ Potential future leaders have been identified.

☐ Potential future leaders have been invested in and developed.

☐ Disciplemaking communities have been multiplied.

Discipleship Focus: Disciplemaking

If you want to plant a church that makes disciples, that initiative needs to start with
you. Reflect on how you are living as a disciple-making disciple.

Inward focus:

  1. What spiritual legacy do you hope to leave?

  2. Who are you currently discipling?

  2. What is your vision for future generations of believers?

Outward focus:

  1. How are you challenging those you are discipling to make more
    disciples?

  2. What bridges that lead from outreach to discipleship need to be
    built (or mended)?

Strategic questions: for you and your coach

- In a diagram of your church, where would you place disciplemaking communities? What do you want your disciplemaking communities to accomplish?
- How will you incorporate—and balance—authentic relationships, sacrificial service, and spiritual transformation?
- What facilitation strategies and approaches do you want your disciplemaking community leaders to practice? How will you model those strategies?
- What are your initial thoughts about how to handle the issue of children in disciplemaking communities? Who could you talk with to get additional ideas? What is your ideal vision for incorporating children into the life of the church as a whole?
- How will you assess whether the DNA is healthy in a disciplemaking community group? What will you be looking for?
- How will you identify, train, prepare, and support new leaders?
- What strategy will you use for the multiplication of disciplemaking communities? How will you get others on board with that strategy?

Discussion questions: for you and your team

- How has our prototype group experienced the essential facets of healthy group life? To what extent have we experienced authentic Christian community?
- What outreach and evangelism activities have we engaged in?
- How have you seen people growing in their faith? How have people been actively participating, both inside and outside official meetings?
- What leadership responsibilities have been assumed by group members?
- How can we help each other accept and celebrate the prospect of multiplication?

Guided prayer: for you personally

And let us consider how to provoke one another to love and good deeds, [25] *not neglecting to meet together, as is the habit of some, but encouraging one another, and all the more as you see the Day approaching. (Hebrews 10:24–25)*

- God, please show me where I need to grow in the area of disciplemaking community participation.
- How can I live in greater obedience to you?
- How can I live in greater transparency to those around me?
- Please give me the strength and wisdom to model disciplemaking community well.

Guided prayer: for use with your team

Pray together with your team through each of these themes:

- How are our disciplemaking communities currently practicing sacrificial service? What are some additional ways we could do so?
- How are our disciplemaking communities currently practicing authentic relationships? What are some additional ways we could do so?
- How are our disciplemaking communities currently practicing spiritual transformation? What are some additional ways we could do so?

Guided prayer: for your intercessors

Please pray that we would form disciplemaking communities that would:

- have healthy DNA.
- practice authentic community in relation to one another.
- practice outward-focused service.
- make disciples.
- transform lives.
- multiply to reach others for Jesus.

Action guide: a place for planning your next steps

1.

2.

3.

Chapter 15:
Launching Public Worship

Not all churches hold a public worship gathering. You can still fulfill all the essential functions of a church without any large-scale gatherings at all. You are still a church even if you don't have public worship. Therefore, depending on the model of church structure you are using and your ministry context, you may opt to skip this chapter if you don't need it.

That said, most planters intend eventually to launch a public worship service of some kind. So one word of caution as we begin: When you approach the point in your church plant where you launch a worship service, the temptation can increase to shift your focus from making disciples to building churches. Remember that Jesus calls us to make disciples, not start worship services. Consider this metaphor adapted from my colleague Dave DeVries:

> Some planters get excited about the cookie jar. You need to build a really good cookie jar to attract cookies, sometimes from other cookie jars. The reality is that you don't need cookie jars if you're not making cookies. If you're not in the business of making cookies, there is no point to having a cookie jar, no matter how nice it may be. Jars are not an end in and of themselves. A lot of churches are more interested in the cookie jar business, as opposed to the cookie-making business.

> Yet the reality is—if you are making disciples, you do need somewhere to put them. Some models of church use disciplemaking communities as their primary option, which I would argue are essential in some form in all types of churches. But one of the most common cookie jars is the public worship service.

Likely you will be planning to have public worship gatherings. Services can be helpful in many ways: for celebration, for teaching, for worship, for bringing in people with some degree of church background, and for casting vision. Even when I led a network of house churches, I put together periodic (but not weekly) times of corporate worship. Many people need to feel like they are a part of something bigger than themselves, and larger gatherings can provide the emotional support and encouragement of knowing many others are on the same journey with you.[6]

Readiness: What needs to be in place before you gather?

If you're going to create a corporate worship service, when will you be ready? What needs to be in place beforehand? From my experience, the DNA gets established before public worship starts. You and your people need to be living into discipleship, engaging, trying, growing, sometimes failing and imperfect, but clearly on that journey. You need to be actively engaged in fulfilling all the core functions of a church: reaching people, making disciples, living as disciples, and forming disciplemaking communities. In many cases, people expect that a public worship service will kickstart those activities, but we have a long history of that not happening.

If you're planting with team members who are used to going to church, here's a simple reality: They'll express a desire to start a public worship gathering right away. This is especially true if they have children. Don't be tempted to a premature birth if you're not ready; there are good reasons to wait. Worship can be done in disciplemaking communities instead. Public worship can be helpful but is not essential. Too often it shifts focus (time, energy, attention, money, leadership) to itself, derailing efforts to multiply disciples.

Here's a good rule of thumb: Whatever you are doing *before* launching public worship will more likely continue *after* starting services. If you're not engaging culture, making disciples, and living in disciplemaking communities before worship begins, the likelihood of those things happening afterward is slim at best.

So how do you know if you're ready to begin a public worship service? Here are three important tests you should be able to answer in the affirmative before launching a public worship service:
1. Are you already making disciples and baptizing new believers?
2. Have you established disciplemaking communities with healthy DNA and have they begun multiplying?
3. Do you have local leaders from the target community who are sufficiently prepared to lead at least part of the worship service?

[6]Dave DeVries, "Cookie Jars and Church Planters," Missional Challenge, www.missionalchallenge.com/cookie-jars-and-church-planters/.

Pitfalls to avoid in launching public worship services:

- *Energy drain.* Often services become an energy drain at a time when energy is more desperately needed in the areas of evangelism and leadership development.
- *People's expectations.* What people think a service is "supposed to be" can get in the way of authentic, culturally relevant worship.
- *Going public too soon.* Launching services before the infrastructure or critical mass is in place is a temptation for many planters.
- *Lack of an assimilation strategy.* Public services without clear assimilation plans can become inundated with attenders who never become part of the community in any meaningful way.

The rest of this chapter is devoted mainly to logistics and planning advice you can put into place once you're *really* ready to start.

The missional/attractional tension

In many ways, the era of needing a worship service to attract people is declining. The days of "come to us" are coming to an end. Society and culture have changed. Churches can no longer expect that worship services will automatically attract people who have no connection with church at all. Our posture, rather, must be, "We're coming to you, just as we are." This distinction is often referred to as the "attractional" church vs. the "missional" church.

In most cases, people are no longer asking, "Is Christianity true?" They're asking, "What works for me?" They have an experiential outlook. In order to understand God, people need to experience him through community, through serving others, and through personal transformation.

However, most churches still place an inordinate importance on the worship service, elevating it above other ministries of the church and channeling an outsized portion of their resources into it. While a very polished worship service may be necessary in reaching some ministry focus groups, reflect carefully on what really speaks most powerfully to the people you're trying to reach.

Consider also how your values play into the emphasis you place on the worship service. Looking at many churches from the outside, you could easily assume that attendance by those who are already believers is a considerably higher priority than, say, serving the community or engaging in discipleship. Others, too, will look at your church from the outside to determine what your values are. What do you want them to see?

As you look at starting public worship services—most easily understood as "come to us"—consider how you're engaging the culture around you. In what ways are you being missional? In what ways are you serving outside the church? In what ways are you providing significant points of relational connection? Regardless of whether you have a worship service or not, regardless of the structure of your ministry, you need to approach the community with a servant's heart. That's why it's important to consider the purpose of your worship service.

> You need to approach the community with a servant's heart.

The purpose of your worship service

Each ministry of the church should have a primary purpose, even though it may serve several purposes. If you could only accomplish one thing through your worship service, what would that be? For example, if observing the sacraments is the main purpose of your worship service, consider when and how you'll do that. If it's casting vision via the sermon, make that the focal point. If it's participatory praise and worship, focus on that. Other areas of the church, such as disciplemaking community groups, can often pick up areas that are not covered extensively during public worship services.

Define what's critical for your worship service, and then allow other aspects to act in a supporting role. Everything should work together to promote the vision and values of the church.

Whatever you do, keep it simple enough that emerging leaders can participate. Worship should begin at the most basic level, and allow all to participate in some way. In one church in Honduras, representatives of families take turns teaching during Sunday worship, simply leading discussion on the same Bible passages they've been discussing with their families during the week.

The clearer you are on your central purpose for worship gatherings, the more likely you are to accomplish it. Rather than feeling pressured into "doing something" by popular demand, consider prayerfully and strategically what you're actually trying to accomplish—*then* consider whether and how a corporate gathering can accomplish that end.

Private vs. public worship services
One in-between option is the private worship service. Not all worship needs to be public. Private worship, or prelaunch worship, plays an important role for the church planting core team. As small groups begin to multiply, a monthly or bimonthly worship gathering for those in the groups can be a good way to begin building unity. Prelaunch worship or private worship will be different in several significant ways:
- It is often held at a time other than Sunday mornings.
- It usually begins as a monthly or every-other-week gathering.
- It can be held in any adequate location, and can move locations.
- People who attend come primarily because they're already involved in groups or teams.
- Its primary purpose is strengthening the groups and teams.
- It's more informal in its presentation than traditional, public worship services.
- No concerted effort is made to advertise to the public.

Having a private worship gathering doesn't mean you can't invite friends. Anyone who hears about it and shows up is welcome. The main reason for keeping the service private is to avoid the energy drain (time, money, and personnel) it takes to pull off a weekly public worship service. Keeping it private also serves to highlight other areas, such as relational evangelism, serving others, group participation, and developing leaders. Keeping a service private, at least for a time, can allow DNA to be strengthened in other areas, making it clear to everyone that attendance at a service is not the main point of church.

When, where, and how often?
If and when you do decide to go public, consider your options for the location, day, and time of your service. Which options might work best for those you are trying to reach?

Once you move from private services to public services, where you meet matters more than it used to. The public is less forgiving than your loyal members. You'll need a place that's easy to find, with good access and adequate parking (if most people need to drive). Space will be needed not only for the worship service itself, but also for any children's ministries you run concurrently.

Having a central place for worship does not imply constructing a building. It may be renting a room for the celebration service, constructing a palm fence around a gathering place, or even something as simple as rolling out a carpet on the ground to give definition to where the church meets. Some churches in California meet on the beach. There are plenty of creative options—you just need to think about what will work best for those you're trying to reach.

If your worship service is primarily a connection time for those already in your disciplemaking communities, you may not want or need to do a lot of advertising. However, if you want to draw new people into your public services, you'll want to do some form of publicity, even if it's just posting temporary signs that notify passersby that the place where you're meeting is—for the next hour (or longer, depending on the culture and your philosophy)—a place of worship.

Internal publicity will include signs that point people to restrooms, nursery, and children's ministry (if applicable). Often churches have a welcome station where someone from the church greets newcomers and answers any questions. Depending on the degree you want to use your public celebration as a door into the church, you may want to do other kinds of publicity, such as newspaper or radio advertising. However, keep in mind that people who come through these avenues will probably not come with your values already in place.

When to hold your services is also an important question to consider. Sunday morning is not the only option. When you meet will depend in part on what facilities are available and in part on your ministry focus group. Traditionally minded people will expect a Sunday service, and their 8–5 jobs may make Sunday the best time for them. Less traditional people may prefer another time such as Friday or Saturday evening. Consider also the length of your services. What will work best for your ministry focus group? How much time do you need to accomplish your intended purposes?

Style
As you begin public worship, be sure to match your style to your ministry focus group. What you choose to do in services and how you present yourself as a church will impact who's drawn to that ministry. Define both your primary and secondary audiences. Will your target audience be primarily those already involved in the church, or those who are new? This decision will affect your style: how you open your services, how you lead worship, and the topics you choose for your sermons.

Consider how your theological stream will affect your style and how that will impact your ministry focus group. Determine appropriate levels of sensitivity to those who are not yet followers of Jesus. If your personal preferences don't match a worship style that appeals to your ministry focus group, you'll either need to adjust your style or consider a different ministry focus group.

That said, worship services are not primarily designed to make things comfortable for those attending. They are about creating an atmosphere of expectancy for meeting God and allowing his Spirit to dwell in our midst. Careful study of the church's ministry focus group will provide clues about what will be meaningful for them in a worship service.

As the community emerges, it should take on the context of whatever environment it is in. We need to allow the church plant to incarnate within its natural cultural setting. The purpose and nature of any church are the same globally, but how that is fleshed out is driven by location and culture.

The church planting process must allow for flexibility and be principle-driven. An all-white, suburban "boomer" church planting model will not work in inner-city Los Angeles; midtown Manhattan; nor in Taipei, Bangkok, or Calcutta. Imagine what Jesus would look like if he were born in these places. He would be the same divine Son of God, but take on the likeness of the people. One helpful question to ask yourself when determining what worship style will work for you is, "What would God's kingdom look like here?"

Children's ministry
In addition to worship style, one of the most significant decisions at this stage of a church plant will be what you do with children in and during the worship service. Planters and their teams should spend significant time in prayer and discernment around this question. Answers can vary widely according to philosophy of ministry, so ensure that you're caring for children in a way that's aligned with your vision, values, and DNA. Too often planters leave this issue as an afterthought.

A major question many parents ask when they consider a new church is, "What does this church have to offer my children?" That question is especially important for those with younger children. Before you start your first worship service, you'll need to train people to lead an effective ministry for children.

Parents—even unchurched parents—look for at least three things: 1) a safe environment where children are cared for; 2) evidence that the children had fun and enjoyed themselves; 3) proof that they learned something. For safety, parents walk into the room and assess for cleanliness, security, adult-to-child ratio, and attentiveness on the part of the adults present. Then afterward, what are the two questions a parent asks a child on the way home?

- **Did you have fun?** If the answer is no, the family is not coming back. When my wife used to teach a Sunday school class for four-to-five-year old children, she would take time at the end of the lesson to review all the fun they'd had together. If the children's ministry passes this first litmus test, the parents will ask a second question:
- **What did you learn?** In response, a very young child may thrust up a paper with cotton balls glued onto it. These are sheep, and this paper is universal proof of Bible learning. Older children may be able to articulate some of what they've learned, but even then it's helpful if they have some form of "proof" to hand to the parent. Even unchurched parents want some proof of learning—that moral education, rather than just childcare, has taken place.

Providing consistent pastoral care and discipleship for children and their families greatly increases a new church's potential for growth. Planters sideline it to their detriment.

Preview services
Once public worship has been planned, most churches take a trial run for a few weeks before advertising to the public. Doing this can function as a type of dress-rehearsal to identify and work out some of the bumps beforehand. Preview services give you an opportunity to get used to a new location, new worship style, and how to provide supporting functions like setup team or children's ministries. Because the worship service is your public face, you want to make sure you're fully prepared by organizing and preparing the supporting ministries.

Preview services are particularly beneficial if you haven't been holding private worship services or if you're radically changing style, format, or location. They are also helpful if you plan your first public worship service to be a big celebration, with much effort having been spent to invite the surrounding community.

Planning

The nature of large events is that they require energy and volunteers. You'll need to do the legwork beforehand of identifying and mobilizing the ministry teams you'll need. Consider the following potential needs you may have, depending on the type of service you want to offer:

- worship team
- intercession team
- children's ministry
- set-up/tear-down
- sound system management
- greeters/ushers team
- welcome ministry for newcomers/assimilation
- coffee and refreshments

Remember, you don't have to offer everything. Some churches are intentionally structured more simply. It all depends on how you clarify your desired outcome. What are you trying to accomplish? You may not need all the bells and whistles to do what you need to do. In fact, they may even be counterproductive in some cases.

After doing some initial thinking, here's a basic planning process you can go through with your team:

- *Brainstorm possible elements that may be needed for the service.* Given what you want to accomplish, consider which are needed and which may be beneficial. Don't be afraid to come up with some bad ideas—you can always discard them. Coming up with a long list of possible options is empowering for the planning process.
- *Confirm key areas to address.* With most plans, there's more than one key area to address. Worship style is a different issue than finding a meeting space, which is a different issue than how to get the word out about a new service. Consider all aspects you'll need to address.
- *Map out a process.* When you're empowered with a range of options to choose from and an array of all key areas, you're positioned to map out a process to follow. Remember, not everything has to happen at once. Rather, consider the most effective order for the various stages of the process. Some decisions may be contingent on previous decisions—so where does it make the most sense to begin?
- *Get specific.* Create a concrete timeline. What are you going to do? Who's going to do what? When will it be done? Specific action steps with who, what, and when attached to them are essential for putting any plan into action.

Assimilation

One important end result of any public worship service is ensuring that people get connected to the community. Worship in and of itself is wonderful, but you've left much of the disciplemaking opportunity on the table if you don't have follow through with people afterward. There is much more to being a part of the living body of Christ than showing up at a service. There are relationships and serving and learning and growing and stretching.

For all of this, you'll want to connect anyone new to your service with a disciplemaking community group. Assimilation is primarily a matter of relational connection. Many people who come through invitation by friends will naturally be able to connect to a group, but you'll need a system in place to ensure that others don't slip through the cracks.

Front-door strategies—like people coming in to a public worship service and then getting connected to smaller communities—are not the only assimilation approach, though. Be aware of side-door entrances too. Often people come in through acquaintances in the community groups or connection to service projects; from there, they eventually work their way into the public worship service. Be sure your assimilation process is flexible enough to serve people who come in at any point along the way.

Evaluating service effectiveness

Finally, determine how you'll measure your effectiveness. A year after your first public celebration, what measurable goals do you hope to have achieved? How will you evaluate the effectiveness of your services? Build evaluation times into your calendar. Set aside time in advance for reflection and evaluation of the worship services. If you don't, the question of effectiveness will often never come up until something is wrong.

I recommend quarterly planning meetings for the services. Have all leaders involved in the service attend the gathering, and spend some time first reflecting on the positives—celebrate successes and affirm one another. Refer back to the specific goals you had before starting the services and assess to what degree, and in what ways, they've been met.

Only then should you move on to the inevitable challenges. What goals are still unmet? What gaps exist? What limiting factors for growth and multiplication have been identified? What training or support do the volunteers seem to need? What common pitfalls are you encountering?

From there, move back to the positive. What ideas do you have? What solutions could your team brainstorm? What opportunities are hidden within the limitations you're facing? What new topics might you address to increase the health of the congregation?

A worship service can—and should—be an exercise in continual growth, improvement, and experimentation as you worship God together and reach out to the community around you.

Journey Guide for Chapter 15
Launching Public Worship

JOURNEY GUIDE

Most church planters intend eventually to
launch a public worship service of some kind.
No matter what size, style, or structure the
planter has in mind, one key to a successful launch is assessing readiness. This
chapter helps planters ensure that all critical systems are functioning before public
launch and provides direction for considering relevant questions beforehand
about what that launch could look like. Ensure all critical systems are in place
before launching a public worship service by working carefully through the
following journey guide.

Checklist: for the road ahead

☐ The need and purposes for a public worship service have been
discerned.

☐ God's timing for public worship, including leadership development
and disciplemaking community multiplication, have been discerned.

☐ Service locations, times, and frequency have been decided upon, and a
place for corporate gathering has been secured.

☐ The worship team has been gathered and trained, and a dynamic and
culturally relevant worship style developed.

☐ Culturally appropriate reproducible methods have been developed and
used.

☐ Appropriate promotion and publicity have been utilized.

☐ People and ministry teams have been mobilized for large group
gatherings.

☐ Preview services have been practiced, if needed.

☐ Newcomers have built relationships and been assimilated into
disciplemaking communities.

☐ Regular (at least quarterly) times of evaluation have been built into the
calendar.

Discipleship focus: Sacrificial Service

As you begin public worship, the temptation is to turn inward. You have a
lot of needs and volunteer slots to fill within the church. Don't give in to that
temptation; continue living with an outward focus of service.

Inward focused:

1. In what ways are you struggling to serve others? What are the
barriers?

        2. What adjustments need to be made (heart, attitude, perspective) in order to engage joyfully in sacrificial service?

Outward focused:

        1. How are you blessing others with your words and deeds?

        2. Who can you invite to work alongside you as your minister to others?

Strategic questions: for you and your coach

- What do you view as the primary purpose of your worship service? What are some secondary purposes? What can you accomplish without a public worship service?
- Consider your options for the location of your service, the day and time, and possible advertising. Which options might work best for those you're trying to reach?
- Considering your ministry focus group, what type of worship styles might be most effective? Give specific examples pertaining to music, theological language, sermon topics, etc.
- Who else needs to be involved in the planning process?
- What degree of sensitivity to those not yet following Jesus do you wish to adopt? Why?
- What is your plan for assimilating those who visit the service into disciplemaking community groups?
- How will you evaluate the effectiveness of your services?

Discussion questions: for you and your team

- What do we want to accomplish through our public worship services?
- How will we know if we have been successful?
- Consider those we are trying to reach. What might be appealing or interesting to them? What might be off-putting?
- What might you personally desire in a worship service that may not work well for those we are trying to reach?
- Who might we involve in the planning process?

Guided prayer: for you personally

After this I looked, and there was a great multitude that no one could count, from every nation, from all tribes and peoples and languages, standing before the throne and before the Lamb, robed in white, with palm branches in their hands. [10] *They cried out in a loud voice, saying,*

"Salvation belongs to our God who is seated on the throne, and to the Lamb!"

[11] *And all the angels stood around the throne and around the elders and the four*

living creatures, and they fell on their faces before the throne and worshiped God, [12] *singing, "Amen! Blessing and glory and wisdom and thanksgiving and honor and power and might be to our God forever and ever! Amen." (Revelation 7:9–12)*

- God, please direct my gaze to the one most important thing we need to focus on in doing a public worship service.
- Help me see how a service fits in with the larger vision you've given for this church plant.
- Allow me to see beyond my own experience and my own comfort zone to recognize the uniqueness you have for this particular worship service.
- In all things, keep our focus on the worship of you.

Guided prayer: for use with your team

Pray together with your team through each of these themes:

- How can we be a blessing to our community through public worship services?
- How can we meet needs and address the questions people are truly asking?
- What are you calling each of us personally to contribute to the team effort that a public worship service will require?
- How can we love and serve people well in a way that draws them into our community?
- What might you be asking us to sacrifice as we move toward a public worship service?
- What do you want us to remember?

Guided prayer: for your intercessors

Please pray for us as we consider whether God is calling us to begin a public worship service. Pray that our team would:

- clearly discern God's voice and direction.
- keep our eyes focused on the mission you've given us of making disciples.
- understand those we're trying to reach and place their needs before our own.
- think creatively, rather than simply repeating what we've seen done before.
- create a worship service that is truly honoring to God, aligned with his purpose for us and for those we are reaching.

Action guide: a place for planning your next steps

1.

2.

3.

Keep Growing: Ongoing Development and Multiplication

When you have formed disciplemaking communities and begun a public worship service (if applicable), you may think you're finished with the planting process. Not so. You need to continue to do the work of ongoing development, and set the stage for church multiplication.

Part 4 covers these chapter topics:

Chapter 16:
Developing Leaders

Full books have been written on the subject of developing leaders; I've authored a few myself. Therefore, this short chapter on the topic should in no way be taken as comprehensive. Rather, I simply wish to highlight a few of the most important principles for church planters to take into account, as you develop leaders within your plant.

A church can only grow as large as its leadership base. As the church begins to expand, cultivating and developing leaders will be one of the primary responsibilities of the church planter. A strong leadership base results in healthy disciples, groups, and churches. In this sense, strong leadership development is the bedrock upon which all other growth rests.

There are also extensive biblical examples. Moses identified and developed Joshua; Elijah identified and developed Elisha; Paul identified and developed Timothy, who developed others, who in turn developed others (2 Timothy 2:2). Jesus, of course, spent much of his earthly ministry identifying and developing the twelve disciples. From the outside, it may have seemed a waste for him to concentrate so much of his energy in so few when he could have spent more time preaching to crowds. But Jesus knew the value of investing deeply in a few leaders. They went on to become the apostles of the early church: the few who reached the many, while developing additional leaders along the way.

Jesus' strategy speaks to our motivation for developing leaders. He knew it would take many more people than just himself to reach everyone.

> *Jesus went through all the towns and villages, teaching in their synagogues, proclaiming the good news of the kingdom and healing every disease and sickness. [36] When he saw the crowds, he had compassion on them, because they were harassed and helpless, like sheep without a shepherd. [37] Then he said to his disciples, "The harvest is plentiful but the workers are few. [38] Ask*

the Lord of the harvest, therefore, to send out workers into his harvest field."
(Matthew 9:35–38, NIV).

We are Christians—little Christs—sent out into the harvest fields to carry on the essential work of Jesus. Leading in this way builds on the reality that people are already engaging the culture, serving others, and making disciples. There is no substitute for that. It's not like people are "on the leadership track now," and therefore no longer have to do "discipleship stuff." We never graduate to not being and making disciples, no matter how high on the leadership ladder we rise—and as planters, we need to model that reality. Never elevate leaders beyond what Jesus sent everyone to do.

Recruiting vs. developing

Probably the most important principle for planters in the area of leadership development is that we must actually develop new leaders, not just recruit existing ones from other places. If we don't develop any new leaders—and other churches don't either—the leadership of the church dies out completely in one generation. Every new generation must pass on the mantle of leadership in order to continue.

One of the challenges is that planters are usually people who want to get things done and get them done yesterday. It's much, much faster to take someone who is already a leader and get him or her to implement the vision. However, it's much less effective. People who are already leaders somewhere else have likely not bought into your vision and are likely to be a DNA mismatch. Even though it takes longer to develop new leaders rather than recruit existing ones, it is much more effective in the long run.

When planters try to solve their leader shortage by recruiting qualified leaders, it's a short-term fix at best. Recruiting from a pool of existing leaders diminishes that pool, leading to more shortages down the road. Temporary recruitment success has the inadvertent side effect of short-circuiting long-term development. The more successful a church plant is at recruiting, the less effort they're likely to put into actually developing new leaders.

Developing new leaders is the long-range solution—and the only way to increase ministry capacity. Although there will be an initial delay between recruitment and deployment, this strategy avoids long-term leader shortages—the number-one blockage identified by Jesus in the passage above. If we invest in development, the supply of leaders is limitless.

Who do you start with?

When you're looking at developing new leaders, where do you look? I recommend starting within the group of people you're trying to reach. Leaders from within the demographic you're serving will be, by far, the most effective leaders. This might even mean looking at potential leaders who are not yet followers of Jesus. Becoming a disciple is, after all, the first step in the leadership development process.

From among those in your target demographic group, look for those who are willing, faithful, available, humble and teachable. *"Whoever is faithful in a very little is faithful also in much; and whoever is dishonest in a very little is dishonest also in much" (Luke 16:10).* Who's doing well with a small amount of responsibility or a small task? That can be an important indicator of future leadership potential.

We tend to start with people who exhibit leadership in business or the marketplace, but don't always vet them to see if they're demonstrating spiritual maturing over time. They don't have to be perfect, but they *do* have to be growing. Do you see evidence of growth? Do you see positive changes in the person's life? Are they spending time with Jesus? Are they becoming more like him? Don't narrow your pool of potential leaders too soon. We disqualify too many people whom God isn't finished with yet. Don't rule out the young, the uneducated, the inexperienced, or those who in the very early stages of their faith journey.

> Leaders from within the demographic you're serving will be, by far, the most effective leaders.

From here, we need to spend some time in prayer and discernment. Who are the new leaders God may be calling us to develop? Again, the most obvious answers are not always the right answers. Who is God bringing to mind? To what degree are you willing to follow his leading?

Prayerfully look around the pool of potential leaders. Who are those who naturally have an influence on others? Which of them demonstrate faithfulness, servanthood, teachability, willingness, and availability?

From this pool of people, we choose those we can invest in developing. We give them tasks and responsibilities that stretch and challenge them, but which are also within their areas of interest and ability. We invite them to join us in moving together toward the reality of God's kingdom.

Identifying the right people to invest in will save you many headaches down the road. If you're not starting with the right people, you're going to hit a lot of roadblocks. Take the time to identify the right people before jumping into a leadership development program.

God is the one who calls leaders, raises them up, and removes spiritual blockages. God is also able to grant you the eyes to see leadership potential in others. Avoid the temptation to look for people who are already leaders, then over-involve them. This approach generally leads to burnout and stagnation, and serves to undercut the development of new leaders.

Skills training and development

Once you've prayerfully discerned those you believe God would have you invest in developing as leaders, talk with them. Ask them what they're hearing from God. Ask what areas of ministry most interest them. Ask what skills they're most interested in developing. The process needs to be relational, flexible, and tailored to the individual from day one. Training is hands-on, life-on-life, learning-by-observation, and experience. This is the way Jesus taught his disciples, and the way we should teach others. We need to provide a relational context, ministry tasks, supervision, and time for reflection and discussion.

Too often we recruit leaders and expect them to start leading. When we skip over providing the necessary training, we find ourselves facing a sky-high burnout rate—not to mention the poor leadership that happens in the meantime. If we want good leaders, we need to invest in training them.

The general cycle of training goes like this: You do the ministry. You model the ministry for others. You do ministry alongside others and provide feedback. Others do the ministry on their own and you get together to discuss it. This method of gradual release creates an effective way to train others to do the work of the ministry. The time spent in reflection and discussion is essential, as it allows for the input of others and time to listen to the Holy Spirit.

After initial development, we must continue to provide ongoing challenges to our new leaders: new tasks, new responsibilities, new skills training. This allows them to continue stretching, growing, and moving into their full capacity as leaders. We also need to release and empower them as leaders in their own right.

Here are three paradigms some planters have found helpful:

The Path	Coaching	Show-how training
Mobilize	What can we	I do, you watch
Orient	celebrate?	I do, you help
Involve	What obstacles are	You do, I help, we
Just-in-time training	you facing?	discuss
Consistent coaching	What are you	You do, I watch, we
Gathering for	learning?	debrief
mutual support	What do you want	You do, someone
	to discuss?	else watches
	What are your next	
	steps?	
	How can I pray for	
	you?	

Ensure that you're raising new leaders in every area of ministry. Apprentices are required for every role and responsibility. Worship leaders should be raising up new worship leaders, children's workers should be raising up new children's workers, coaches should be raising up new coaches, and church planters should be raising up new church planters. Apprentices are much more than assistants or helpers—they're leaders-in-training. These emerging leaders need mentors or coaches to guide them, and safe arenas for practicing new skills (often a small group).

Jesus first got his disciples involved in ministry, *then* taught them what they needed to know. The difference is significant. See Mark 9:14–29 for an example: Once the disciples had tried and failed, they were much more receptive to what Jesus had to say on the matter. The information was immediately relevant and useful. Real leadership development is hands-on and experiential.

Example: Training a small group leader
Let's take the example of training a new leader in how to facilitate a small group. The first step—orientation—is simply a conversation. It is sharing the vision for this ministry and establishing a common understanding of what's supposed to be done and why. It is seeing whether there is interest and agreement on becoming a part of that vision.

If there is, you could invite them to observe you facilitating a group, and then have a conversation afterward where you unpack their observations and answer their questions. People absorb at least twice as much this way as they do in classroom training; plus, they have a concrete picture of what the ministry looks like. They may make adaptations, but they can model their own group after yours.

From there, move to involving—transitioning the leader-in-training from an observing posture to a helping posture. You're still there, you're still leading, but they're now helping. They can do ministry alongside you with close supervision and guidance, as they move through the middle three points of the show-how training model:

- I do, you help—we talk

- You do, I help—we discuss

- You do, I watch—we debrief

In a small group facilitator training process, you could give the leader-in-training various tasks of increasing difficulty. One week they could lead prayer time. Another week they could lead the study, or plan a group service project. Eventually, they would do all of the pieces of facilitating a small group.

Then move to the debriefing stage, where the leader-in-training asks questions, shares insights, and reflects on learnings. These are the over-coffee conversations after the group has ended. Because the leader-in-training has been knee-deep in ministry already, they know the questions to ask and are primed to pay close attention to the answers: "What should I do when that guy is monopolizing the conversation?" "How can I gain more buy-in for the group service project?"

As the new leader becomes more and more proficient in leading the group, the equipping stage moves seamlessly into a coaching relationship. You're no longer attending the group; instead, you're coaching the leader in his or her own ministry. Ownership—and leadership—has been passed on.

How can you bring your leaders together? Forming leadership communities
Ongoing support of leaders involves not only coaching but also peer support. Leaders often gain some of their best insights from interaction with their peers. Be intentional about setting aside time for leaders to gather. Some churches call these gatherings networks, or leadership communities. Whatever you call them, the function should be the same: allowing designated time for leaders to share their learnings, struggles, and successes with one another and to pray together.

Remember that this time is relationally based, not teaching time. Resist the urge to change leadership community gatherings into training sessions. One way to avoid this temptation is to come with only a topic and some open-ended questions, but no prepared material. Ask your leaders the questions—and then let them process. Resist the temptation to step in with answers; they should be doing 90 percent of the talking.

A leadership community needs to share life together. Disciples must view their leaders and one another in the context of real life, watching how they relate to God and others, how they deal with spouses and children, and how they go about ministry activities. Jesus' inclusion of his disciples in on-the-way training was a key relational component. He lived and traveled with his disciples, and did ministry with them. Following this example, relationship and interaction in a whole-life format is essential for forming and training your new leaders in the context of community.

A comprehensive system of leader-care and development

Coaching at every level, and connection with peer leaders, forms the bread-and-butter of a comprehensive system of leader care. The goal is an ongoing, reproducing system of challenge and support for everyone; people need to be stretched and challenged for optimal growth.

Coaching leaders is perhaps the single most important activity for the church planter, and has the most profound impact on leaders. Continued care for leaders is critical to the ongoing life of the church. Every level of leadership needs someone they can turn to for support and encouragement. Few leaders who don't receive ongoing support will be able to continue over the long haul. If your leadership dropout rate is high, review your support structures.

At the same time, church planters who continue to do all the coaching will soon stretch themselves too thin, resulting in a leadership crisis. Orient and deputize others. Simply having someone who'll ask a new leader what he or she has planned, and then follow up by asking how it went, goes a long way toward creating a competent leader. Coaches come alongside leaders to help them develop their potential. Therefore:

- Observe your leaders in action regularly.
- Celebrate small wins.
- Give specific, positive affirmation.
- Highlight one key area for improvement.
- Provide training as needed.
- Help leaders spot new potential leaders.

As you create pathways for leadership development, keep in mind those leaders who'll soon be walking beside them and training others. All methods and materials need to be reproducible. Leadership needs to be modeled in such a way that those who are being trained will be able to easily pass necessary skills on to the next generation of leaders. The same goes for new coaches. Creating a process such as this systematizes the way a church raises up new leaders, increasing efficiency for everyone.

The only way a church will continue to have enough leaders is if existing leaders continue going back into the harvest fields. Most future leaders aren't yet believers—they can only be raised up if someone first goes into the harvest fields to reach them.

How do you know if it's working?
You can tell your leadership development system is working if it's multiplying at all of these levels: Harvest > discipleship > leadership > coaching. Therefore, you'll need ongoing development and growth in each of these four areas.

Creating or maintaining a multiplication mindset can be bolstered by developing a system-wide apprenticing process. Apprenticing should not just be limited to planters. Extend the concept to every area of the church multiplication system —coaches, trainers, group leaders, worship leaders . . . any area that will need to reproduce. The movement will break down if vital training and support cannot be passed on from one generation of leaders to the next.

Remember that a leader, by definition, has apprentices. Without this central concept, the multiplication process will be limited to a linear progression—addition as opposed to multiplication—and may die out within a few generations as available personnel are used up. One way to ensure that leaders have apprentices is to make it a nonnegotiable part of leadership expectations. An important note, however, is that having apprentices means giving them freedom and responsibility—and giving up your own control.

All systems must be able to reproduce in a "fractal mode"—reproducing in all directions—not just in a tightly defined, linear way. As a need arises in one part of the system, the system itself should be able to produce the needed element. An organic, reproducing system will help keep the momentum for church multiplication going. Systems like this generally require a good deal of adaptability.

Leaders need to spend time thinking about what they do to raise up other leaders, and whether those actions have a positive or a negative impact. Sometimes apostolic leaders successfully coach and release others without being aware of all that they do to facilitate that process. In those cases, it may be helpful to have a coach come alongside those leaders, to help them analyze what they're doing —what works and what doesn't—so they can strengthen and streamline those areas that are working best.

When you're evaluating a successful leadership multiplication system, look beyond the numbers of leaders multiplying. Although that's certainly important, make sure those numbers reflect healthy leaders and a healthy leadership culture. Are your leaders growing as disciples? Are they living in a spirit of humility and mutual support? What qualities are viewed as important and worthy of imitation? How do you see authenticity, servanthood, and vulnerability playing out? Is there an unspoken assumption that "leaders are people who don't sin?" Such expectations can foil honesty and growth moving forward. Everyone needs safe places, and safe people with whom to share.

Also, what basic qualifications do you have in place for leaders—regarding who they're accountable to, what connections they have to other leaders, and how they're engaged in ongoing learning or development? Make sure your own expectations of leaders communicate the right messages. For instance, how much are you asking each leader to do, and in what areas? The meetings and time you commit them to should reflect your ministry priorities, as well as not burn them out.

The power of listening well in developing leaders

An essential but underrated skill in developing leaders is the ability to listen well. It's the single most effective way to develop others. Ask people open-ended questions— then be sure to listen. It's amazing how often people ask questions and then don't listen to the answers. We are too busy preparing our next statement or question in our minds to really listen.

Listening is hard work. It may look like you're doing nothing, but it requires focus and concentration on someone other than yourself. What do they need next? What might God be calling them to? Good listening allows you to put yourself in someone else's shoes—even when that person may be very different from yourself.

If you want to reap the vast benefits of listening well as a leader, you'll need to listen well in these three ways:
- Listen to others.
- Listen to your intuition.
- Listen to the Holy Spirit.

Good listening means paying attention. Too many leaders think leading means talking rather than listening. Listening is sometimes viewed as passive or weak. On the contrary, it's one of the most effective development tools there is. Before you can lead people and develop them, you need to listen to them. You need to find out what they need, what they think, what motivates them. You need to understand them. And you need to listen to find out where God is leading next.

> Here are a few good exercises to help you practice and hone your listening skills:
> - Ask someone an open-ended question about something they care about. Allow yourself to respond only with additional follow-up questions, not with statements of your own. See how long you can listen.
> - Next time someone comes to you with a complaint, resist the urge to defend yourself. Instead, ask questions to get at the core of their concerns.
> - Spend fifteen minutes with God, only asking questions and listening. Write down what you're hearing from him.
> - For one week, set aside fifteen minutes each evening to journal on this question, "What did you notice today?"

Growing yourself as a leader

One of the most important elements to take into consideration as you're developing leaders is how you yourself are growing in both leadership and discipleship. That's a prerequisite to developing others. How are you spending time with Jesus? How are you serving others? How are you growing holistically—not just in your theological understanding or ministry skills, but personally and relationally? How are you working with a coach or mentor who'll ask you the tough questions about your marriage, your friendships, gossip, pornography, overeating, addictions, and all other manner of maladaptive coping skills we turn to?

Periodically, we all need to reflect on our own lives, get input from others, and take time away to hear from God. If you aren't doing that, you can hardly expect those you're developing to do so.

Another significant personal challenge is to know when to step back and give over incremental control to new leaders. Think of it this way: The only way you can really train someone to preach is to sit down and let them preach. They may make mistakes, and you can give feedback, but at some point you have to get out of the way and let them lead. Too often, existing leaders wait until there is no other choice but for someone new to take the reins. No one else preaches until the senior pastor dies—and then there's no one to provide essential feedback and coaching and incremental support.

Releasing new leaders must be intentional. Succession and the passing of authority must be clear. To fully release new leaders, you must let go of the reins. It can be challenging to decide precisely when to release new leaders; we can err by doing it too early or too late. But whenever you sense from God that it's time to release, make the leadership succession clear, public, and intentional.

**Journey Guide for Chapter 16
Developing Leaders**

JOURNEY
GUIDE

A church can only grow as large as its leadership
base. As the church begins to expand, cultivating
and developing leaders will be one of the primary
responsibilities of the church planter. A strong leadership base results in healthy
disciples, groups, and churches. This chapter takes a look at how planters and their
teams can be intentional and effective at developing new leaders. The following
journey guide provides a checklist and questions for walking you through that
process.

Checklist: for the road ahead

- ☐ Commitment has been made to developing new leaders, rather than
  recruiting existing leaders.
- ☐ Disciplemaking has been fully integrated into the leadership
  development process.
- ☐ Potential new leaders have been identified.
- ☐ New leaders have been raised from the harvest, through prayer and
  apprenticing at all levels.
- ☐ On-the-job training and coaching have taken place for all leaders, using
  reproducible methods.
- ☐ Vision and values have been reinforced through the example of leaders.
- ☐ Regular times have been established for leaders to gather for sharing,
  prayer, and encouragement.
- ☐ Active listening skills have been practiced, modeled, and taught by the
  church planter.
- ☐ The leadership development system has been evaluated for effectiveness.
- ☐ Personal commitment to ongoing development has been made.

Discipleship focus: Generous Living

As a planter who is developing new leaders, you'll need to operate out of a spirit of
generosity rather than scarcity. That requires a strong personal faith that God will
provide.

Inward focus:

1. To what degree are you willing to invest in developing new
   leaders as opposed to hoping or expecting that ready-made
   leaders will join you?
2. What does the word "empowerment" mean to you?
3. What will it cost you to empower others?

Outward focus:

    1. Who might God be calling you to invest in?

    2. How can you hold them loosely even as you invest in them?

Strategic questions: for you and your coach

- Where are your strengths as a leader developer? In what areas do you need to improve?
- How are you training and coaching emerging coaches? What reproducible process are you using?
- How often will you schedule coaching sessions with your leaders?
- How will you provide special care and support in times of crisis?
- How will you identify and develop new potential coaches?
- How will you know if your leadership development system is working?
- How are you personally modeling healthy leadership?

Discussion questions: for you and your team

- How could we mobilize emerging leaders?
- Who are some untrained people with potential who could be mobilized? What people who don't yet know Jesus might be potential leaders?
- What methods could we use to train leaders? List as many as you can:
    - hands-on experience
    - modeling
    - mentoring and coaching emerging leaders
    - instructional teaching
    - leadership community meetings
    - retreats
- How are we integrating evangelism and leadership development? What else might we need to implement in order to achieve holistic training?
- Looking at all roles of responsibility within the church, where do you see apprentices functioning and where do you see them lacking?

Guided prayer: for you personally

But the student who is fully trained will become like the teacher. (Luke 6:40b, NLT)

- God, give me eyes to see the leaders I don't yet see, and give me the vision to develop them to their full potential.
- Please help me model healthy leadership to the very best of my ability, to rely on you, and be honest with others when I fail.
- Help me create an environment where people are motivated to try new things and risk failure in the service of growth and development.

Guided prayer: for use with your team
Then Jesus went about all the cities and villages, teaching in their synagogues, and proclaiming the good news of the kingdom, and curing every disease and every sickness. [36] When he saw the crowds, he had compassion for them, because they were harassed and helpless, like sheep without a shepherd. [37] Then he said to his disciples, "The harvest is plentiful, but the laborers are few; [38] therefore ask the Lord of the harvest to send out laborers into his harvest." (Matthew 9:35–38)

Pray together with your team through each of these themes:
- Open our eyes to the potential leaders all around us.
- Who are you calling us to invest in?

Guided prayer: for your intercessors
Intercessors stay motivated when they hear how their prayers are making a difference. Share answers to prayer; flag special needs. Also, find ways to thank and celebrate your intercessors. Reinforce your utter dependence upon God through prayer, during each phase of the church plant's development.

Please pray for us to develop new leaders in every area of ministry. Pray that our team would:
- reach out to and invest in those who are not yet followers of Jesus.
- discern those God would have us develop as new leaders.
- provide opportunities for growth and development—and even failure.
- create an environment of sharing, mutual support, encouragement, and prayer.
- know when to give up our own control and step back, so God can work through others.

Action guide: a place for planning your next steps

1.

2.

3.

Chapter 17:
Organizational Evaluation and Development

I remember a season early in my church planting experience when I was feeling burned out. It didn't make a lot of sense, as things seemed to be going well and the church was growing. I prayed to God, looked for unconfessed sin, took sabbath days, but I continued to feel the same. Then I had a prompting: "Draw an organizational chart." I thought, "Well, since God isn't answering my prayers, I might as well."

In doing so, I discovered that I had twenty-seven people directly reporting to me. There it was on paper: Twenty-seven lines, going directly to me. No wonder I was feeling burned out. I was having a Moses problem (see Exodus 18 for the full story). I'd been doing all of the work myself and it was past time to restructure.

As you get overloaded, it's a sign to develop others. As you grow, there will be needs to reorganize. Even when your strategy seems to be working well, the very growth your success generates will lead you toward change. What worked effectively in one stage will lead you to a blockage in the next stage; some things will need to change. You'll need to evaluate, right-size, adapt, reorganize, and shift gears in order to keep working at optimal effectiveness.

Constant reevaluation—and making the changes based on it—is what will increase your capacity for the next level of growth. You'll need to continually assess so you can continually grow. It's like adding layers: workers, team leaders, supervisors, an overseer. Doing this allows you to work *on* the ministry rather than *in* it—you can keep the big picture in mind and avoid getting bogged down. So delegate: What are you doing that could now be done by someone else?

Also be sure to update job descriptions accordingly. You'll want clear job descriptions for every role, so people know where their areas of responsibility begin and end and how they interface with other people's roles. Regularly evaluating and reorganizing will help you adjust and adapt effectively as the church grows.

The need for evaluation

The reality is that you're doing some type of assessment, whether you're aware of it or not. It may not be intentional or proactive, but you likely still have in the back of your mind some sense of what you're looking for that indicates whether it's working or not. The difference is that if you don't do it intentionally, you won't have any very clear set standards you're measuring the success of your plant against, nor any clear data to back up any assessment.

Unsurprisingly, in most church planting settings, unintentional assessment comes down to attendance numbers: If more people are attending your events and giving financially, things must be going well. If few people are attending, you must be doing something wrong. When you look at this type of assessment from the outside, there are some easily spotted flaws. However, it's much harder to see when you're the planter, and looking out over a sprinkling of people in a large auditorium.

Questions also arise over who you're comparing yourself with. True, your church doesn't look like that well-known megachurch whose podcasts you listen to. But stop a minute to think. . . . *Should* it? The best assessments compare yourself not against other churches but against your own vision of what you want this new church to look like.

The best assessments also look at that picture incrementally. You're not there yet—true—but what progress has been made? What does today's picture look like, as opposed to last month's picture? You don't need to do everything at once and you don't need to get there overnight. Take snapshots in time and measure progress over the long haul. These types of benchmarks are much more helpful than all-or-nothing approaches. We all need something to celebrate and build on.

How are you measuring success?

One of the most important things in evaluation is making sure you're measuring the right things. What are you tracking? What determines success? If your goal is making disciples and you're measuring how many people show up on a Sunday morning, consider whether one is necessarily an indicator of the other.

I once asked a German church planter, "How large is your church?" He replied that they had ninety people gathered in cell groups (what I call disciplemaking communities). They also had a weekly worship service, but for this planter, church meant active engagement in cell groups rather than service attendance. He was measuring what he considered important according to their values and philosophy of ministry.

Now, I do advise tracking how many people attend on a Sunday morning if that's when your main gathering is. That information can be very helpful to you. But consider what additional things you can measure that correlate more closely to your values. How can you tell where people are in their discipleship journey? How can you tell how well you're doing at raising and supporting new leaders? How do you know if you're effectively serving the surrounding community? How do you know if your people are loving others? Get creative in what you track and measure.

Reflect on your values and on your vision. First ask: What do you want to end up with? Then ask: What indicators would show that we're moving toward that? Consider whether you might want to measure the following areas and, if so, how you could go about doing that. Be sure you're measuring the results or impact, and that what you measure shows your priorities.

Potential area to measure	Ideas for how to measure
Percentage of people involved in discipleship relationships	
Percentage of people in disciplemaking communities	
Percentage of people using spiritual gifts in ministry	
Baptisms (conversion growth)	
Development of apprentices and new leaders	
Growth in number of new groups started	
Quality of existing groups	
People (time) serving inside the church	
People (time) serving outside the church	
Personal discipleship growth	
Worship attendance	
Financial giving	
Other	

Using evaluation to help you modify as you go

Life seldom goes according to plan, no matter how good the plan may be. It's the same with churches. As planters, we need to continue to monitor and evaluate progress, then use the resulting data to help guide our decisions. If some areas are going well, how can we make best use of that momentum? What principles can we apply to other areas? How else can we invest in what's working? Likewise, if some areas aren't progressing as hoped, how can we improve them? How can we determine the core problem? How might we redirect our energy?

We also need to adapt to continually changing circumstances and environments. The world in which we are carrying out our plans is not static. What seems like a good strategy one day may be a terrible strategy the next day if the situation has changed. Say you've planned a celebration, but a national tragedy takes place the day before. You'll need to modify. That could mean canceling the event, rescheduling it, or changing the way you present it. Context and conditions matter, and sometimes we must shift course in response.

When you have clear snapshots of where your church is in time, you can use that data to help you navigate the unexpected. Let's say you've been doing well financially, but not as well with outreach. How could you redirect funds within your organization to help? How could you engage in sacrificial giving to other ministries, charities, or new church plants?

Many mistakes have been made by creating and implementing a plan—and then sticking to it even when it's become clear that the plan isn't working. Rather, we need to periodically assess and reevaluate the plan so we can make needed changes. Setting intentional time aside for this type of reflection helps us listen to the Holy Spirit more intentionally and effectively.

Here's a great starting point for a full evaluation. Together with your coach, work through these five questions:
- What's working?
- What's not working?
- What are you learning?
- What needs to change?
- What's next?

Leadership and pastoral evaluation

As you evaluate your ministry, don't forget to look at senior leadership. Depending on where you are in the planting process, that could be just you as the planter; it could be you and a core team, a board, and/or a staff team. How are you going to grow, change, and become more effective?

I recommend some type of staff/senior leadership assessment at least once a year. Often the board can evaluate the pastor, while the pastor evaluates staff. Feedback from the congregation—often in the form of focus groups or congregation-wide surveys—can be taken into account as well. Constructive feedback is then given, and a personal development plan is made for each individual.

Whatever type of tool you use, some evaluation of senior leadership needs to be done. It reflects values of personal development, ongoing improvement, and being the most effective we can be—not to mention providing an opportunity to model humility and openness to feedback.

Many leaders feel threatened by the prospect of evaluation, but it should be framed as a standard practice and an opportunity for growth. When you look at the list of leadership requirements in 1 Timothy 3, no one can say they have completely arrived and perfectly meet every requirement. Rather, we should foster a culture that encourages constructive evaluation, so we can keep growing toward that ideal.

Take time for celebration

Finally, evaluation should not primarily focus on the negative. Usually that's what people think of when they hear "evaluation," and it's part of what people worry about. But the best evaluations yield plenty to celebrate.

The old rural American tradition of barn raising provides a great example of celebration of progress. Neighbors, families, and friends joined together to build a barn in one day. This fun event was almost like a party—a break from everyone's regular daily routine. Typically the barn raising began with a breakfast together, during which everyone shared the great anticipation of what they planned to accomplish.

After breakfast, work commenced. Everyone had a role to play. Grandma might take care of the little children. Older children had assignments like gathering loose nails or carrying water to the workers. Teens and adults brought supplies, nailed or sawed boards, or supervised the construction, according to their skills.

Together, they raised the barn in one day.

Then the people celebrated with dancing and an evening meal together—something that had also been worked on all day. The barn raising illustrates three important phases of doing ministry: anticipation, performance, and celebration. This is the cycle of ministry that keeps us going.

Always take time to stop and celebrate wins. We and our teams need the encouragement that comes from celebrating past progress—even when everything isn't going according to plan. What *is* going well? What can you celebrate? There's usually something.

It's also good to confirm what's working: Even if what's working is something as simple as teamwork among members—affirm it. That's important, and it's important for people to hear. If you've invested in outreach or service efforts—even if you're not sure those efforts yielded what you hoped for—that's still something to celebrate. You might try different options next time, and you'll certainly learn from these experiences, but effort alone is well worth celebrating. Whatever's working, highlight it.

> Always take time to stop and celebrate wins.

Evaluating and developing in light of priorities

Here's the recurring theme that runs through this whole chapter: The specific ways you choose to adapt each ministry area depend on what your priorities are. There are no *right* answers, per se. You only need to be sure you've addressed each ministry area to make sure it's in full alignment with your mission and vision of how this church will be. The choices you make can shape your ministry in important ways. Your priorities can be primarily identified by how you spend your time and your money. What do you want to be known for?

As you consider organizational structure and priorities, revisit the idea of giving money away—to the last and the least of these, and to other church planting efforts. It's easy to push giving off until you feel you have enough money to be self-supporting—but the challenge is, that day never really comes. There will always be needs and places to invest in. Make it a habit from the very beginning to give away a portion of your funds and resources to ministry outside your own plant.

When the apostle Paul was sent out to reach the Gentiles, James, Peter and John made only one specific request: *"They asked only one thing, that we remember the poor, which was actually what I was eager to do" (Galatians 2:10).* What you give may not feel like much, but the amount isn't even really the important part. The important part of giving is what it will do in you, in the heart of your congregation. It will provide a posture of open hands and generosity that you can build on for many years to come.

Journey Guide for Chapter 17
Organizational Evaluation and Development

JOURNEY GUIDE

As the church plant grows, the organizational structure needs to grow and develop along with it. This means setting aside regular time for evaluation of what's working and what's not, how actions are aligning with values, and what midcourse corrections might need to be made. Celebrating and reinforcing the positives should also be made a priority. You can use the questions below to rethink your organizational structure and how to be proactive about moving to the next level of growth most effectively.

Checklist: for the road ahead

- ☐ Regular time has been set aside for evaluation.
- ☐ Intentional choices have been made about what to evaluate.
- ☐ Connections have been made between your values/vision and what you're evaluating.
- ☐ Appropriate tools for evaluation have been selected.
- ☐ Outside help, if needed, has been obtained.
- ☐ Evaluation results have been used to shape and develop the organization, as needed.
- ☐ Senior leadership has been evaluated regularly.
- ☐ Humility and openness to feedback have been modeled.
- ☐ Time has been taken to celebrate the positives.

Discipleship focus: Experiencing God

Allowing your ministry to grow and multiply means letting go of control. It means opening your hands to what God may want that you haven't seen yet. Take some time now to worship and recognize the vastness of God.

Inward focused:
1. In what ways do you feel like you bring your whole and true self to God? In what ways is that hard?
2. How do you process your disappointment or anger with God?
3. When did you last sit in awe of God? Describe that experience.
4. In what areas might you have to let go of control?

Outward focused:
1. How can you partner with your faith community to carry the knowledge, grace, and peace of God out into the community?
2. In what ways can you expose your surrounding community to worship?

Strategic questions: for you and your coach

- What ministry efforts do you have currently in process that need evaluating?
- What questions do you need to ask to evaluate accurately? What fears or concerns do you have around evaluating?
- What will you measure? How do those elements connect with your values as a church?
- What evaluation methods might be helpful?
- Who might be able to give you helpful data or perspective?
- What approach could you take to evaluate yourself and your own leadership effectiveness?
- After you've received evaluation results:
  - What can you celebrate?
  - Based on current progress, how might you need to redirect energy?
  - What changes need to be made?
  - Who do you need to have on board in order to modify effectively?
  - What action steps are you sensing God would have you take?

Discussion questions: for you and your team

Read this passage aloud with your team:

> Now during those days, when the disciples were increasing in number, the Hellenists complained against the Hebrews because their widows were being neglected in the daily distribution of food. [2] And the twelve called together the whole community of the disciples and said, "It is not right that we should neglect the word of God in order to wait on tables. [3] Therefore, friends, select from among yourselves seven men of good standing, full of the Spirit and of wisdom, whom we may appoint to this task, [4] while we, for our part, will devote ourselves to prayer and to serving the word." [5] What they said pleased the whole community, and they chose Stephen, a man full of faith and the Holy Spirit, together with Philip, Prochorus, Nicanor, Timon, Parmenas, and Nicolaus, a proselyte of Antioch. [6] They had these men stand before the apostles, who prayed and laid their hands on them. [7] The word of God continued to spread; the number of the disciples increased greatly in Jerusalem, and a great many of the priests became obedient to the faith. (Acts 6:1–7)

- What could we learn from this example of the early church, regarding putting structures in place to make the ministry more effective?
- In what ways are the structures of our church planting helping us further our mission of making disciples?

- Where do you see gaps?
- What additional structures might we put into place to help us live out our mission more effectively?
- Who could help us?

Guided prayer: for you personally

By wisdom a house is built, and by understanding it is established (Proverbs 24:3)

- God, please give me the humility to be evaluated.
- Please give me the openness to hear constructive feedback.
- Give me a vision for an organization that would allow this church plant to serve your purposes to the fullest.
- Provide wisdom and counsel as I—together with my team—make decisions about how best to structure our ministry.
- Please help me sort out what is truly important from your vantage point— and major on that.

Guided prayer: for use with your team

Pray together with your team through each of these themes:

Please reveal to us how you are working and how you want to be working in our . . .

- service to others.
- sharing of the gospel.
- financial generosity.
- prayer and worship.
- engagement with Scripture.
- relationships with one another in our disciplemaking communities.

Please guide us toward becoming and living as the local body of Christ that you would have us be. Amen.

Guided prayer: for your intercessors

Please pray for Spirit-led wisdom as we shape an organization that is pleasing to God. Pray specifically that our team would:

- see ourselves clearly, with honesty and transparency.
- see our strengths clearly, as well as our weaknesses.
- engage in assessment with a spirit of openness.
- ask for help when and where it's needed.
- learn from past mistakes and from past successes.
- set a helpful course for future growth and improvement.

Action guide: a place for planning your next steps

1.

2.

3.

Chapter 18:
Planning Strategically

As we follow the leading of the Holy Spirit, we can begin to think strategically about what he may have next for us and where we should be focusing our energy. Planning and relying on the Spirit are not opposites; rather, they work together. As we listen for the voice of God and see where he is already at work, our direction often becomes clearer. We can see possibilities and then gear our actions to move toward those ends.

Taken together, this concept is known as discernment. Success is finding out where God is working and joining him there. We make our plans, and God directs our steps. We need discernment to figure out how that fits together. This discernment—listening to the Holy Spirit—is both proactive and responsive. We seek, we listen, we take steps, we listen again.

Within some Christian circles, planning is viewed with suspicion, or even considered unspiritual: "God's plans are higher than ours—he is in control and is powerful enough to accomplish his will. He is the one who brings renewal and revival—not us." As true as that is, it's only one side of the story. The question remains: Will we cooperate with what God is doing? Are we positioned to take full advantage of the opportunities he provides?

The way I see it, planning and relying on God fit together perfectly. Strategizing is a way of looking toward the future with faith; it gives us a practical handle on how to implement the vision God has given us. Through our strategic planning, God is at work through us. Consider David's strategy as he fought Goliath, Joseph's years'-long planning as he won Pharaoh's favor, or Nehemiah's planning and strategy as he sought to rebuild the walls of Jerusalem.

Plans may work or they may not work, but we're not going to get very far without them. When we're in a bind and/or something needs to happen, making a plan is the best chance we've got. We can also learn from our past planning efforts. Didn't work last time? Try something different. Worked last time? Try something similar, but adapt for a new goal.

We need both prayer and planning. The Spirit of God is the primary component, but God calls us to become active participants in his work. Strategy includes purpose, goals, plans, and resources—all in the context of what God has called us to do. The more clearly and prayerfully we can define our purpose and goals, the more practical, realistic, and Jesus-centered our plans will be. The spiritual and the practical are both essential in planting churches that are structured, reproducible, and Spirit-led.

Planning for multiplication

Reproducibility is an important component. Organize everything for optimal multiplication. The structures of your ministry should continue to support the development of life. If your structures aren't enhancing life, they could be restraining new life from forming.

Think reproductively. Any plans you make should be:
- *repeated easily.* Anyone should be able to pass on the DNA and concept of your plan with a simple explanation.
- *reproduced strategically.* Plans should be readily applied to different ministry areas and different ministry forms.
- *translatable cross-culturally.* The plan should—with some adaption— translate and transfer into other languages and cultures.

A basic planning process

How can you engage in an action planning process? The basic process below can be applied to almost any area of ministry. Also, having a connection with a good coach, to help you shape the plan along these lines, is indispensable at this stage.
- *Clarify the outcome.* What are you trying to accomplish? If you know your desired outcome, you can create a more effective plan.
- *Brainstorm possible strategic initiatives.* Given what you want to accomplish, think of some possible actions that might get you there. It's okay if not all of them are good ideas. Some will be. You can pick and choose, but coming up with a long list of options is empowering for the planning process.
- *Confirm key areas to address.* With most plans, there's more than one key area to address. There may be one major initiative, but you'll also need to think through issues—especially getting buy-in, supporting the

leaders who'll be implementing it, and bringing in any needed resources. Consider all aspects that you'll need to address.

- *Map out a process.* When you're empowered with a range of options to choose from and an array of all key areas, you're also positioned to map out a process for the plan to follow. Remember, not everything has to happen at once. Rather, consider the most effective order for the various stages of the process.
- *Set SMART goals.* SMART goals will be discussed in more detail in the next section. This is where you create clear and specific goals.
- *Get specific.* What exactly are you going to do? Who's going to do what? When will it be done? Specific action steps with "who, what, and when" attached to them are essential for putting the plan into action.

Goal setting and SMART goals

There's an old Yiddish proverb: "Man plans and God laughs." Certainly that may be true at times. Our plans—and the goals they reflect—may be far from the mark of what God has in mind for us. Other times the goals we have in mind *are* the right ones . . . but God has a more circuitous route for getting us there than we'd like.

So what does this mean? Should we not set goals because God may have something else in mind? Not at all. Goal-setting, even when we don't have the right goal in mind, sets us in motion. God can better direct our steps when we're in motion than when we're doing nothing. A goal is actually a statement of faith. When God guides us in a particular direction, a goal clarifies what we sense God wanting to accomplish. Even if that goal changes over time, it sets us in motion so we can continue to act in obedience and discern God's direction.

We should set goals, trusting that God will reveal his will. Discernment—seeing where God is working and joining him there—is an important part of that process. If we take a posture of listening to the Holy Spirit and being open to new directions as we hear from him, God will guide our steps . . . even if it doesn't always look like it at the time. And yes, almost certainly the path will not look like what we expect.

Without setting a clear goal that maps out where you want to go, the chances of getting there—or anywhere—are slim. A good goal is a SMART goal. The acronym stands for these five qualities:

- *Specific*: A good goal will be specific. It's not "lose weight," but "lose ten pounds by doing X, Y and Z."
- *Measurable*: Any goal that is specific enough will be measurable. How do you know if you've met your goal of losing ten pounds? You use a scale

before and after to track it.

- *Achievable*: Any helpful goal must be realistic. That doesn't mean that all you ever want to lose is ten pounds, but starting with a goal of fifty pounds may be too overwhelming to be helpful. Start with an achievable goal; then when you meet it, celebrate and look toward any new goals you may want to set.
- *Relevant*: A good goal should be relevant to your basic mission. To what degree does this goal line up with your overall mission of, say, health?
- *Timelined*: Set a deadline to see if you've met your goal. Write it down. If you didn't meet the goal, you can readjust, but not having a timeline makes goals difficult to track—and therefore less effective.

Assessing your plan for simplicity and alignment

When you have a draft of a plan, take time to look at it critically. Generally speaking, the larger a plan grows, the more complex we make it. When aiming for reproducibility, simplicity is better.

Each training, series of meetings, or process needs to be developed in such a way that someone else could come along behind you, pick up the template, and basically do the same thing. Creating things this way takes a lot more effort, but it can make the difference between one successful leader or group and a whole network of successful leaders and groups. It's worth it. A well-designed plan:

- empowers ordinary people to do extraordinary things.
- increases the growth potential of the ministry.
- multiplies your outreach without sacrificing quality control.
- allows a ministry to function well and smoothly.
- frees leaders to lead rather than to produce.

In addition to simplicity, check any potential plan against your values. Does it align with what you want to be about—who you want to be? For example, if your ministry places a strong value on relationships, is your plan sufficiently relational? Any plan must be a good fit with the values and culture of the group it's supposed to work within.

Reflect on your initial vision. When you look at your plan, are you keeping the main thing the main thing? Are you staying aligned with your mission? Every ministry needs to set aside time regularly to check their alignment—and when it gets off-center, fix it.

Establishing a planning rhythm

Always be in a cycle of planning. Planning should be a rhythm as you plan in advance, monitor how it's going, consider the community, assess and make corrections as needed, and reengage in new planning. The plan itself is nothing. Planning as a process is everything.

Healthy, reproducible systems don't just happen without considerable forethought. The best time to engage in an intentional, reproducible planning process is when your ministry is basically stable and functioning. Of course, no ministry is ever fully stable and functioning; none of us are problem-free. However, find a time of relative stability. Even if you find your church plant going from crisis to crisis, it might be a symptom of something that needs to be addressed through better planning, so set aside some time to engage in a planning process. Sometimes a weekend away with your leadership is in order, so that you can prayerfully plan without interruption.

> The plan itself is nothing. Planning as a process is everything.

As you work with your team, be aware of two different ways people have of coming up against a problem: macro-thinking and micro-thinking. The macro approach asks, "What would this look like if it were completely fleshed out?" They want the big picture in mind first, then build from bottom up. Those taking the micro approach find this either overwhelming or incomprehensible. They want to start smaller, take some basic steps, make the impact they can, and build as they go. Both approaches are valid and can move toward the same goal; it just depends where you want to start. You'll likely have both macro and micro thinkers on your team.

Also be sure to engage in both some long-term as well as some short-term planning. We tend to overestimate what we can do in a short period of time, and underestimate what we can accomplish over a long period of time. Consider your plan for the next few months. What can you reasonably hope to accomplish in that time? How about your plan for the coming year? For the next five years? Plan for all of these options, even if you know you may have to come back and revise the plan according to your actual progress.

Calendaring with the community

Context is everything, especially when it comes to ministry planning. Know the community you're serving and plan around it—or rather, plan for it. This is an essential part of your planning rhythm. Be aware of when community activities are taking place, so your church can plan for and participate in what God is doing.

One church plant planned to do a Halloween alternative event, then realized that neighborhood elementary schools were already doing it. Instead of sponsoring their own, they realized they could strategically partner. The same is true with Christmas events and Easter-egg hunts. Community-wide activities also have the advantage of drawing in a wider variety of people than would likely attend a church-sponsored event.

Be aware of other big events in your community. Do people celebrate Cinco De Mayo all weekend in early May? How could you be a part of that? How about the Super Bowl—or a big Harley festival? Know what's important to your community and be a part of it.

Taking factors like these into account can also tell you when not to plan other events. If the target demographic in your church is out of town all of August, that's not the best time to plan an event. Some churches cancel regularly scheduled activities during that season so as to not unnecessarily crowd people's calendars. Conversely, if your demographic tends to have more time off in the summer, with less to do and not enough money to go on vacation, that's the perfect time to plan more events—especially events involving kids. Instead of extracting your people from their culture, partner with them and integrate them into the community.

Adjusting as you go

Change is easier when a church plant is small. As the plant grows and expands, people will become more resistant to change. We'll deal with the challenge of change more in the next chapter, but for now, be aware that you'll need to adjust as you go. Whatever plans you make, be sure to build in flexibility, so you can adjust for optimal effectiveness as your ministry grows.

In short: Planning should be an ongoing spiritual process involving listening prayer. Follow this mantra: Pray, plan, act, evaluate, and adjust.

Journey Guide for Chapter 18
Planning Strategically

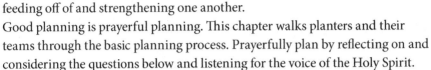

JOURNEY GUIDE

Although often positioned as opposites, prayer and planning work together symbiotically, feeding off of and strengthening one another. Good planning is prayerful planning. This chapter walks planters and their teams through the basic planning process. Prayerfully plan by reflecting on and considering the questions below and listening for the voice of the Holy Spirit.

Checklist: for the road ahead

- ☐ The purpose of planning has been clarified, and integrated with spirituality and prayer.
- ☐ A goal-setting process has been established.
- ☐ The basic planning process has been created.
- ☐ Tools and resources have been selected.
- ☐ Time has been set aside for planning.
- ☐ Long-range and short-range planning have been considered.
- ☐ Planning processes have been oriented toward multiplication, and assessed for simplicity and reproducibility.
- ☐ Plans have been assessed for alignment with values.
- ☐ Community events and seasons have been taken into account.
- ☐ Room for adjustment as the plant grows and develops has been built in.

Discipleship focus: Authentic Relationships
As you plan, don't forget to pray. Continually fostering a rich and authentic relationship with the Lord will sustain you for the road ahead.

Inward focused:

1. How would you describe your prayer life?
2. What settings are most conducive to prayer for you?
3. What are some creative ways you can branch out in your prayers?

Outward focused:

1. Who or what do you feel compelled to pray for regularly?
2. How do you practice corporate prayer?
3. In what ways can you bring prayer out into your community?

Strategic questions: for you and your coach

- What are you hearing from God?
- What is your current planning moving toward?

- How do your previous two answers intersect?
- How is your plan aligned with your end goal?
- What other ends do you need to create a strategy to move toward?
- How are you praying for wisdom in your planning?
- What action steps are you sensing God would have you take?

Discussion questions: for you and your team

- Is your inclination to grow without planning, or to plan without adjustment? What steps will you take to find the right balance?
- How is God directing your personal plans? How much time are you devoting to prayer for those plans?
- How do your personal plans intersect with your involvement in church planting?
- What obstacles could you foresee getting in the way of your planning?
- List some of the dreams you've had for ministry. How have those dreams changed or shifted over time?

Guided prayer: for you personally

- What have I learned in the past about how God comes alongside me as I move toward goals I've set?
- What goals do I currently have foremost in my mind?
- To what degree do those goals dovetail with God's specific calling for this church? With God's specific calling on my life?
- What would success look like for me in this case?

Assignment: Read the book of Acts, paying special attention to how the apostle Paul planned and adjusted to changing circumstances and opportunities throughout his ministry. What lessons can you take away from Paul's example?

Guided prayer: for use with your team

Pray together with your team through each of these themes:

- Show us the ways you're currently at work in our community.
- How can we best cooperate with what you're doing?
- Where do we need to focus our energy next?
- What changes might we need to make as we move forward?
- Help us hear from you and listen to your guidance, as we plan ways to accomplish the mission you've given us.

Guided prayer: for your intercessors

Please pray . . .

- that we would continue to engage with God and listen for his voice throughout our planning process.
- for sensitivity to God's leading, and for willingness to shift direction accordingly.
- for us to be open to the wisdom of others, and resources that become available.
- that we would ultimately settle on a plan that is pleasing to God and in alignment with the mission he has for us.

Action guide: a place for planning your next steps

1.

2.

3.

Chapter 19:
Navigating Growth and Change

If there's one thing I want you to take away from this chapter, it's this: Change is not an announcement. Here's a common scenario as one church planter experienced it, about three years into her plant:

> We used to have kids be a part of the worship service, and then be dismissed just before the sermon. Eventually we ran into space constraints and decided we needed those chairs for visitors and new people. We organized a children's worship in a different room, and considered the space problem handled. However, the transition was not processed well. We did not let people in on the process—simply made an announcement of the change—and consequently ran into significant resistance.

This chapter is all about change dynamics—how to lead through change and transitions. That's not just an issue with older people and older churches; it's more connected to being used to the environment you're already in. You can be twenty and resistant to change if it's not what you're socially or culturally comfortable with.

It's especially difficult for people to navigate change that's forced on them. Dictatorial leadership is bad in any context; you need to take the relational dynamic into account, address concerns, process people, create buy-in, and bring in change incrementally.

Think of it this way: People are all relationally connected to one another, like a spider web. They feel threatened when you take away some aspect of what they have or what they're used to, and then the effects radiate throughout that spider web. In the case of a new church plant that grows from a core team of eight to a worship service of fifty, people can begin mourning the fact that they'll no longer have the same kind of connection with those eight people the way they used to, now that they need to broaden their relational bandwidth. The same thing will happen again when the church grows from fifty to two hundred. Most people can meaningfully interact with less than fifty people; now they're in a position where some people in the service are merely acquaintances. That's not necessarily a bad thing, but it does need to be managed, and the growing pains need to be addressed.

No matter what type of change you're leading, here are my top seven coaching questions for helping people guide the change process:

1. How will you free up time and energy to focus on the change process?
2. Who are the key people who can work with you to facilitate the change process?
3. Who are the key influencers who need to embrace the vision and/or be included in the discussion/planning process?
4. What permissions need to be secured, and from whom?
5. What are the people/groups most affected by the proposed changes? What impact will each face?
6. What can you do to help people embrace the change?
7. How will you strengthen relationships during the change process?

Creating ownership for change

The single most important skill for leading change is creating ownership and buy-in from everyone impacted by the change. It's not enough to make and announce a decision; you need to ensure that others are actually on board with that direction— as committed to it as you are. They need to "own" the vision for change, and feel it is their own. How we go about doing this is a great test of leadership.

Creating ownership takes time. There's no way around it, no shortcut through it. You simply need to invest the time needed in a lot of conversations, a lot of vision-casting for change, and a lot of listening. We need to process people. That means talking with key leaders one-on-one about the idea, listening to their concerns and questions, allowing them time to think. Here are some important points to keep in mind for the most effective ways to create ownership:

- *Involve people in the process.* Don't hole up in a monastery, and then come down to declare the vision. People are committed to what they help develop. Involve them in the visionizing process.
- *Identify the opinion leaders.* There are always some people with outsized influence—those that others naturally look to in order to see what they think about a given idea. If these opinion leaders are on board with your vision, you have a much greater chance of getting others on board. Figure out who these people are in your circles.
- *Process people one-on-one.* Once you've determined who your opinion leaders are, talk one-on-one with them. Get their thoughts, hear

their perspectives, give them a chance to air their concerns. These conversations are essential for getting people on board. Don't start with a big meeting. If an opinion leader says "no" there, almost everyone else will too and the plan is over.

- *Dialogue with all parties involved*, not just official permission-givers. Just because the board approves something doesn't mean your people will support it. Focus groups can be an effective way to facilitate conversations and gain feedback and input.
- *Reframe people's perspective*, as needed. What will it mean if we don't change? What do we have to gain by going in this new direction? People need to be in touch with a sense of need and a sense of urgency.
- *Integrate feedback.* Listen to the feedback you're getting, and take it seriously. See if there are ways you can integrate it into the vision. Doing so will both strengthen the vision and increase ownership.
- *Go slowly.* This process of gaining ownership takes a long time. Don't skip over it or rush it; you'll just end up paying later. Take the time to process people well and hear them out. It's worth it.

Truly creating ownership means we've brought people to the point that even without us, they would still continue toward this new vision, because it's become their own. Take the time necessary to build true ownership. It's essential and worth the extra investment of time and energy.

When do you need to shift gears?

As you go, roles on the team will shift. Span of care will broaden, and structures will need to be adapted. You'll need to evaluate regularly and decide when to pass more responsibility on to others as the ministry grows. Planters can find these shifts difficult, as it means more delegation and less direct control. Yet transferring more and more of the decision-making responsibility to the people group you're reaching will ensure the church's long-term survival.

People will also leave during the course of the ministry—for all different reasons: moving, calling to other ministries, unresolved conflicts. Those you start the church with aren't necessarily those you grow the church with. Some core team members you grow close to will leave. Those who are starters are often not builders. This dynamic can be painful, but it's simply a reality. It's okay to grieve, but keep pressing on. Try not to take it too personally in the cases where it isn't personal.

There are also times when the planter is called to move on. Leaders with planting skills are not always well-suited to pastoring a church over the long haul—they're significantly different roles. Understand how you're wired and talk with your coach. Many planters leave a few years too late, and inadvertently do damage to the plant in the meantime, because they're dissatisfied working within existing ministries rather than startups.

As you and others shift roles over time, remember who you are loyal to: God and his calling, not any particular local church or people.

Transitions in the planter role

As the church plant develops, the planter will need to adopt appropriate leadership styles in each phase. Often the very things that made a planter successful in the first stage of the church plant can sabotage efforts in the next stage.

At the beginning of a church plant, the planter will be more directive; he or she will make most of the decisions alone or with a small group of leaders. As the church develops and its leaders mature, the planter will invite more people into the leadership process. At this point, the planter will shift to a collaborative style of leadership that allows others to take more initiative in their areas of responsibility.

The planter also ought to periodically reevaluate roles and responsibilities. Most planters will eventually pass on many functions to others as they move more into coaching and overseeing. Depending on the structure of the church, the progression of the role for the planter can look something like this:

- learner
- evangelist
- team leader
- equipper
- resident coach
- itinerant coach

As groups and ministries begin to multiply, you'll need to move incrementally from direct ministry to coaching. This shift could also be described as moving from a doer role to a leadership-developer role. In almost all cases, additional leadership is needed to grow in a church plant. The methods and style of leadership you used to launch the church plant may not be the same ones that will make the church successful in the next stages of growth. Change *will* be required—you might as well make it intentional change.

The wise planter will help people navigate these expectations. If you emphasize small groups and discipleship, that's where people's primary relationships will be formed. If you emphasize corporate worship services, you develop people who feel more relationally connected with you and with the worship leader. Watch out for the risk of having more people depending on you than you can reasonably shepherd.

Yet even as the church grows and you focus on developing other leaders, the planter most often maintains a small group of people he or she is close to and personally shepherds. You'll still have close relationships with the people you knew from the early days of the plant, even if they're not leaders. Those who come later will never have the level of relationship with you that the earlier people have. It's the same way a great-grandchild is different than a child—you have more of a relationship with those with whom you've shared more experience.

Long-range leadership

In your short-term planning, don't forget the long game. Make sure the steps you're taking now are ultimately leading in the right direction, even if they may look different at the time. Leading change well requires maintaining long-term focus on where you want to go. How committed are you to getting there? The process is lengthy and difficult. Real change will require a deep, long-term commitment of time and energy.

With consistent focus, the seeds of transformation in an existing organization can be established in a three-year period, but then those seeds must be cultivated in years four to seven, so that in years eight to ten the change can be truly established as a part of the organizational culture.

In a new church, results will appear faster but not instantaneously. Getting there means maintaining focus on the end goal, even in the midst of organizational leadership changes. So count the cost—it is high. But for those who are willing to pay the price and embark on the journey, the results can be astounding: long-term transformation.

What common obstacles can you avoid?

When leading change, what to avoid is almost as important as what to do. Here are some common barriers and blockages to leading change well:

Corporate ADD: Sometimes organizations are afflicted by corporate ADD (attention deficit disorder). We engage in a pattern of starting something, losing focus, starting something different, and so on. When we behave this way repeatedly, we're essentially training our people not to take us seriously.

Convoy mentality: As church plants, we tend to believe that for change to take place, we must first get everyone on the same page, ready to move along in the same direction. Until everyone is ready to move, no one moves. However, that's simply not realistic, and the common result is that *no one* moves. So instead, like Gideon, take a coalition of the willing and allow others to opt out.

Education beyond obedience: A common breakdown occurs when we try to cram everything someone could possibly someday need to know into their orientation or training. We overload them with information, and their practice doesn't have a chance to catch up. Rather, we need to give them just enough to get started—bite-sized pieces—and give them time to live into it.

Event-focusedness: If seminars could do the job, we'd be done by now. We don't need another event. What we need is the follow-up that takes us the rest of the way through the process. One major mistake we make is to think that events by themselves will accomplish our goals. Providing support and follow-up, resourcing, and coaching, is what empowers people to experience true change over time.

Working in isolation: Many planters get roadblocked on their way to reaching their goals simply due to lack of connection with others. It sounds simple, but it's essential: We need other people along the way with us. Without intentionally creating an environment that allows connection with others—something with set-aside time—many good intentions come to nothing.

Too high too fast: Often we set the bar too high too fast. An athlete training for the high jump wouldn't start with the bar seven feet high; he or she would start much lower and work their way up. Setting the bar too high too quickly results in people failing and feeling discouraged, overwhelmed, and frustrated. By building up to the goal with smaller, more manageable steps, we create an atmosphere of encouragement and momentum.

The piecemeal approach: We can't accomplish long-term change by doing it piecemeal. We are often tempted to just focus on one area, as if that one thing will fix everything—maybe just prayer or relational connection or vision. But any one of those without the others will be incomplete. We need a holistic, principle-based approach.

Agenda disharmony

Any planter who listens even marginally well has run into agenda disharmony. Those are the times when someone on your team speaks up and you're thinking, "Wait, I thought we were on the same page." One common example arises when the planter tries to multiply the leadership team, and the people on said leadership team view that move as "splitting" and damaging relationships rather than fulfilling the mission. In this case, the planter and the leadership team may have differing values or vision, or even different understandings of topics like outreach and relationships.

These differing perceptions can spring from lack of clear communication early on by the planter. They can spring from the personal histories and agendas of team members. They can spring from a desire for control on either part.

The first step toward addressing agenda disharmony is listening well and asking questions, to discover people's expectations and understandings of where this church plant is going. Your understanding of what's "normal" may be different from the understandings of others. We all come in with preconceived ideas, and this is where listening and vision-casting come in.

Constantly reinforcing the values and vision of the church is an essential and primary leadership function. Often planters do that with their initial core team, but taper off as the church plant becomes more established. Yet new people continue to come in, so the vision needs to be cast and recast. Create the environments, relationships, and processes you need to bring people on board with the vision as they come into the church.

Reinforcing the vision can be done through sharing stories, recognizing contributions, affirming efforts, or large-scale vision-casting. When the church is small, this process will happen more spontaneously, but as the church grows and the planter/pastor no longer has a close relationship with every attender, increased intentionality will be necessary.

Not only will newcomers need a variety of ways to hear and connect with the values and vision, but regular attenders and members will need to be continually reminded of how their ministry involvement is accomplishing the overall purposes for this church. Taking a proactive approach along these lines will help cultivate commitment to vision, values, and long-term direction.

The role of trust

Trust is a key ingredient of leading change well. Having trust speeds up change; not having it throws up additional barriers. The degree to which people trust you has a direct correlation to your ability to lead change effectively. So as a leader and planter, how will you gain and keep trust?

The most important starting point is to keep your word: Do what you say you're going to do. Don't equivocate. Don't overpromise. Know what you're going to do and not do, and follow through consistently.

Also, gather people around you who are trustworthy. You don't necessarily need to know everything about financial decisions, but you should have someone on your team who does and can validate the feasibility of a plan. It's helpful to have others involved who are also faithful (1 Corinthians 4).

Broken trust takes a long time to get back. If you haven't been faithful in the little things, how can you expect people to trust you in the big things?

> "Whoever is faithful in a very little is faithful also in much; and whoever is dishonest in a very little is dishonest also in much. ^{11} If then you have not been faithful with the dishonest wealth, who will entrust to you the true riches? ^{12} And if you have not been faithful with what belongs to another, who will give you what is your own?" (Luke 16:10–12).

Trust and respect go hand in hand toward the ability to lead change. They require a track record of consistency and authenticity, listening well to others, being authentic, and resolving conflicts as they arise rather than letting them fester.

Staying connected to the vision

Keep the main thing the main thing. Continually connect back to your redemptive mission and vision. Recalibrate and change tactics when necessary, but orient everything around the primary vision God has called you to. Make disciples. Stay connected to the culture around you. Continue in prayer. Keep learning. Maintain an attitude of humility. Practice listening for the voice of the Holy Spirit.

> Trust and respect go hand in hand toward the ability to lead change.

Keep your eyes on the goal: What do you really want?

That should remain the same, even as how you go about getting there remains the same. The "what" stays the same, even as the "how" changes. The lack of a sense of urgency is the number-one reason missional transformation doesn't happen. If we're satisfied with the status quo, there is no motivation for change. We need passionate commitment to a vision—a vision that is clear and compelling. Picture what new things will be emerging—for the vision is for starting new things, not just for revitalization.

Look ahead fifteen to twenty years. If God had his way, what would look different? Once you have this clear and compelling vision in mind, you'll need to paint that picture for others. You'll need to help them uncover their dissatisfaction with the status quo. You'll need to talk about the vision in such a way that it takes hold of people, and so they respond by wanting to make the sacrifice and take the risk by moving toward this new vision of a preferred future.

As you go, keep the main thing the main thing: growing disciples who make disciples who, in turn, make disciples.

Journey Guide for Chapter 19
Navigating Growth and Change

JOURNEY GUIDE

Every planter will be required to navigate various seasons of change. Even positive changes, such as growth, require the use of leadership skills in leading change. This chapter provides ways for planters to continue developing and strengthening these relationally intensive leadership skills. Leading change is a challenge for all leaders. Make use of the resources in this journey guide to help you navigate the process. You can return to it time and again as you continue running up against needs for change.

Checklist: for the road ahead
- ☐ Listening to the Holy Spirit for direction has been a regular and faithful part of the process.
- ☐ Ownership has been created among the congregation.
- ☐ When necessary, "gear changes" have been made.
- ☐ The span of care has been delegated and expanded.
- ☐ The leadership team has been expanded and developed.
- ☐ The planter's leadership style and role have shifted as the church has grown.
- ☐ Long-range goals have been clarified, including identifying and planning around potential obstacles.
- ☐ Agenda disharmony has been addressed.
- ☐ Trust has been cultivated and maintained.
- ☐ New goals have been connected back to the vision and mission.

Discipleship focus: Community Transformation
Leading change well means opening up our hands and heart to what God may bring that is new. What has been may not be what will be.

Inward focus:
1. What changes ahead do you expect might be difficult for you personally?
2. What might God be asking you to let go of?
3. What will be required of you personally?

Outward focus:
1. How can you help others cope with change? What might they need?
2. What steps can you take to build greater awareness for the feelings of others?

Strategic questions: for you and your coach

- What new directions do you currently have in mind that will require gaining ownership? What benefits would full ownership give you moving forward?
- How do you plan to build buy-in for those new directions? Who are the key opinion leaders you need to talk with? What concerns might you need to address?
- How has your time allotment for various roles and activities changed in the last six months?
- How well are you balancing your leadership responsibilities with your family responsibilities? Would your spouse agree?
- What changes do you need to make at this stage of development to be more effective?
- How do you expect your time allotment for various roles and activities to be different six months from now?
- What action steps are you sensing God would have you take?

Discussion questions: for you and your team

- What direction do you sense God wanting us to move as we reach more people?
- How might your own role shift as we move in that direction?
- What excites you about that? What concerns you about that?
- What can you do to build trust with those you're leading?
- How can you remind people of the vision?

Guided prayer: for you personally

Beloved, I do not consider that I have made it my own; but this one thing I do: forgetting what lies behind and straining forward to what lies ahead, [14] I press on toward the goal for the prize of the heavenly call of God in Christ Jesus. (Philippians 3:13–14)

- God, please help me hold this new church with open hands, giving over control to you.
- Give me the grace to live a life worthy of trust.
- Bring team members and leaders I can trust, and give me the faith to delegate not only tasks but responsibilities.
- Even in the midst of day-to-day ministry, help me keep my eyes focused on what you have for us long-term and help me move us as an organization toward that goal.

Guided prayer: for use with your team

Pray together with your team through each of these themes:

- Lord, please guide us toward the future you have for us, and give us the courage to move forward into it.
- Help each of us to be a light and guide for others, as you call them to move closer to yourself on their journeys of discipleship.
- Grant us patience and the gift of listening as we strive to live lives worthy of trust.
- Help us be wise as we follow you.

Guided prayer: for your intercessors

Please pray for us to develop new leaders in every area of ministry. Pray that our team would:

- receive a clear vision from God for the road ahead.
- have the faith to step into that vision, even if we can't see every step along the way.
- be willing to relinquish control and delegate, recognizing that you are the true leader of this church.
- build one another up as we seek to move forward together making disciples.

Action guide: a place for planning your next steps

1.

2.

3.

Chapter 20: Multiplying Movements

Most of the challenge of multiplication is setting everything up for it when you first put things in place. If you've followed everything prescribed in this book, multiplying should be assured. Ideally, you've designed your discipleship process to multiply disciples, your leadership development process to multiply leaders, your disciplemaking community structure to multiply disciplemaking communities, and so on. Everything—every aspect of what you do—should multiply.

It's very unlikely that you'll be able to multiply new churches if you're not already multiplying disciples, leaders, and groups. That's like skipping to the end without putting any foundations in place beforehand. A multiplication movement needs to see multiplication happening at the smallest level. You can't truly be a church planting movement if you're not first a disciplemaking movement.

The biblical roots of church multiplication

We see this running theme of multiplication throughout the Bible. Jesus multiplied disciples. Moses multiplied leaders. Paul multiplied churches. We see this multiplication extending to the fourth generation and beyond: *"and what you have heard from me through many witnesses entrust to faithful people who will be able to teach others as well"* (2 Timothy 2:2). If I'm discipling you, I haven't succeeded until you've discipled someone who has discipled someone else. That's when I can see the fruit of multiplication.

Jesus seems to have organized his earthly ministry along these lines. He spent time with his chosen twelve disciples, then left them with the Great Commission— essentially a charge to pass along his influence, his spiritual DNA, his family tree. As individual believers, we are called to make disciples and multiply.

What's true of individual believers is also true of churches: We are called to multiply our groups, and ultimately our congregations. That's the story of the book of Acts.

Only through multiplication could Christianity go from being a few hundred outlaw followers of Jesus to the official state religion of the Roman Empire—its influence felt worldwide—all within its first three hundred years.

Church planters and pastors should be told from the beginning that healthy churches reproduce—it's a biblical concept. A general rule of thumb is that new churches should plan to plant another church within the first three years of their life as a church. The likelihood of a new church planting another church diminishes significantly after three years. If you don't plant by then, you probably won't—and that breaks the chain of multiplication.

Multiplication is inherent in the creation principle: Everything reproduces after its own kind. The true fruit of an apple tree is not just an apple, but another apple tree. A person can count the number of seeds inside one apple, but only God can count the number of apples inside one seed. Just as disciples reproduce disciples and ministries reproduce ministries, churches reproduce churches.

The power of multiplication over addition
We talk about *multiplying* churches rather than *planting* churches for a reason. Even if every single church in existence plants (adds) just one other church, that doubles the number of churches. That's great—but it's not nearly as powerful as multiplication.

If you put one grain of wheat on one square of a chessboard and multiply it by every square (2, 4, 8), how many would you have by sixty-four? Enough wheat to cover India by a depth of fifty feet. Consider also taking $1 and doubling it each day rather than adding to it. What do you have after just thirty-one days? More than a billion dollars: $1,073,741,824. The exponential concept makes a big difference.

In the same way, planting three churches is good. Planting three churches that each also go on to plant three new churches takes you a huge leap forward. When you tally it up, the long-term potential is astounding. Most pastors think about growing healthy churches or growing large churches, but typically don't think of growing multiplying churches. A significant paradigm shift is required—for the best way to reach the harvest isn't through large churches, or even through planting more churches, but through churches that multiply—whatever their size.

Laying the groundwork for multiplication
So where do you start? What foundations need to be in place to facilitate optimal multiplication? I'd say these four aspects form the cornerstones:

- keeping a laser focus on the *vision*
- putting *coaching* in place at all levels
- praying, and expanding the base of *prayer*
- being willing to *empower* others

Come back to the vision and remember what you're about. Don't get caught up in being the biggest or the best. Remember, you and your church are just one small part of God's kingdom. What can you do—not to contribute to your own church plant, but to contribute to the greater kingdom of God? Keep your eyes on the vision.

From the outside, coaching can be one of the least visible components of a church multiplication movement. Yet behind the scenes, it provides that essential strategic and relational element that brings life and direction to key leaders in those movements. Without leaders at every level being empowered through coaching, continued multiplication will not happen. Consider all the essential levels of ministry that require coaching: discipleship, leadership, disciplemaking community groups, ministry teams, new church plants, existing congregations, parent churches. Build your coaching capacity accordingly.

> True multiplication cannot happen apart from empowering others.

Pray. Nothing happens apart from prayer. You can do everything right and the ministry may not grow or multiply, because all transformative power comes from the Holy Spirit. Continue to communicate with your intercessory team. Continue to pray yourself. Continue to weave prayer at all levels into the DNA of your church. *"He also said, "This is what the kingdom of God is like. A man scatters seed on the ground. [27] Night and day, whether he sleeps or gets up, the seed sprouts and grows, though he does not know how. [28] All by itself the soil produces grain—first the stalk, then the head, then the full kernel in the head" (Mark 4:26–28, NIV).*

True multiplication cannot happen apart from empowering others. If you want to be able to control something, you'll need to keep it small. By definition, a church multiplication movement will grow beyond your own reach as you empower not only other leaders and planters, but other churches and ministries as well.

Where can you multiply? Vision for the scope of church planting
As you think about planting new churches that will plant new churches that will plant new churches, consider both local and long-distance options. When Jesus was giving his mission to the disciples, he clarified the scope of that mission in Acts 1:8: *"But you will receive power when the Holy Spirit has come upon you; and you will be my witnesses in Jerusalem, in all Judea and Samaria, and to the ends of the earth."* That means everywhere, but let's break it down and look a little more closely.

- *Jerusalem*: This is the heart and center of the movement. This is where Jesus was crucified and resurrected, and where the disciples gathered together and became the church. Planting in "Jerusalem" means planting right where you currently are.
- *Judea*: This is still familiar territory culturally, but it includes the outlying districts and towns. Today it might be akin to the suburbs or small towns within driving distance—not far, but not right next door either.
- *Samaria*: This is where things get challenging for most churches. Samaria represents the "commutable" areas, but those that are different culturally, religiously, and/or socioeconomically. Samaritans are the people you may see regularly, but do not normally have fellowship with because they're outside your regular circles—in today's terms, the people on the other side of the tracks. They're reasonably close physically, but distant culturally.
- *Ends of the earth*: This is everywhere else—everywhere that you'd need to pick up and move to in order to reach the people living there. This is what we normally think of when we hear "missions." That has traditionally been Africa, Asia, or South America, but increasingly applies to major secularized metropolitan areas in the United States and Europe as well. The "ends of the earth" require studying the culture, being called and gifted by God to reach that culture, and then picking up and going there.

Any church desiring to start a multiplication movement should consider all of these areas. In some cases, you may start with just one, but in other cases you could be mobilizing new planters and new churches in multiple areas at one time.

Many reasons exist for pastors to resist planting in these different spheres. Usually, Jerusalem and Samaria feel like the most threatening places to plant, while Judea and the ends of the earth feel more manageable. The reality is that all four places have people who need to be reached for Jesus.

Jerusalem can feel threatening to plant in, due to fears that the new plant will harm the livelihood of the mother church. Will it simply draw people and funding away? If church planting is done well, new people will be reached, rather than just reorganizing people who are already in churches. Samaria can feel threatening for different reasons. Samaritans are often people that—culturally, racially, or economically—we have been taught to fear or dislike. Planting in Samaria often means addressing various forms of prejudice internally.

Judea can seem a better option for planting: people who are similar culturally, but not close enough physically for many of them to switch churches. Many churches can send a small team to plant nearby, often made up of people who already live in that area and have been commuting. The ends of the earth can also feel like a good planting choice: You can send a mission team far away from the mother church to work in a completely different culture. In many cases—but not always—the economic cost for doing work overseas or far away is less than it would be closer to home.

Pastors must be committed to church multiplication—wherever that may be. Otherwise they can become the chief blockages in the process.

One other important point about the scope of planting efforts is clarifying timelines. If you're financially subsidizing a new church plant, a clear plan must be made for it to become self-supporting in order to avoid long-term dependence. It's much healthier for a church to be independent financially, even if it means leaders are working bivocationally. The task is like that of a midwife: The role is not to stay, but to provide a safe delivery and then move on to help with other births.

Helping new churches retain the vision

Churches committed to multiplication will have it in their "genetic code." In other words, the development of leaders for the purpose of multiplication will be clearly present in vision and plans, and actions will be consistent with statements about multiplication. Incorporating the idea of ongoing multiplication of disciples, leaders, and groups into basic church planter training can go a long way toward building a strong genetic code for the future.

Seek out practical, creative ways to keep multiplication foremost in the minds of new churches. Some movements use a highly visible apprenticing system. Every new church plant begins with both a planter and an apprentice planter, who is expected to plant the next church. The same is true of disciplemaking community group leaders. The more roles that have apprentices in place, the more likely they are to multiply. Designating apprentices right from the beginning builds multiplication into the DNA in a way that provides a visible reminder to all who are involved.

The risk of an outward focus

One of the key pieces of DNA that needs to be modeled, practiced, and passed down is maintaining an outward focus. Doing that can feel like a big risk, along with all that goes along with it: the fears of your own finances not being enough to meet your internal needs, the risk of giving people away, the risk of shifting your focus away from your own congregation. Yet dying to self-focus is part of what Jesus calls us to:

> *"Therefore I tell you, do not worry about your life, what you will eat or what you will drink, or about your body, what you will wear. Is not life more than food, and the body more than clothing? [26] Look at the birds of the air; they neither sow nor reap nor gather into barns, and yet your heavenly Father feeds them. Are you not of more value than they?" (Matthew 6:25–26)*

That's the primary shift in thinking that is required for churches to be intentionally engaged in multiplication—turning from an inward to an outward focus. Even brand-new churches that are small, struggling financially, and not yet ready to multiply can find creative ways to be involved in new church planting efforts.

Just months after launching, one church knew it didn't have the resources to become a parent church yet, but they committed to sending prayer teams into neighboring communities where the groundwork was being laid for new church plants. Later they volunteered to lead worship for a new plant during its first three months of public services, while training some of their laypeople who had gifts in that area. By being involved from the very beginning and actively looking for ways to help new church plants in any way they could, the people in that congregation kept their focus outward and their hearts open to the idea of multiplying. They focused their vision on church planting and regularly asked themselves, "What's the best way for us to participate in that vision right now?"

Seven ways to become a church planting church:

1. Pray that God would raise up workers for the harvest fields. Look out over the harvest fields and ask God to break your heart over what breaks his heart. Encourage others in your congregation to pray as well. God may even begin to give you direction regarding how to invest in people in order to reach the harvest.

2. Start new churches with apprentice church planters. Just like you start a small group with an apprentice leader, why not start churches with apprentice planters right from the

very beginning? That method communicates clearly that the church is designed to reproduce, just like groups are designed to reproduce. Identify potential church planters in your midst.

3. Use your church as a training ground for developing potential church planters. Offer training and ministry experience to potential planters. This method can be used whether you're recruiting existing leaders from within your own congregation, raising leaders from the harvest, grafting them in from outside the church, or any combination.

4. Hive off a group from your church to start a new church. Just like you can hive off a group of people from one small group to start another one, you can do the same thing at a congregational level. Pastors often become threatened when it comes to giving away people and leaders to a new church. However, consider applying the principle of tithing and generous giving to the church itself. Make it a practice to release the best of the best in your congregation for church planting. Give away 10 percent of your people—and watch God bless the remaining 90 percent.

5. Start and multiply groups in a new area. It only takes one leader to go out, start a group, and see it multiply—and you could congregationalize that group into a new church. Think of it as group planting. Groups that grow and multiply could be organized into new churches.

6. Raise leaders from the harvest. Evangelize, disciple, and raise leaders while you're starting and multiplying groups. That is the most powerful and efficient way to start a church multiplication movement.

7. Send mission teams to multiply churches cross-culturally. Certain gifts are required for successful cross-cultural ministry. Bicultural interns can be especially helpful.

Becoming a parent church

The right timing is certainly key in church planting and multiplication. Although all churches can be involved in contribution toward the vision of multiplying churches, not all churches are ready to become parent churches. So how do you know if you're ready to plant? Consider your current DNA and disciple reproduction.

What's in your DNA? Who and what have you raised up so far? Are you multiplying disciples, groups, leaders? Are they healthy? That's what needs to be measured rather than the number of years you've been around, the number of attenders you have, or the size of your budget. Those are false indicators. Look rather to the quality of the DNA that you see being reproduced. You need to see some evidence that you're raising up leaders who could take over an existing church or start new ones.

Dream big and don't limit your thinking. Even a modest contribution toward church planting, made consistently over time, can bring important dividends, both for the church plant and for the health of your own congregation. God is ready to do bigger things than you can imagine.

Personal transitions for the planter

The stage of development when a church plant becomes a parent church can bring about significant changes and growing pains. Very often, church planters are not suited to remain indefinitely as pastors of the churches they have planted. So how do you know when it's time to go? I have asked many planter/pastors this question, and they all had a similar answer: You'll just know. It does help to have people around you asking you questions to help you discern that timing.

Some planters stay on too long, especially if they're truly relationally connected to the community. Even though I was planning to spend the rest of my life in the church I had planted, and to continue planting churches from there, the Lord had other plans for me.

I had an associate pastor, Rob Acker. Every year, I'd pray about what challenges to give him to further his development. One year, I couldn't think of any new assignment that would help him develop further that did not involve calling him to become a senior pastor. Maybe God was calling him to plant a church and become a senior pastor somewhere else? That would be difficult for me because of how valuable he was in his current role, but I was committed to church planting and willing to let him go.

So God said, "Yes, you're right, Bob. Rob is ready to be a senior pastor, so you're out of here."

"Wait, me?" I thought. "*I'm* out of here?" Through a series of events, circumstances, and the persistent leading of the Holy Spirit, God made it abundantly and inescapably clear to me that it was time for me to go to the seashore to help other planters. Remember the seashore? I had promised God way back that if he helped me plant this church, I would help other church planters navigate the process. It was time to fulfill that vision, and that meant I needed to go.

Some planters do stay at the church they plant for a lifetime, but others are better in a catalytic role. The key issue is to find out what God is calling you to do, and then do it.

You never know what God may choose to do through you—or through others. For this reason, I urge all planters to begin looking for their successors early on in the planting process. In 2 Timothy 2:2, Paul talks about raising other pastors. But in the first century that meant raising up church planters. After all, there weren't already existing churches in need of new leadership.

Whether you're called to stay long-term or to move on to another ministry role, you'll eventually need a replacement. It's better to be prepared before you need to leave rather than wait until it's imminent. None of us ever knows when God may call us on, whatever that may look like.

> *You have heard me teach things that have been confirmed by many reliable witnesses. Now teach these truths to other trustworthy people who will be able to pass them on to others. (2 Timothy 2:2, NLT)*

Journey Guide for Chapter 20
Multiplying Movements

JOURNEY GUIDE

Everything—every aspect of what a church plant does—should multiply. That includes disciples, groups, leaders, planters, and congregations. Multiplication of ministry is the end game of any church plant. The roots are founded in obedience and vision and the fruit is generations upon generations of new disciples. The journey guide below has been designed to help planters and teams ensure that every aspect of ministry is growing and multiplying effectively.

Checklist: for the road ahead

- ☐ Prayer for church multiplication has been established, and a kingdom perspective cultivated.
- ☐ The number of unreached people and people groups has been reviewed.
- ☐ A vision for planting churches beyond the local area/people group has been cultivated and embraced.
- ☐ Decisions on where to multiply have been made, and readiness for becoming a parent church assessed.
- ☐ Coaching, and a general culture of empowerment, has been put into place.
- ☐ Blockages have been addressed.
- ☐ Outward focus has been confirmed.
- ☐ New leadership has been commissioned in the new community.
- ☐ A vision for church planting has been imparted to new church plant.
- ☐ The planter has made any needed personal transitions in his/her roles and responsibilities.

Discipleship focus: Take inventory

In this last chapter of the book, pause to look back and take stock of where you are right now and how far you have come in the multiplication of ministry.

Inward focused:
1. Has your vision for church planting changed? If so, how?
2. Describe the current state of your life balance?
3. What changes might God be calling you to make?

Outward focused:
1. How have you witnessed the fruit of multiplication in your ministry?
2. How have you celebrated this multiplication?
3. Who else could you empower for ministry multiplication?

Strategic questions: for you and your coach
- How can you cast vision for church multiplication?
- How can you know when your church is ready to become a parent church?
- How can you be involved in church planting in the meantime?
- How will you ensure you are moving toward multiplication rather than addition? What will be your limiting factor(s)?
- What do you have in place for:
  - prayer?
  - coaching?
  - empowerment of leaders?
  - vision-casting?

Discussion questions: for you and your team
- How do we see the principle of church multiplication at work in the book of Acts? [Engage your people in a study of some relevant passages in the book of Acts that speak to your situation.]
- What fears do you have surrounding planting and multiplying churches?
- What could be gained from planting and multiplying churches? [Spend time in prayer listening to the Holy Spirit]

Guided prayer: for you personally
And day by day the Lord added to their number those who were being saved. (Acts 2:47b)
- God, give me a vision much larger than my own church.
- Give me enough confidence in you and your guidance that I can be generous and supportive of new churches starting up.
- Help me see blind spots that may prevent me from seeing the full range of the harvest you want to reach.
- Grant me the clarity to see what you have next for me personally.

Guided prayer: for use with your team
Pray together with your team through each of these themes:
- Open our eyes to the harvest fields.
- Who needs to hear about you who is right here near us?
- Who needs to hear about you who is far away from us?
- Who needs to hear about you who is physically nearby but culturally distant?
- Please break our hearts over what breaks your heart.

- Who are you calling us to invest in? What will we have to give up?
- What might you want to do through us for the greater kingdom?

Guided prayer: for your intercessors
Intercessors stay motivated when they hear how their prayers are making a difference. Share answers to prayer; flag special needs. Also, find ways to thank and celebrate your intercessors.

Please pray for us to plant churches that plant churches that plant churches. Pray that our team would:
- avoid the trap of selfishness and self-focus.
- embrace a kingdom vision that is much larger than our own church plant.
- provide solid foundations upon which to birth new ministries and churches.
- listen to the Holy Spirit and strive to live in loving obedience.

Action guide: a place for planning your next steps

1.

2.

3.

Acknowledgments

The Church Planting Journey is a legacy work. To create it, I have drawn from many of my past works, and therefore from literally hundreds of people who have influenced me along the way. It's impossible to create a comprehensive list of everyone who has contributed ideas over the years that have found their way into this work, so my apologies. As much as possible, I have tried to credit people within the text as I wrote.

Yet I would like to acknowledge some who worked closely with me on this project: Tara Miller, who collected materials and formed them into a readable manuscript; Marcy Bradford, who kept me organized and sane along the way; Colin Noyes, who gave me formative feedback; Carl Simmons, who edited the manuscript; Bev Browning, who volunteered her excellent proofreading skills; Julia Michaud who formatted it and added graphics; and Michelle Coe, who created the cover design. I'd also like to thank the following church planters who took the time to provide feedback on the manuscript: Dennis Bachman, Tim Clark, Josh Miller, Colin Noyes, Albie Powers, and Gary Reinecke.

Most of all, thank you to those who are reading this book with an eye toward planting churches that plant churches that plant churches that plant churches. You are the people who make it possible for me to fulfill this vision God gave me many, many years ago, to do all that I can to help other church planters succeed.

> *Now to him who by the power at work within us is able to accomplish abundantly far more than all we can ask or imagine, to him be glory in the church and in Christ Jesus to all generations, forever and ever. Amen. (Ephesians 3:20–21)*

Suggested Resources

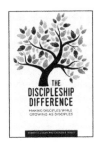

The Discipleship Difference lays out an intentional, holistic, and relational approach to discipleship that is individualized to meet each person wherever they are.

Guide for Discipling (digital and print) a comprehensive curriculum to help you on your personal discipleship journey. Invite others to study with you and encourage disciples new and old to Love God, Love Others, and Make Disciples.

These guides have also been adapted to reflect the culture of several denominations. Look for your denomination at https://loganleadership.com/guides, or to inquire about the development of Discipleship Guides for your ministry context, contact us at admin@loganleadership.com.

Becoming Barnabas - This short book sets forth the biblical basis for coaching—tied to the story of Barnabas—and describes how it can transform your ministry through the everyday practice of basic coaching skills by laypeople and clergy alike. Learn more by visiting: www.loganleadership.com/BB

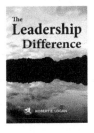

Leadership Difference - A book providing practical guidance on developing essential leadership skills within a coaching paradigm. To learn more or purchase this resource visit: www.loganleadership.com/LD

Made in the USA
Middletown, DE
29 July 2019